THE TEUTONIC MYTHOLOGY
OF
RICHARD WAGNER'S
THE RING OF THE NIBELUNG

Volume III
The Natural and Supernatural Worlds

Part 1

William O. Cord

Studies in the History and Interpretation of Music
Volume 18-A

The Edwin Mellen Press
Lewiston•Queenston
Lampeter

Library of Congress Cataloging-in-Publication Data

Cord, William O.
    The Teutonic mythology of Richard Wagner's "The Ring of the
Nibelung" / by William O. Cord.
      p.   cm. -- (Studies in the history and interpretation of
music ; v. 16-18)
    Contents: v. 1. Nine properties -- v. 2. The family of gods -- v. 3. The
natural and supernatural worlds.
    Volume 18 ISBN 0-88946-443-X (Part A & Part B)
    1. Wagner, Richard, 1813-1883. Ring des Nibelungen.
2. Mythology, Germanic. 3. Legends--Germany. I. Title.
II. Series: Studies in the history and interpretation of music ; v.
16, etc.
ML410.W15C7   1989   782.1   89-12612
                                                      CIP

This is volume 18A in the continuing series
Studies in the History & Interpretation of Music
Volume 18 ISBN 0-88946-443-X
SHIM Series ISBN 0-88946-426-X

A CIP catalog record for this book is available
from The British Library.

The Edwin Mellen Press   The Edwin Mellen Press
P.O. Box 450   Box 67
Lewiston, NY 14092   Queenston, Ontario
USA   CANADA L0S 1L0

The Edwin Mellen Press, Ltd.
Lampeter, Dyfed, Wales
UNITED KINGDOM SA48 7DY

Printed in the United States of America

To my parents . . .
To Mierl, who hears
Wagner's song,
and to Owen, my father,
who has journeyed on to
his Valhalla.

"...and the thing shall sound in such fashion that people shall hear what they cannot see."

Richard Wagner

TABLE OF CONTENTS

A Prologue in Verse[*]

O hearken, ye who speak the English tongue,
How in a waste land ages long ago,
The very heart of the North bloomed into song
After long brooding o'er this tale of woe!
Hearken, and marvel how it might be so,
That such a sweetness so well crowned could be
Betwixt the ice-hills and the cold grey sea.

So draw ye round and hearken, English folk,
Unto the best tale pity ever wrought!
Of how from dark to dark bright Sigurd broke,
Of Brynhild's glorious soul with love distraught,
Of Gudrun's weary wandering unto naught,
Of utter love defeated utterly,
Of grief too strong to give love time to die!

William Morris

---

[*]   First and sixth of six stanzas of the poem that prefaces a translation from the Icelandic of *Volsungasaga* by Eikikr Magnusson and William Morris, London, Walter Scott Publishers, 1888.

ABBREVIATIONS

AS -   Anglo Saxon (England, 5th-7th centuries)

Goth -   Gothic

LG -   Low German (Northern Germany, since 16th century)

ME -   Middle English (England, 11th-15th centuries)

MHG -   Middle High German
(Central and Southern Germany, 12th-15th centuries)

MLG -   Middle Low German (11th-16th centuries)

Mod E -   Modern English (England, since 1600)

Mod G -   Modern German

OE -   Old English (England, 7th-10th centuries)

OF -   Old Frisian

OHG -   Old High German (Prior to 12th century)

OLG -   Old Low German (Prior to 11th century)

ON -   Old Norse (Scandinavia, prior to middle of 14th century)

OS -   Old Saxon (Northwest Germany until about the 12th century)

PREFACE

This volume is intended to serve as a complement to the two volumes of this series previously published:

Volume I   *Nine Dramatic Properties*

Volume II   *The Family of Gods*

The reader who is familiar with either or both of these cited volumes will note immediately the radical change in format that the current work has acquired. There is a reason for this format, albeit it personal and thoroughly rationalized.

Over the years I had spent an inordinate amount of time involved in matters of Teutonic mythology. This time included study, examination, consideration, analysis, observation, and even journeys of intense inquiry to Germanic lands. At the same time, I was realizing a direct experience with Richard Wagner and his *Der Ring des Nibelungen*. In all, I was privileged to attend no less than twenty-seven performances of five distinct productions of this monumental work. Slowly, there emerged from the natural association of these two activities the realization that despite the mountains of voluminous materials written about Wagner's Teutonic drama, the *totality* of mythical matters in that landmark work had never been singularly presented. Again and again, as I read the myths and assorted tales of the gods, and as I learned about the Valkyries, about the Norns, about life in Valhalla, and about the fated destruction that would end the universe, I was drawn more and more to Wagner's drama, garmented as it was, in its own cloak of that ancient Germanic thought. I became more and more aware that the mythical coloration of the poem was more extensive, much more intense, much more thorough than the general society of Wagnerian followers had ever acknowledged. If it was true that most of the figures of the drama of the *Ring* had been drawn from early Teutonic religious thought, and if it was true that many of the incidents of the *Ring* had their sources in the early tales of myth and legend, so was it also true that literally each word, each action, each property, each setting, each concept, each idea of this lengthy work was awash in one way or another in Teutonic mythical ambience. Even those matters that were obviously of relatively insignificant dramatic or thematic importance reflected a mythical garb that Wagner had woven into his work, an attire that he had gathered from the several years in the 1840's that he had devoted to the study and understanding of the thought and belief that had dominated the ancient Germanic peoples and their culture.

In the course of time, the realm of the Teutonic gods, the adventures of Sigurd, the cunning of Loki, indeed, the gamut of societal thought of the early Germanics, and the tale that Wagner weaves in his *Ring* merged, fused that is, into a single entity, a kind of offering that my intellectual capacity could savor and my emotional being could easily indulge and thoroughly enjoy.

As I continued to make my joyous way through the seemingly fathomless reams of materials, I was slowly but certainly overcome by an insistent and persistent urge. Why not attempt to fill that mythical gap that had existed for so long in the *Ring's* history by preparation of a work that contains the totality of mythicalness that is to be found in the *Ring*, a work that included mythicalness that would range from the obvious to the obscure, from the import of a Wotan as Supreme God of the universe, and his ultimate destruction, as well as that of the world itself, to the equally significant if relatively unimportant topic of altar stones for the gods, or the ingredients of a magic potion! I understood that such a work would be an immense undertaking and that the finished product, if it were to be completed, would not easily adjust to the literary format of regular and acceptable divisions within a manuscript. Such a work would be, rather, of an encyclopedic nature because there would be an seemingly endless number as well as variety of entries, some to be presented in as short a space as a single, brief paragraph, while an acceptable depiction of other subjects would require many pages. In such a study, matters of prime import would range in line with others of scant significance, yet, in such a format, each and every item would have its rightful niche within that overall presentation of the mythicalness of the *Ring*.

I began my literary mythical adventure with eagerness, with enthusiasm, coupled with the highest of investigative ideal. As time passed, the notes that I accumulated, the ideas that I had conceived, the pages that I had written, all began to mount, to grow, to increase to limits that I had never dreamed. The whole of the proposed study grew in size to unimaginable dimensions. I soon was forced to conclude that time and subject probably would not allow me the pleasure of a finite end to my work. After all, I did not possess the Teutonic apples of eternal youth, the apples that Wagner puts in the charge of his goddess Freia.

It was then that I decided to divide my undertaking into smaller bits, somehow to prepare individual volumes that could stand alone should my larger task not be completed. The first volume was one that relates to the present three volumes only indirectly. I had discovered that there was no primer for newcomers to the *Ring*, no place where the neophyte could begin to understand the artwork that had attracted him. I prepared such a primer, a handbook that presented Wagner's drama from its inception in the composer's mind to the present day. That work was generously received.

Then came the second step, a direct path into the mythology of Wagner's poem. At once, two significant subjects for study became obvious. The first was that of the major properties of the *Ring*, that is, Valhalla, the ring itself, Freia's apples, and Wotan's spear, among others. After a lengthy period of time Volume I, *Nine Dramatic Properties*, was completed. The second inclusive theme pertained to the divine hierarchy that Wagner had placed in his poem. As before, this was a single topic that settled well into a volume. In time, Volume II, *The Family of Gods* resulted.

The materials that now remained were numerous, individual, diverse, and varied beyond imagination. What to do with those many items of mythical flavor that remained but which did not fit appropriately into either of the first two volumes and yet were fundamental to any total comprehension of the mythicalness of the *Ring*? It was at this point that the concept of an encyclopedic format again came to the fore!

An encyclopedic format became the best of all format worlds. In such a work all items would be appropriate. So, too, the variety of subjects, those that might be lengthy as well as those of brief substance or quantity, could easily be accommodated. An encyclopedic format did not limit theme or subject, and this format with its system of alphabetization would also allow ample space for placement of linguistic matters, as well as those that were of literary or historical interest. Everything pertinent to the subject could be included, regardless of dramatic, theatrical, or musical significance of any item. Each word of such a format could only bring me closer to that end that I had once proposed to myself, a presentation of the totality of Teutonic mythicalness of Richard Wagner's *Der Ring des Nibelungen*.

Hence, this, Volume III! In brief, it is hoped that it will inform, perhaps entertain. It probably will irritate some readers, even agitate certain well-fixed ideas to shake their dramatic dust. Perhaps this volume, and its companion pieces, may somehow challenge the neophyte as well as the sophisticated follower of the Wagnerian art. In all events, I ask only that the reader accept the work for what it simply purports to be.

The logistic turmoil that this work has stirred makes it quite possible, in fact probable, that some study has been overlooked, some depictions have incorrect facts, or spellings, or interpretations, or any number of matters of detail. If any errors of these or any other kinds come to the surface, only the author is to blame. I will do all possible to make necessary changes as these matters come to my attention.

Rohnert Park, California   W. O. C.

TO THE READER

Many of the Teutonic mythical matters that Richard Wagner brings to *Der Ring des Nibelungen* are overt, absolute, entirely observable, and easily recognized. At the same time, however, much of that drama's mythology is subtle, delicate, sublimated perhaps, ever potentially imperceptible. Then, too, not all that passes for mythology has been gathered from the ancient thought. Indeed, some matters of the *Ring* that are believed to be reflective of early Germanic beliefs are artistic creations of the composer himself. Other matters of a mythical nature have come under Wagner's artistic scalpel, the result of which is fundamentally Teutonic, but uniquely Wagnerian. Yet, always, throughout his lengthy drama Wagner was essentially true to his native past, faithful to the concepts and beliefs of his ancient Germanic culture.

It is not unusual for a follower of Wagner's *Ring* to accept the matter of the drama's mythology simply as a matter of fact. The obvious is acknowledged. It is also more usual than not for Wagnerites to be essentially unaware of the thoroughness and completeness of the mythical ambience that Wagner develops in his tetralogy. The *Ring's* mythical content is so extensive, so quantitative, and so substantive that its forces immediately impress themselves on the consciousness of every individual who takes it up, either as a literary work or as a music drama. It is this very mythical content that nourishes the dramatic, indeed, even the philosophical insights of those with whom it comes in contact.

It may be true, as some followers of the Wagnerian way insist, that the *Ring* is something more than a drama based on Teutonic mythology. Rather, these patrons claim that the drama itself is myth, that the drama is mythical in every warp and woof of its fabric, mythical even in every metaphor and alliteration that abound within its lines. Surely such a statement may boast of some exaggeration, but, nevertheless, the mythicalness is very much there, throughout the piece, there where it is to be absorbed almost by literary osmosis, slowly, ever so slowly, much of the time unnoticed. Perhaps there is no other artwork of man's creation that has so seduced those who have come into its presence.

The above said, permit me now to offer some suggestions regarding the reader's approach to the contents of the work at hand:

To the extent possible, the names of those figures and properties that appear in the *Ring* are presented in their German form, much as Wagner did in his drama. It is overwhelming to envision the confusion that would result if the variations of a given name that are to be found in each of the works consulted were used, not to mention the compound confusion that would come with the additional forms that arise because of linguistic or language needs. One would read a Siegfried as Sigfrid, Sigfrit, Sigurd, Sigurth, Seyfrid, Seufrid, Sifrid, Sifrith, and even Sivard! Of course, the original spelling of a name is presented when such is first used, but from then on, in most cases, the German spelling takes over.

It seems natural that in due time a reader may begin to skip about in this volume, stirred, stimulated, or otherwise moved by his own personal wants and wishes. So be it! A word of caution, however, Each entry is meant to be digested individually. That concept automatically infers that some mythical matters may be repeated elsewhere in other entries, perhaps more than once, in order that each may be understood completely. However, every attempt has been made to rearrange materials, to alter emphasis according to the primary matter under consideration, and on occasion to include an additional exclusive detail or two.

Included in the entries is a separate linguistic discussion of each proper noun that is found in the *Ring* drama. Many, perhaps most, of these presentations, which immediately follow the textual presentation concerning that figure or object, may not be mythical in and of themselves. However, it is only seldom that there is a name in the *Ring* whose linguistic history does not make some valuable, often vital, contribution to the whole that is the *drama*. Each of these linguistic presentations is indicated by the specific name as a title, followed by (Name).

At the termination of an entry a reader may see See: and/or See also:. The former is reference to an entry that serves in lieu of the topic title that it follows. The latter suggests entries that are related in one way or another to the topic title that they follow.

The names and titles of Wagner's sources are used repeatedly throughout this volume. In order to understand these sources more thoroughly, and thereby comprehend better certain matters in the entries of this volume, the reader is referred to Supplement B, "The Sources of the *Ring*," that is found in Volume I of this series.

A summary of the Teutonic world and its mythology and some specifics of that mythology are to be found in Supplements A and C of Volume I.

THE TEUTONIC MYTHOLOGY
OF
RICHARD WAGNER'S
THE RING OF THE NIBELUNG

Volume III
The Natural and Supernatural Worlds

Part 1

-A-

AIR   See: *Elements*

ALBERICH

The figure of Alberich in Wagner's *Ring* is a composite of the entire race of dwarfs that ranged throughout Teutonic mythology. Wagner formed the basic characterization of this supernatural around the Alberich that is found in the celebrated German epic *Nibelungenlied*. The Alberich in this work is a dwarf who is the guardian of a treasure of gold that belongs to King Nibelung. When the king dies, the treasure, which is stored deep in a mountain, goes to his two sons, Schilbung and Nibelung, who in turn later lose it to Siegfried.

Alberich's role in the German poem is really most secondary. He serves as warder of the hoard, yet he is forced to serve as a vassal to Siegfried when the latter takes the treasure as his. At such time as Siegfried became owner of the gold, Alberich was also forced to give over to the hero a whip of gold that had seven heavy balls at its end, and the *tarnkappe*, the cloak of invisibility that Siegfried will later wear as he lends his aid to Gunther. The only description of the dwarf that the poem includes is that Alberich is a "wild" dwarf and that he has a beard.

The physical aspects that Alberich has in the *Ring* are essentially those of the dwarfs in the mythical world of the early Teutonic peoples. He lived in the bowels of the earth, and came to the surface of the earth only when the sun was not shining. (Dwarfs were turned to stone by the rays of the sun.) It is for this reason that Wagner's dwarf is called *Nacht-Alberich*, or Night Alberich. In the drama as in the mythical tales, Alberich is a dwarf whose foremost trait was that of a craftsman in precious metals. Like the mythical dwarfs, he is short of stature, ugly, foul, and a hairy imp whose back is humped. He is very much like the Black Dwarfs of Teutondom whose skin becomes a ghostly grey, or even black, from the soot and smoke that dominates their home underground.

If Wagner took the name of his dwarf from an epic poem and if he gave his figure the form of the dwarf of the Germanic myths, there is no doubt that he was influenced if not inspired for much of his argument by a single mythical poem that has a dwarf as a principal figure. The poem is titled "Reginsmol" ("The Ballad of Regin"), and much of its story will ring familiar to followers of Wagner's *Ring*.

Wotan (Odin), the god Hoenir, and Loge (Loki) are on a journey. The trio arrives at Andvari's waterfall which is located in the mythical world of the dark or black dwarfs, Svartalfaheim, and in which there are many fish. Andvari, who is a dwarf and the son of Oin, was forced to take the form of a pike and to live in the waterfall by an evil Norn. Andvari guards a great treasure of gold that lies deep in the water. (This treasure was originally the Nibelung treasure that is a factor in the German poem *Nibelungenlied*. As the tale made its way into the Nordic regions of Teutondom, Alberich the dwarf became Andvari the dwarf, and the gold became the latter's property, and had its home in Andvari's waterfall.)

One of the nearby residents was Hreidmar, whose three sons were Otr, Regin, and Fafner (Fafnir). Otr often went to Andvari's waterfall where he would take the form of an otter, catch a salmon, and sit on the bank to each his catch. Otr always ate with his eyes closed so that he would not see his food diminish in quantity. Otr had gone to the waterfall this day and as he sat on the bank, eating his fish and with his eyes closed, he was unaware of the three travelers who were approaching. When the trio neared the greedy Otr, Loge picked up a stone and threw it at Otr. The stone hit its mark and Otr was killed. Wotan thought that what Loge had done would bring good luck and so the trio skinned Otr.

That night the three travelers sought lodging with Hreidmar, to whom they showed their booty. When Hreidmar saw the skin of his son he went into a rage. He immediately seized the three travelers and declared that their ransom would be enough gold to fill his son's skin and to cover him from sight. The gods sent Loge to the waterfall where the cunning Loge fashioned a net and caught the dwarf. Loge told Andvari that he would die unless he gave up the treasure of gold that was in the waterfall. The frightened Andvari did as he was ordered, but he held back a ring. This ring was known as *Andvaranaut* ("Andvari's Gem"). Loge saw what the transformed dwarf had done and demanded that he give up the ring or die. Andvari succumbed to Loge's demands, but as he turned the ring over to his captor he placed on it a curse of death and declared that no owner of the ring would ever know happiness.

The mythical tale continues. The gods took the gold that Loge had obtained from Andvari and stuffed Otr's skin and then placed the gold so that Otr was hidden from view. Hreidmar was called to looked at what the gods had done. Everything had been done correctly except that Hreidmar could see a single whisker on his son's face. Hreidmar demanded that the whisker be hidden. Wotan takes out Andvari's ring and covers Otr's whisker with it. Later, Hreidmar's son Fafner killed his father, stole the gold, and went to Gnitaheid where he transformed himself into a dragon in order to guard the gold. Ultimately, Siegfried (Sigurd) slays Fafner and takes the treasure for himself.

Wagner's Alberich is, of course, a separate and individual being of the *Ring*. His actions are all tempered to fit smoothly into the argument of the drama. Yet, Wagner's principal dwarf is very much a supernatural that is drawn from the mythical tales that formed much of ancient Germanic belief. The *Ring* Alberich's looks and his appearance, his temperament, and his nature, are all mirrored by the dwarfs that lived in the ancient past. It remained for Wagner to take the humble and most untoward figure of his culture's past and bring him to a prominence that placed him on a level with even the King of the Gods.

See also: *Alberich's Curse*
          Dwarfs

————————————

ALBERICH (Name)

The name *Alberich*, in terms of modern language, means literally "Elf King." Yet, the historicity of the term suggests a more extended meaning, one that supports more appropriately the mythicalness that Wagner gave to the figure in his drama.

Wagner took this name for the principal Nibelung dwarf of his *Ring* from that of the dwarf who is the guardian of the Nibelung treasure in the first part of the German national epic *Nibelungenlied* (*Song of the Nibelungs*). Wagner's choice of the name *Alberich* quite probably was the result of a consideration of the Nibelung dwarf in that story as well as his keen linguistic awareness of the mythological history of the prefix of the dwarf's name, *Alb*.

The prefix *Alb*, which was derived from ON *alfr* and which frequently is paired with the variant *Alp*, once denoted a happy, small figure who lived deep in the earth. This being, the *Alb*, became the *elf* of English and German folk culture (OE – *aelf*; MLG – *Alf*). In time, however, the Germanic society lost the concept of *elf*, and *Alb* took on the meaning of an evil, harmful figure, a being that was cunning, shrewd, and not to be trusted. This small, devilish character still lived in the bowels of the earth and was now famed as well as feared because of his bad or evil spirit. In time, this awesome creature, this *Alb*, became known as *Alp*, a variant that remains in the modern German language. The word *Alp* (and frequently the word *Alb*) translates in modern language as "nightmare" or "incubus," that harmful spirit that descends upon helpless women while they sleep. A compound form, *alpmännchen*, means "hobgoblin."

The development in English of the original Old Norse *alfr* was *aelf* in Old English, which became *elf* in modern language. As has been inferred, this separate development in English was accompanied by a meaning that was quite different from that of the Teutonic *Alb* and *Alp*. If a strict semantic application is applied, the name *Alberich* therefore translates as "Elf King," and perhaps such a name may be somewhat appropriate for the Alberich of Wagner's *Ring* because he is the 'king' of the Nibelung dwarfs. Yet, given the character and nature of that Alberich, and given the role he plays in Wagner's drama as well as the manner in which that role is carried out, perhaps the earlier semantics of *Alp* should apply, in which case the translation of "Evil King" becomes uppermost.

ALBERICH'S CURSE

The curse that Alberich the Nibelung dwarf makes is a dramatic moment in the final scene of *Das Rheingold*. This pronouncement of gloom, unrest, and ultimate death for all who come into possession of the ring that he had fashioned from the gold of the Rhine and which was stripped from him by Wotan, is one of the major dramaturgical elements of Wagner's tetralogy. As with much else in the *Ring*, the dramatist-composer found both the inspiration and the source of his curse in the mythical literature of the early Germanic culture as well as in the culture itself.

There is both a ring and a death-curse in a poem that is part of *The Poetic Edda*. The poem is titled "Reginsmol," which translates as "The Ballad of Regin," but which at times is called "The Tale of Otter." It is a treasure of gold, a ring, and a death-curse in the stanzas of this work that set into motion a series of events that Wagner was able to adapt to his version of the Siegfried story. This relatively short poem tells of Loge (Loki) who forcefully takes a hoard of gold from the dwarf Andvari who lives in a waterfall in the form of a pike fish. The treasure is to be used as ransom for the lives of two gods. When Loge discovers that Andvari has withheld a gold ring, he forces the dwarf to add it to the hoard. The angered dwarf then pronounces his vile curse. In *The Prose Edda* and in the *Volsungasaga*, in which four of the original stanzas are quoted, Andvari places the death-curse on the ring itself, as does Wagner's Alberich in the first drama of the tetralogy. In the Eddic poem, however, the death-curse is laid upon ten figures who, if not specifically named in a given stanza, ultimately die in the course of the tale: Regin and his brother Fafner (Fafnir), Siegfried (Sigurd), Gotthorm, Gunther (Gunnar), Hagen (Hogni), Attila (Atli), Erp, Sorli, and Hamder. Much like the path of the curse in Eddic poetry, Wagner's curse of death is not placed on a single being, yet it exercises itself on each and every being who comes into possession of the ring, and even upon those who covet the jewel: Fasolt and his brother Fafner, Siegfried, Brünnhilde, Mime, Gunther, Hagen, Wotan.

The laying or placement of a death curse did not hold great prominence in the mythical life of the early peoples of Teutondom. The belief in such curses, if not extensive, was essentially particular to the northern Germanics and did not appear in any substantial manner in the mythology of the continental people. However, if Wagner accepted this mythical feature for his own thematic ends, and expanded it into a continuous, inciting undercurrent that runs throughout his *Ring*, he was supported in his decision, at least indirectly, by a belief of rather secondary nature that was held by some of the tribes. This belief held that the dwarfs, the metalsmiths of the pagan world, were capable of putting a curse on weapons that they had made. The curse could be of any kind and was not restricted to one of death. The gold ring in Wagner's drama is not a weapon in the usual sense of the word, yet it was an object that was fashioned from metal and brought into existence by a dwarf who, in his turn, lays a curse on it.

The ring and its death-curse are primary to the development of the argument of Wagner's drama. As part of the aura that is attached to the evil magic of the ring, Wagner incorporated into his work three separate but essentially related ways by which the fatal curse could be removed. Each is a dramatic device of Wagner's creation, one that is not found in either the mythical literature or as a societal belief within the culture itself. This trio of possible releases is revealed in the last of the four *Ring* dramas (the first in order of composition), and each is disclosed by a different figure. In the third act of *Götterdämmerung*, Siegfried, who has become separated from his hunting party, encounters the Rhinemaidens. The nymphs tell him of the death that awaits the wearer of the ring, and they ask that he give it up, that he return it to them. They tell the hero that they will take the ring to the depths of the Rhine, whose waters alone can wash away the curse that has been placed upon it. The haughty hero gives little heed to the words of the three water spirits. In his fearlessness, Siegfried replies that if the Norns have woven such a strand, such a pronouncement into the Cord of Destiny, his sword, Notung, the sword that splintered Wotan's spear of authority, will sever that thread of fate.

It is Brünnhilde who tells of the third manner by which the curse of the ring may be erased. This revelation comes in the climactic scene that brings about the doom and downfall of the gods and the destruction of the universe. During Brünnhilde's lament for the slain Siegfried, she removes the ring from the hero's hand. She holds it high in order that the gods who sit in Valhalla can see it. She then offers it to the Rhinemaidens, telling them that the fire that is about to consume her and her beloved will cleanse the curse from the ring. She then adds that the three daughters of the Rhine may retrieve the ring and wash it pure with the waters of its home.

Alberich's curse in the drama of the *Ring* is really Andvari's curse in the *Edda*. In this sense, there is in the drama the mythical ambience that Wagner sought. It remained only for Wagner to shape his source in order that it have its place and its effect according to the needs of his argument. In this later sense there is the genius ability of Wagner's dramatic mind.

See also: *Curse*

ALTAR STONES

The stage directions that Wagner gave for the second act of the fourth drama of the *Ring*, *Götterdämmerung*, include among other things what are obviously *sacred stones*. There are three of these stones, one each dedicated to Wotan, Donner, and Fricka. Wagner's word for these stones is *Weihstein*, a word that is generally rendered in English as *altar stone*.

Wagner's use of altar stones for three of his gods was a dramatic replication of such stones, their functions, and their uses as they existed in the beliefs of ancient heathen Teutonic culture. In that early society, these stones, in the main, were more *consecrated* stones in that they were generally a part of a larger sacred place, usually a grove of trees within a forest. At times, sacrifices of animals were carried out on these stones if their size permitted such ritual. In the later years of Teutonic beliefs, images were carved into the stone, and eventually these stones were used to produce crudely carved statues of the gods. There is some historical evidence that prayers were offered to these stones and statues.

Wagner showed dramatic caution when he designated which of the five gods that appear in his *Ring* were to have altar stones in their honor. His selection of Wotan, Donner, and Fricka was made in order to manifest the divine stature and rank of these gods within the divine hierarchy that existed in Germanic thought. The size and the placement of these stones would reflect that intent. The stone that honored Wotan, the Allfather and King of the Gods, was to be larger than the others. This god's stone was to be located on a level that was higher than that of the stone dedicated to Fricka, wife of Wotan and Queen of the Gods. Such placement of these two stones symbolizes the greater authority and command that Wotan held in the divine world. It should be noted, however, that Wagner directed that the stone that was dedicated to Donner was to be placed at the side of that for Wotan. Such placement would be an indication that Donner was of equal divine rank as Wotan.

Over the years both the mythical literature as well as the practices of the people accorded to Wotan principal rank among the gods. Yet, there were certain occasions or situations in which Donner was looked upon as having equal divine status. Such occasions were related to the divine powers that the god had, forces that allowed him to reign over rain, lightning, and thunder. In some regions of the Teutonic world Donner's rank frequently superseded that of the great god Wotan. Such stature is noticeable in the later literature and, in religious terms, especially in Norway where Donner (Thor) was recognized as the dominant figure.

Wagner's exclusion of Froh and Freia, the two other gods in his drama, from his thoroughly mythical method of demonstrating divine rank and status was not because of any personal or secular reason or idea. The exclusion of this mythical brother and sister pair of deities was a dramatic necessity that had its source in the Germanic mythical history as revealed in the Eddic literature that served the composer as the primary source for his *Ring* argument. This literature states that in the primeval times of the

Teutonic peoples, there were two races of gods. One of these races was known as the *Aesir* and the other was the *Vanir*, occasionally referred to in English as the *Wanes*. The first named race of gods, which included Wotan, Donner and Fricka, was a warrior clan, and the latter was a race of gods of fertility that flourished in the region of the Baltic Sea, especially in Denmark and in Southern Sweden. According to mythical beliefs, these two divine races early on engaged in a great war against each other. This war, which was the first battle of the universe, became a struggle in which neither side could gain an outright victory. The two divine races finally agreed to a peace that would include the exchange of hostages. As part of that exchange, the Vanir gods gave over Froh and Freia, who then were accepted into the Aesir clan. Froh and Freia retained their godhood as gods of fertility, and they became principal gods of rank and status in Asgard, the land of the Aesir deities, even to the point of stimulating invocation and having a cult. Froh gained a considerable cult among the Scandinavian people, particularly among the Swedes, a cult that was similar in intensity and scope as that of Donner in Norway. Yet, the two gods were never thought of as true Aesir deities in the same sense in which Wotan and his divine colleagues were viewed as Aesir deities. These Aesir, with Wotan as the Supreme God, continued their dominance throughout the vast region of Teutondom, and especially so in continental Teutondom, which included Germany. In this southern region, Froh and Freia figured as gods, but deities of a lesser status than Wotan, Donner, and Fricka. Wagner was keenly aware of this hierarchy among the gods and his statement regarding the size and the location of the altar stones was obviously an accurate reflection of the mythical history of the ancient Germanic gods and their relative positions in the divine pantheon.

ANIMAL SACRIFICE See: *Sacrifice (Animal)*

ANIMALS

The matter of animals, both in Teutonic mythology and in Wagner's *Ring*, is one of primary importance. In the times of the early Teutons, animals held a significant place in the peoples' lives, and these people were on more familiar or intimate terms with the creatures that essentially surrounded them than are humans of the modern age. Likewise, those ancient peoples lived in what may be called a 'forest' society, primitive, even wild, and without the developments that would come as civilization made itself felt in the world. It is probably logical, then, to assume that the appearance and the role of animals within that early culture obviously was more to be expected than in modern times. It is then of little surface curiosity that *The Poetic Edda* is replete with references to animals, with the naming of animals, with use of animals in routine divine matters. At the same time, however, it may come as somewhat of a surprise to serious followers of Wagner's *Ring* to learn that the composer cites almost as many kinds of animals in his drama as are to be found in the Eddic literature, and in certain ways brings about the Germanic animal ambience much more persistently than does the Eddic writings.

A presentation, side by side, of the kinds of animals that appear in each of the works offers an interesting comparison:

Ring	*Edda*
Bear	Bear (Berserkers)
*Birds (General)	Birds (General)
Boar	Boar
-----	Cat
Deer	Deer
Dog	Dog
Dogs (Pack)	-----
*Dragon	Dragon
*Eagle	Eagle
Finch	-----

Fish (General)	Fish (General)
*Forest Bird	Forest Birds
Fox	Fox
Goat	Goat
-----	Hawk
*Horse	Horse
-----	Pike
-----	Salmon
Ram	(Sheep)
*Raven	Raven
-----	Rooster
Serpent	Serpent
Sheep	Sheep
Steer	-----
-----	Squirrel
Toad	-----
*Wolf	Wolf

It is interesting to note that the variety of animals in both works is not limited. Of equal interest is the fact that those animals before whose name there is an asterisk are animals that Wagner used in his drama in a fashion that duplicates identically or almost identically the use to which that animal is put in the *Edda*.

It is not necessary to present in detail the data that is available in the two works about each and every animal that appears in the listings. Those that are of primary importance will receive the necessary treatment and consideration in their own right elsewhere. Suffice to offer here a few select pairs of lesser creatures to demonstrate how aware Wagner was of the need to fill his drama with the matter of animals and that at times it would be to his advantage to take an animal and its functions from mythical beliefs, and bring that animal and as much of its function as possible into his drama.

The hound or dog is one of the creatures of mythical tales that makes its way into Wagner's drama. In a scene in *Siegfried* it is Alberich who tells his brother Mime that he would rather see the gold ring that they both covet so sincerely go to a mangy dog than to him! That single dog is a pack of dogs when the *Ring* argument relates the tale of Siegmund and Sieglinde. It is in the first act of *Die Walküre*, that the fleeing Siegmund tells of his plight to Sieglinde. He says that he was chased by a pack of dogs. In the following act, as Siegmund and Sieglinde flee Hunding, it is Sieglinde who says that she hears the bay of the dogs that are tracing them. Then, as Hunding closes in on the couple, he shouts that the pack of dogs will down the Volsung!

Wagner's use of the dog is singular to his *Ring*. There is no similar appearance or function of dogs in mythical literature. The dog, however, is found in that literature, and the fact that these animals are given names in the mythical tales indicates that their existence is something more than mere routine. There are two dogs that stand in front of Wotan's Hall, which would be his dwelling Valaskjolf ("Shelf of the Slain"). These dogs are named Gif ("Greedy") and Geri ("Avaricious"). A third dog that makes its way into the mythical thought of the early Teutonic peoples in Garm, the hound that guards the gates at Hel's kingdom in the underworld. It is Garm's loud bark that is heard as *ragnarök*, the fated destruction of the world, begins.

One mythical creature that Wagner deemed necessary to his drama was the *serpent*. He brings that creature into his work in *Das Rheingold*, in the scene in which the dwarf Alberich demonstrates to Wotan and Loge that the Tarnhelm allows him to transform himself into whatever form he chooses. Then, as the two look somewhat in wonderment at what is happening, the Nibelung changes himself into a "Riesen-Wurm," a "giant serpent." (Wagner uses the word *wurm*, which translates as 'worm' or 'grub' or 'maggot.' However, that same term, when used in a poetic sense, acquires the meaning of 'serpent' or 'snake.' Elsewhere, Wagner uses the term *Riesen-Schlange*, which can translate as "giant serpent.")

The concept of giant snakes or serpents was a prominent notion in early Teutonic thought. These serpents seemed to exist in all regions of the Teutonic mythical world, and they were always large, ugly and usually harmful to man. It was a common thought that these serpents could kill, and even eat mortals. The ancient Germanic myths makes reference to numerous serpents. In one Eddic poem Atli (Attila) orders that Gunnar (Gunther) be thrown into a pit of serpents. In a lay of the gods there are six serpents, all named, that gnaw on the twigs and branches of the World Ash Tree. These creatures are symbolic of the destruction that is rampant in the universe. There is also Nidhogg ("Dread Biter"), the giant serpent that lies beneath the World Ash Tree and eats away at the tree's root. This act, too, symbolizes the elements of destruction that exist in the world.

There is, however, another serpent that is without doubt the most renown and celebrated creature of all of Teutondom. This animal is *Jormungandr*, perhaps better known as *Midgardsorm* or "World Serpent." This monster was one of the three offspring of Loge (Loki) and the giantess Angrboda. The other two offspring were Hel and Fenrir, the wolf. When these three were born, the gods became aware of the danger that they signaled, of the real possibility that they could do harm to the gods. The deities met in council and decided that each of this trio should be sent far away from the land of the gods. Hel was sent down into the netherworld where she tended the dead. Fenrir was caught and bound with the famed necklace Gleipnir, and Jormungandr was tossed into the sea. In time, Jormungandr grew so large that his body circled the world and he could bite his own tale. It is because of his encirclement of the world that he became known as the World Serpent.

The serpent Midgardsorm had a role in the fated downfall of the gods and the destruction of the universe. It was this creature who fought Donner (Thor). In the combat, Donner slays Midgardsorm with his famed hammer, Mjollnir ("Crusher"). However, as the god walked away, the giant serpent drooled some poisoned spittle on him, and Donner fell dead as he took the ninth step.

The deer is a third of the lesser animals that are found in the *Ring* as well as in mythical literature. In Wagner's drama, it is Siegfried who makes reference to this animal. In the first scene of *Siegfried* the youth is desirous to learn about his father and his mother. He reminds Mime that even animals have mates and offspring, and that these creatures live together as families. He cites the deer as one such animal.

There are no less than five deer in the myths of Teutondom, and all are named! There are four, Dain, Dvalin, Duneyr, and Dyrathror, that nibble away at the leaves on the World Ash Tree. There is also Eikdyrnir

("The Oak Horned"), the animal whose antlers are compared to an oak tree, the deer that stands by Wotan's dwelling, eating the leaves of the tree Laerad.

It would seem that Wagner's mind was not only well aware of the matter of the animals in myth, but also well versed in the kinds and their respective functions. As he brought much of the mythical creatures of old into his drama, he was not necessarily intent on absolute duplication. Such duplication was essentially impossible because of the thematic differences between the *Edda* and the argument that was developing in his mind. What was evident to him was the fundamental need to bring about an argument which, if not totally awash in animals, was nevertheless an argument that presented a society that was closely associated with animals, a tale that made animals almost as natural in their existence as were the mortals and the supernaturals. The drama that was ultimately realized out of these thoughts is clear and obvious evidence that he was capable of such work and, of equal importance, the drama also reveals that he was always obedient to the ancient concepts regarding animals, and respectful of the numbers as well as the kinds and the functions that flourished within that societal mind of long ago.

See also: *Sacrifice (Animal)*

ANVIL

The stage setting of the first act of *Siegfried* is dominated by a large forge and the necessary anvil upon which the forging of the metal is accomplished. As the act comes to an end, Siegfried the Volsung has taken the two pieces of his father's sword that he has forced from Mime and has begun to reforge them into a sword for himself. As the frenzied dwarf watches, Siegfried works diligently and feverishly on the sword that his father, Siegmund, had named *Notung* ("Child of Need" or "Child born of Need"), the sword that Mime was unable to reforge. In due time, Siegfried finishes the sword and in his moment of triumph, he shouts at Mime to look at the sword, to see how the new sword cuts. With those words he brings the new sword down sharply on the anvil. The sword is so strong and so sharp that the anvil is split into two pieces! Wagner took the action for his scene of Siegfried, the sword, and the anvil from the Teutonic myths. In a poem titled "Reginsmol" ("The Ballad of Regin") that is found in *The Poetic Edda*, Regin ("Counsel-Giver") is a guide and companion to Siegfried (Sigurd). He is the son of Hreidmar and brother of Fafner (Fafnir). (Regin is described in some of these early myths as an intelligent and cunning dwarf.) Regin made a sword that was named Gram ("Wrath") which he gave to Siegfried. When Siegfried tried the sword for its sharpness and strength, he "cleft asunder Regin's anvil." There is a similar scene in *Volsungasaga*, another of the sources for his *Ring* argument that Wagner consulted.

The scene of the reforging of a sword in *Thidrekssaga* is at once similar but also unique in its own way. The young Siegfried (Sigfrid) had grown to manhood as a fierce and unruly person. This same Siegfried had become better skilled at smithing than his mentor, Mimir. Once, he smote with such strength that he split the anvil in two, and he broke the tongs of the trade.

Wagner's scene in which Siegfried forges the sword and then splits the anvil with it is the composer's adaptation and blending of the actions that are found in two of his sources. The matter of Siegfried as a person capable of reforging a sword was taken directly from the saga that focuses on the deeds and adventures of Dietrich (Thidrek) of Bern, while the concept that the sword was sharp and strong is found in Eddic literature and in the *Saga of the Volsungs*, which is essentially a prose paraphrase of *The Poetic Edda*.

APPLES See: *Freia's Golden Apples* (Vol. I)

ASH (Tree) See: *The World Ash Tree* (Vol. I)

BEAR

The early Germanic peoples viewed the bear as the king of beasts, king not so much as a beast of royal bearing, but rather as the most forceful, the most powerful of animals. The bear was considered to be the most savage of all animals, yet the people also believed that this animal was endowed with a certain rationale, a special power that caused that society to look upon the creature with definite awe as well as dutiful respect. The kindred clans and tribes of ancient Teutonic peoples did not consider the bear to be a sacred animal and it had no cult, but this creature nurtured a kind of worship principally because of the fear that it instilled. There were few persons who would purposefully stand to fight against a bear because it was believed that this animal ate humans, and when it became riled it was a ferocious monster of death and destruction.

The concepts about the bear that the ancient heathen society had held for a long period of time were, in turn, also associated with certain warriors. It was not unusual for warriors who were about to go into battle to work themselves into a state of frenzied emotion. Over a period of time these warriors could become so maddened that their actions were uncontrollable. They became incoherent. They howled like wild animals. Quite often their eyes reeled back in their heads, and they frequently foamed at the mouth. It was believed that these raging warriors were invulnerable to weapons, and because of that belief they entered battle quickly and fought relentlessly and wildly. This agitated and explosive physical and mental condition came about because, as the people believed, these warriors had changed themselves, inwardly at least, into bears! Evidence of the scope and intensity of this belief is found in the words that were used to refer to these warriors, *bjorn serkr*. Those Old Norse terms translated as "bear shirt" and the merged words remain in modern English as *berserker*.

Despite the fact that the bear was an animal much to be avoided, the people also had good reason to seek it out. There was no religious association with this creature, and it was not an animal that was a part of any ritual or sacrifice, yet in its own way, the bear held a kind of power over the people. It was believed throughout Teutondom that the bear could be involved in good or evil, and could be instrumental in the affliction of that good or evil upon some person. According to the beliefs of the ancient peoples, the bear was a creature on whose feet runes could be written! The Germanic runes were certain charms which, when 'worked' properly, were thought to bring about some predetermined end. These runes were very special to the Teutonic peoples. Since one part of a rune was its own unique mark, that mark had to be inscribed, often carved, on something before the rune could be effective. Those places on which it was deemed possible to place runes were locations that for one reason or another had some special meaning or value within the Teutonic scheme of things. The feet of a bear were just such appropriate place for inscription of the runes of Teutondom!

Wagner fused the majority of the early Teutonic concepts of the bear into the argument of his *Ring*. His method was sometimes subtle, but the results were always accurate. In the opening scene of the second drama of the *Ring*, Siegmund strays into Hunding's dwelling. Exhausted, he falls to the floor, as Wagner's stage directions indicate, onto a bear skin. This item suggests the manliness, the fearlessness of the hunter and slayer of this animal. Of course, the item clearly indicates that Hunding is that hunter. The bear is again a factor in the *Ring*, this time in *Siegfried*. In the opening scene of that drama Mime laments his inability to forge the pieces of the sword Notung into a new weapon. As the dwarf whines about his misfortune, Siegfried enters their cave, leading a live bear that he has caught in the forest. Mime is frightened by the animal, and he attempts to hide. Siegfried declares that the bear is a better companion to him than the dwarf. When Siegfried finds interest in other matters, he sets the animal free and sends him scurrying into the woods. This short scene was probably inspired by a scene in the German national epic *Nibelungenlied* (*Song of the Nibelungs*) in which Siegfried captures a bear and then frees it among the men of a hunting party. It would seem that Wagner had two objectives in mind when he wrote these activities into his drama. The capture and binding of a live bear obviously demonstrates the fearlessness, and perhaps the strength, of the hero. At the same time, the appearance of this animal as a stated property item suggests the existence of popular attitudes about the bear while also equating those attitudes with the black qualities of Mime's nature.

Wagner included references to the bear in two additional scenes of his tetralogy. In the second act of the third drama, Siegfried plays his reed pipe in a vain attempt to communicate with a bird. The disheartened hero then says that he is better at blowing his horn than he is at blowing the reed pipe, even though the only thing that act can attract is a bear or a wolf! The obvious sense of aversion for the bear that is apparent in the scene in Mime's cave is echoed, again by the Volsung hero, in the last of the four dramas of the *Ring*. Siegfried has become separated from his hunting party, and the furry creature that he had captured has escaped. The youth then encounters the three Rhinemaidens who implore the Volsung to give the ring to them, promising in return the creature that he had captured. Siegfried asks why should he do as they request. Why, he wonders, should he exchange the ring, for which he fought and slew a dragon, for the worthless prize of bear paws? If Siegfried considers the paws of a bear a worthless prize, his mention of them does bring to mind the matter of runes and magic that can be worked by one who knows the necessary secrets. Siegfried obviously is not the one who has that supernatural knowledge.

Each of the several references to the bear that Wagner has written into his *Ring* drama mirrors in one way or another one of the prevalent mythical concepts that the early Teutonic peoples associated with this animal. These bits of dramatic action, in their totality, are not only a reflection of certain aspects of the ancient culture, but they also give accurate evidence of the prominence of the animal in that society. Wagner's references to the bear are essentially inconsequential in the thematic development of his drama. This animal is in no way associated with the larger matters of the work. Yet, nevertheless, these relatively minor actions contribute effectively to the composer's intent to include in his work the flavor, the atmosphere, the sense of the authentic Germanic past. The *bear* in Wagner's *Ring* is no stranger in early Teutonic culture, and neither is it loosely used in the drama.

See also: *Animals*
      Sacrifice (Animal)

BIRD (Waldvogel) See: *Woodbird*

BIRD LANGUAGE

Cultural beliefs of the early Teutonic peoples held that all of nature, plants and trees as well as animals, had *life* much in the manner that humans had life. These beliefs held further that as a part of that life all creatures, small and large, were able to understand human speech, and plants and trees were capable of knowing physical sensations. If, however, animals understood the speech of humans, it was only certain mortals who were gifted with the power to understand the language of animals and birds. Many of the accounts of such incidents that are included in the principal codices and manuscripts of the age, as well as those that were part of the oral tradition, indicate that this gift could be obtained only by eating some special food, most often a certain species of white snake!

There is a Eddic poem that tells of the warrior Kon who had learned "bird chatter" and was able to communicate with a crow. In another poem of *The Poetic Edda* young Atli, a messenger and servant to Hjorvard ("Sword Guardian"), King of Norway, had learned bird language, and once, while on a mission for his master, he carried on a conversation with a bird. (The verses do not specify a species.) There is also an Eddic statement that Guthrun (Gutrune) came to understand the language of birds! Most scholars of the myths agree, however, that the statement is really an incorrect one that was placed in a margin of the Eddic manuscript at some time in the distant past by some unknown annotator.

The most celebrated episode that depicts the matter of an individual who comes to understand the language of the birds is that in which the hero Siegfried is the principal focus. This tale is that in which he meets and eventually slays the dragon and which is a story that Wagner sensed would be integral to his *Ring* drama. There is a version of this facet of the Siegfried legend that is to be found in each of the major literary works that were written or compiled in the middle medieval period (900-1400) of the Teutonic peoples. These works include: *Nibelungenlied (Song of the Nibelungs)*, *The Poetic Edda*, *Thidrekssaga (The Wilkina Saga)*, *Volsungasaga (Saga of the Volsungs)*, and *The Prose Edda*. Wagner consulted each of the aforementioned works, except *The Prose Edda*, as he developed his story which, like each of the others, is unique. The modifications that Wagner made are minor, yet his final version complements most appropriately the thematic development of his story of the gods.

See also: *Woodbird*

BLACK DWARFS See: *Dwarfs*

BLOOD

Despite the dramatic primitiveness that permeates the *Ring*, an ambience that Wagner intended for his drama, there is little of the carnage and gore of battle and combat that is regularly associated with such a background. Massive slaughter is not a factor in the drama, and an effusion of blood seldom has any a relationship to death and dying. Rather, in both the *Ring*, as well as in the several works that served the composer as sources for his poem, there are few situations in which blood is a factor, and even then, the blood that plays a role usually has none of the baseness that can so easily be associated with it.

Wagner's *Ring* has but one scene in which blood is of significant import. The single scene develops in the first act of *Götterdämmerung*, at that time when Siegfried the Volsung and Gunther the Gibichung will swear an oath to be true to each other. The drugged Siegfried and Gunther agree that Siegfried will use the Tarnhelm to disguise himself as Gunther, and will go to the fire-girded mountain to bring back Brünnhilde as Gunther's bride. For his services, Siegfried is to have Gunther's sister, Gutrune, as bride. To seal the agreement, the two take an oath, an oath of blood-brotherhood.

The oath of blood-brotherhood apparently had a certain standard ritual in early Teutonic society, one that Wagner had encountered in *Volsungasaga* (*Saga of the Volsungs*), and an action that he attempted to replicate in his drama. The stage directions of the *Ring* state that Hagen is to pour wine into a drinking horn. Then, individually, Siegfried and Gunther each is to prick his arm with his sword, and then to hold the arm over the horn in order that a drop of blood from each of the arms may co-mingle and mix into the wine. Each of the pair then lays two fingers on the horn, two being the number of persons involved. Each takes his oath of fidelity to the other, and in his turn, drinks from the horn. After each has drunk, Hagen breaks the horn in two, a symbol of the sanctity of the oath itself and also to indicate that no other oath may be taken on that horn. (The consumption of blood was not an exceptional ritual among the Germanics. It was a frequent and common practice to mix the blood of an animal that had been killed, especially one that had been sacrificed, with the flesh of that same animal, and then to consume that result. Both celebrants and witnesses participated in such a practice. The sacrifice of animals terminated with the advent of Christianity, yet the preparation of such dishes continued to be prepared and consumed by the Teutonic peoples. The preparation and consumption of such dishes continues in the modern Germanic world of today.)

Wagner had the *Saga of the Volsungs* as a guide in the matter of an oath of blood-brotherhood. Although there is no similar rite depicted in *Nibelungenlied*, the German national epic that frequently goaded the composer as he composed his poem, there is in that work a scene that may be looked upon as one that can be associated, if only indirectly, with the scene of Siegfried and Gunther.

Grimhild (Kriemhild) has mourned the death of her husband Siegfried for thirteen years. She then accepts Attila's (Etzel) invitation to marry. She accepted that proposal because she imagined that it would be easier as Attila's wife to take revenge on those who had slain her hsuband, that is, Hagen who had done the actual killing and her brother Gunther who had been a part of the plan. At the end of thirteen years of that marriage, Grimhild finally devises a plan to avenge Siegfried's death. She convinces her husband that the Burgundians should be invited to visit Hunland and the Huns. The Burgundians and the Huns have been enemies for some time, and Hagen and Gunther hesitate to accept the invitation. In the end, however, they cautiously agree to make the journey. Once the Burgundians are in Hunland they are invited to come into Attila's Great Hall. Secretly, Attila has ordered 20,000 of his warriors to enter the hall and slay the startled men. The soldiers would prefer to fight in the open, but Grimhild refuses their request because she believes that the Huns would lose such a battle. Grimhild then orders the Hall set afire, and soon a huge conflagration is raging all about and from which few can escape. Only 600 Burgundians will survive. However, the soldiers of Hagen and Gunther fight as best they can in the seething, searing flames, but all realize that they have been entrapped. The men become desperate as they fight. Soon, their strength has been sapped and they have great thirst. At this point, Hagen tells his men to drink the blood of their comrades, that this blood will not only quench their thirst, but will also give them renewed strength because this is the blood of brave and valiant warriors!

The scene in *Nibelungenlied* that features blood is very much different than the scene of the *Ring* that has blood as one of its dramatic components. Yet, if the matter of setting and actions can be momentarily stalled, and if the idea of thematic argument is temporarily removed, the overall concept of *blood* is essentially the same in both scenes. Blood is not a sign of violence, and it is not a symbol for wanton carnage or unwarranted physical violence and death. Rather, blood represents a kind of nobility, a specific and definite moral aspect of mortal life. The blood in both these situations is a symbol of human vitality, a symbol of the basic and fundamental factor of life itself. In the case of the *Ring*, Wagner knew what blood and the oath signified in the ancient culture, and he brought all elements together into a situation that was paramount to the theme and drama of his poem and, in the end, another demonstration of his keen understanding of early Germanic society.

See also: *Altar Stones*
        Oaths

BOAR

The boar, as a thematic property, is found on two occasions in the *Ring*. Those two appearances in the drama, however, illustrate Wagner's thorough knowledge of early Teutonic culture, and also his awareness of the extensive repute that this animal had generated in that society. In addition, by means of the two appearances of the boar, the composer was able to enhance, if subtly, the totality of the Teutonic mythical ambience that he wished his drama to have.

The heathen people of ancient Teutondom looked upon the boar as a sacred animal. It was the animal that was associated with the god Froh. This animal was named Gullinbursti (Gold Bristle), and was one of the finest creations of the metalsmith dwarfs who had forged the animal in such a way that the gold bristles on the his skin lighted up the night as if it were day. The association of the boar and the god Froh was a most natural one. Froh was the mythical God of the Fields and the warder of the fertility of the land, and it was from the boar and its constant rooting in the earth that the people had learned both the skill and the benefit of plowing, an action that allowed the god to work his magic. Thus it was that both the god and the boar that had much to do with the crops, their harvest and their abundance.

The boar was regularly and frequently consecrated in the ritual of sacrifice. It was an animal that met the two basic and fundamental requirements that were necessary in order to permit such action: It had some form of association with the divine world, and its flesh was edible. (The blood of swine was regularly an ingredient in the 'magic potions' that the *volva* or prophetess prepared.) Among the people themselves, on each New Year's Eve, the holiest day of the heathen Teutonic year, a boar was slain and prepared as part of a sumptuous meal. Before the animal was consumed, the god Froh was invoked while the participants laid their hands on the animal's body as a vow and a pledge of loyalty to their divine leader.

The sacredness of the boar is also evidenced in the Eddic poetry as well as in cultural practice. It is this animal's flesh that is considered as the only food that is worthy of the fallen heroes who have been raised and now reside in Valhalla. Each day the boar of the gods, Saehrimnir (The Blackened), is slain, after which he is prepared by the cook Andhrimnir (Sooty-Face) in a special caldron named Eldhrimnir (Fire-Sooty), and then served to the members of Wotan's army. Then, each night the animal is raised by divine powers in order that he may be offered again as food on the following day.

Wagner disregarded part of the mythical belief that concerned itself with a boar, but he also accepted another element that had to do with this animal. He was unconcerned about the boar as food, a consideration for which there was no significant regard in his drama. He accepted, however, the practice of the sacrifice of a boar and its consecration to the god Froh. This latter action takes place in *Götterdämmerung*, in that scene in which the wedding of Gunther and Brünnhilde is anticipated. It is Hagen who orders that animals be slain to honor the gods, to assure that their blessings will come to the marriage that is about to be realized. To reflect the concepts and beliefs as they had existed in the earliest of Teutonic times, Wagner caused his Hagen to order that a boar be slaughtered in honor of the god Froh, an act that was certain to bestow joy and happiness on the couple through the fertility that would now come to them.

If, in the Teutonic mythical mind, the boar was an animal of divine association, an animal worthy of sacrifice, and the food of celestial inhabitants, the boar was also known to be a wild and savage beast, the only untamed animal possessed by the gods. Mythic belief held that the boar was a regular participant in *The Furious Host* (*wütende heer*), that incredible phenomenon of a vast army of specters and ghostly spirits that swept through the skies in the black of night, creating a roaring, frightening din. (In the mythology, Wotan was the leader of this army, a factor that Wagner acknowledges in his drama when, on two occasions, the Supreme God is called "Heervater" or "Father of the Host.") A facet of this phenomenon was to be found in the belief that Froh's boar could run through the air and over water faster than a horse, and when he raced across the sky the wheels of the chariot made a noise so loud that it could be heard by all below on earth.

Wagner made every attempt to interpolate the several mythical concepts of the nature and the character of the boar into a thematic device that accounted for the death of Seigfried. He fused the violent, fierce, and savage attributes of this creature with its respected rank as an animal of the gods, and he then associated that animal with the greatest of heroes. Thus it is that in the last of his four dramas, Wagner causes Hagen to state that the planned death of the Volsung could be reported as the result of a frenzied charge of a wild boar. Then, in the final act of his lengthy poem, after Hagen himself has slain the Siegfried, Wagner has the murderer announce that indeed the hero has been killed by a wild boar. This representation, adopted from a similar presentation that Wagner had found in *Thidrekssaga*, is an acceptable dramatic expedient because it pictures an action by a beast thoroughly capable of rendering death, yet an act realized by an animal that is a part of the divine world upon the greatest of heroes, a mortal who in mythical eyes could never die ignominiously.

There can be no doubt that the boar is a relatively inconsequential, even inconspicuous element in the full and complete dramatic order of the *Ring*. However, the subtle references in the drama to this animal are of such nature that they parallel the Germanic mythical concepts that focus on it and, at the same time, provide evidence of Wagner's serious intent to render as accurate a mythical portrait of the pagan culture as possible as he dramatized his story of Siegfried and the gold of the Rhine.

See also: *Animals*
　　　　 Sacrifice (Animal)

BRAUNER

Braun, correctly declined as *Brauner* (*Die Walküre,* Act III, Scene 1), is used as a name for the horse that belongs to the Valkyrie Helmwige.

See also: *Horses*

BRAUNER (Name)

The word *Braun,* which Wagner declined correctly in his text (*Die Walküre,* Act III, Scene 1), means *brown,* or perhaps in this case, as the name of an animal, *Brownie.*

BRIDGE See: *The Rainbow Bridge* (Vol. I)

BRÜNNHILDE

The name Brünnhilde, which has several different spellings, like that of Siegfried, is one of the most celebrated names in all of Germanic literature. This name means literally "Warrior Maid in Mail Coat," and the *Volsungasaga* (*Saga of the Volsungs*) states that she was called Brünnhilde because she always traveled with her helmet and bryny and eagerly went into battle. She is, nevertheless, a prominent and principal figure in the celebrated Siegfried legend that originated in the region of the Danube in southern Germany and steadily made its way north, through all of ancient Teutondom, as far as Iceland. As this favorite story slowly traveled orally from person to person, from clan to clan, from tribe to tribe, it was only natural that it would be altered, modified, changed, or enhanced by the people who recited it. In time, the tale of Siegfried became quite varied, even disjointed, because of numerous versions that were both inaccurate and often incomplete when compared to the original. However, as a result of those decades, indeed centuries, of oral popularity throughout all of Teutondom, it was also inevitable that the tale eventually be put into writing. Hence it is that *The Poetic Edda*, the storehouse of Teutonic myths, contains one version of the tale and another is found in *Nibelungenlied* (*Song of the Nibelungs*), the national epic poem of Germany and the German people, both of which served as important sources for Wagner as he composed the argument of his *Ring*. These two versions, which are the principal ones that are available in the modern day, are at once the same story with the same characters and numerous similar actions, yet they are also versions that are quite distinct and different in several ways. These versions are known respectively as the northern, sometimes called the Nordic version, and the southern or South Germanic version. Remnants of the tale range from an almost complete story that is found in *Volsungasaga,,* to another that is far less than complete in *Thidrekssaga* (*Dietrich's Saga*).

Brünnhilde's role in the several works that are extant varies according to the whims of the people who gave it poetic substance. In the tale that was prominent in the northern region of Teutondom Brünnhilde is very much a human, the sister to Bekkhild, and Oddrun. In an even older version, she is sister to Atli, who is better known as Attila. These four are the children of Buthli. Bekkhild is the wife of Heimir, in whose home Brünnhilde lives. Despite this very mortal family, there is one Eddic poem that tells that Brünnhilde is so fearless a maid that her father once made her wear a helmet in order that she could become a "Wishmaiden." This is the first hint that Brünnhilde is really something other than mortal woman because a "Wishmaiden" in Nordic mythical thought was a Valkyrie, a supernatural being whose time was spent, at least in part, serving the warrior heroes in Valhalla in whatever their pleasure. In other Teutonic myths, Brünnhilde is not known as a Valkyrie but rather is identified as a *swan maiden*, one of those beautiful maidens who sits by the water's edge and lures unsuspecting men to their deaths.

There are other northern poems that reveal that there is a fair, rich maiden who sleeps in a hall that is completely surrounded by fire. This maiden, who is not named but who is identified in other verses as Brünnhilde, is called a "battle maid," a term that is frequently used to describe Valkyries. This maid sleeps on *Hindarfjoll* ("Mountain of the Red Deer") which is located deep in the forest known as *Skatalund* ("Warriors' Wood"). Still another poem, which identifies this maid as the daughter of Buthli, states that she sleeps not in a hall but on a rock. This as yet unnamed maid, whose horse is called *Vingskornir* ("Bringer of Victory"), was put into a deep sleep because she had disobeyed the Allfather Ygg, one of Wotan's many names.

The full story of the maid's sleep and her awakening can be pieced together by excerpts that are gleaned from several Eddic poems, one of which is more inclusive than all others. The poem in question is called "Sigrdrifumol," or "The Ballad of the Victory-Bringer." The principal figure throughout these verses is a Valkyrie who is called Sigrdrifa ("Victory-Bringer"). This term as used in this Eddic work, that is, *sigrdrifa*, is really an epithet for Brünnhilde that the unknown poet misused as a proper noun. Hence, when the word *Sigrdrifa* is used, it more properly should have been *Brünnhilde*.

According to the details of these stanzas, Ygg was made quite angry by an action of Sigrdrifa (Brünnhilde). The Allfather god had promised victory to an old but mighty warrior, King Hjalmgunnar, in his battle with King Agnar. When Agnar announced that he had no one who would shield him, Sigrdrifa came to Agnar's aid by slaying Hjalmgunnar. Wotan was furious and announced that Sigrdrifa must be punished for her act. The Allfather of Teutondom then pricked the Valkyrie with his sleep-thorn, an act that would cause her to fall into a deep sleep and also would take from her all of her supernatural powers and render her a mere mortal. Before Sigrdrifa closed her eyes in sleep, the supreme god spoke to her and told her that never again would she know victory in battle, and that one day she would awaken as a mortal who would become a bride to the man. Sigrdrifa responded by saying that she would never wed a mortal man who knew the meaning of fear, and Wotan then repeated those words!

In due time, Siegfried (Sigurd) comes to the spot where Sigrdrifa lies asleep. Siegfried had been told of the sleeping maid by a nuthatch. He believes that the person who lies before him is a man, but when he cuts away the breastplate he discovers that the figure is a woman. Siegfried awakens the sleeping figure who then elegantly greets the day and the sun. Siegfried sits beside the maid and asks her to give him wisdom. Sigrdrifa responds by revealing to the youth a lengthy series of charms, healing signs, good spells, and runes. Siegfried then vows his love and fidelity to Sigrdrifa who now offers him numerous counsels which end the poem.

In this northern version of the Siegfried theme there is a serious question as to when Brünnhilde and Siegfried exchanged their vows of love. The myths are forthright in their statement regarding this matter, but there are at least two versions of this single point. The original, that is, the southern version, has Siegfried as the guest of the Gibichungs (Gjukungs) before he has heard of Brünnhilde. The first time that he sees her is after he has changed forms with Gunther (Gunnar) and is to woo her on behalf of the Gibichung. (The myths state that Grimhild, the mother of Gunther and Gutrune, taught Siegfried and Gunther the "art" of transformation.) A second version of the initial meeting of Brünnhilde and Siegfried that became popular in the north reveals that the Volsung came to where the maid had been put to sleep, awakened her, after which he went to the Gibichungs. While with Gunther and Gutrune (Guthrun), their mother, Grimhild, gives Siegfried a magic draught which causes him to forget Brünnhilde and to desire Gutrune as a wife. So powerful is his desire that he agrees to go to Brünnhilde and to woo her for Gunther if he can have Gutrune as his bride. Another Eddic poem states that it was not a magic potion that worked its way on Siegfried, but rather that Grimhild "tricked" him into doing her bidding.

Siegfried's association with both Brünnhilde and Gutrune becomes another detail in the story that stimulates several northern versions. After the Volsung's sojourn with Brünnhilde, Gutrune reproaches her severely for having slept with the hero, and for so long a time. One verse puts the time that the two were together as eight nights, while another states that Brünnhilde and Siegfried slept together for three nights. It is Brünnhilde who says that the time she and Siegfried spent together was passed as if they were brother and sister, and yet another version tells how Siegfried placed his sword between them when they slept. However, when Brünnhilde learns of Siegfried's association with Gutrune, she is angered and declares that she has been betrayed. She berates Gutrune by saying, "May the witch now hope for husband and children...." In turn, Gutrune refers to Brünnhilde as "that woman ill...." Gutrune's brothers, Gunther (Gunnar), Hagen (Hogni), and her half brother Gotthorm, then seek revenge on Siegfried. They state that because Siegfried has been with Brünnhilde he has broken the oath that he had taken. It is Gotthorm who eventually slays the hero while he sleeps in his bed.

Brünnhilde is grieved by the death of Siegfried. One poem states that as she weeps in sorrow, she orders that eight thralls and five serving women be put to death in order that they may serve Siegfried in his afterlife. Then, in order to join the slain hero, Brünnhilde kills herself with her sword. A second Eddic poem states that after Siegfried's death, two pyres were made. Siegfried was burned on the first pyre and then Brünnhilde was placed in an elegant coach and went to her death in the flames of the second pyre. In her afterlife, Brünnhilde travels on her coach down Hell-Way, the road to Hell, where she meets and talks at length with a giantess. It is to this giantess that Brünnhilde vows that she and Siegfried will live together forever. (There is yet another Eddic verse that states, as does the version that is found in *Volsungasaga*, that Siegfried and Brünnhilde were burned together on the same pyre.)

The Southern or South Germanic version, that is, the original tale that originated in Germany and then traveled northward, is to be found in *Nibelungenlied*. This is the only wholly German work that Wagner used as a source for his argument of the *Ring*. The storyline of this epic poem, at least that part of the work that features Brünnhilde, is told in the first nineteen chapters of this national art work, the second part of which deals essentially with Siegfried's widow and her eventual revenge of her husband's murder.

In *Nibelungenlied*, Brünnhilde is a queen whose kingdom lies across the sea from the domain of King Gunther of Burgundy. Brünnhilde's land is called Isenland and she lives in a palace that is named Isenstein. Brünnhilde is a beautiful queen who is known both for her cruelty and for her amazon-like feats of strength. Many have been the suitors who have sought Brünnhilde's love, all of whom have lost their heads. It seems that it had been decreed that whoever sought the queen's love must defeat her in three distinct physical acts. These "games," as they were called, were hurling or tossing a heavy stone, leaping a great distance, and shooting or throwing the lance as if in combat. If the suitor had not bested Brünnhilde in these three feats, his head was severed from his body by the queen's soldiers.

King Gunther admired Queen Brünnhilde and decided that he must win her for himself. It is evident enough that Gunther would lose in the three contests that he would have to wage with Brünnhilde. At that point the princely Siegfried pledges to help Gunther if he can have Gunther's sister, Grimhild (Kriemhild), whom he much admires, as his bride. Siegfried says that he will travel as Gunther's servant in order that he will not be conspicuous and that the magic cloak that he took earlier from the dwarf Alberich will help him in his task. This cloak will give him the strength of twelve men and will also allow him to become invisible. Gunther agrees to the arrangement.

King Gunther and his entourage make the journey to Isenland. The necessary details are resolved and the time comes for Gunther to attempt to win out over Brünnhilde in the three acts of physical might. Siegfried has told Gunther that he will make himself invisible and will be at Gunther's side all the times. Gunther is only to go through the motions, to pretend that he is performing the actions, and Siegfried will actually perform the acts. Brünnhilde then calls for the great spear that is so heavy that it requires three men to carry it to the starting line. The queen picks up the spear, summons all her strength and hurls it at Gunther and the invisible Siegfried. The spear pierces the shield that Siegfried holds. Gunther then goes through the motions while Siegfried takes the spear and turns its blunt end toward Brünnhilde because he does not want to kill the queen. Siegfried then musters his strength and hurls the spear at Brünnhilde with such force that it strikes Brünnhilde's shield and knocks the queen to the ground. Gunther had won the first contest. The next feat was that of tossing the stone, a rock that weighs so much that twelve men are needed to lift it and place it before the two contestants. Brünnhilde lifts the stone and throws it a distance of seventy-two feet (twelve fathoms). Gunther then steps to the line and again, as he had done before, imitates the act of throwing the rock as the invisible Siegfried actually picks up the boulder and throws it farther than the queen' had done in her turn. The disturbed Brünnhilde then makes a great leap and lands well beyond the spot where her stone had hit the ground. The invisible Siegfried then gathers Gunther in his arms and takes a tremendous leap, landing well beyond Brünnhilde's mark. Gunther has defeated Queen Brünnhilde in the contests and the queen was now obliged to become his bride. However, she is unwilling to consummate the marriage until after they have reached Gunther's castle in Worms.

Siegfried and Grimhild take their wedding vows at the party that is held for Gunther and Brünnhilde. Brünnhilde is puzzled as to why a lady of the court like Grimhild would take a servant like Siegfried as a husband. The queen senses that she does not have all the information and so, that night, in the bridal chambers she tells Gunther that she will not lie with him until he tells her the entire story. When Gunther makes advances toward his bride, she rejects him and then binds him with a girdle and hangs him on a nail that is in the wall. Gunther then promises her that he will not touch her, at which Brünnhilde takes him from the wall and frees him. Later, Siegfried vows that he will help Gunther to overcome the maid, just as he had done in the three contests. Siegfried uses the magic cloak to become invisible. He then goes into Brünnhilde's chambers after Gunther had entered. With all the candles extinguished, Siegfried attempts to force himself upon Brünnhilde. She refuses again, and in the struggle she squeezes his hand so tightly that blood runs from beneath his fingernails, and then she hurls Siegfried across the room. Gunther can hear all that happens and he is concerned about the clamor that is raised. The invisible Siegfried becomes quite angry, and he summons all his strength to press the bride against the wall until she cries out in pain. Brünnhilde finally surrenders. Gunther is then left to his pleasures as Siegfried departs, taking with him a ring and a girdle.

Siegfried then travels with Grimhild to the Netherlands where his father, Siegmund, is king, and his mother, Sieglinde, is queen. Siegfried is made king and when Sieglinde dies, Grimhild becomes queen. Siegfried, Grimhild, and Siegmund are invited to visit King Gunther and Queen Brünnhilde in Burgundy. When Grimhild and Brünnhilde meet, a heated argument breaks out. Brünnhilde accuses Grimhild of having given herself to a bondsman, a servant. Grimhild then accuses Brünnhilde of having lost her virginity to Siegfried, and she then produces the ring and girdle that Siegfried had taken from Brünnhilde's room long ago. As Hagen then demands that Siegfried die because of his actions, Brünnhilde fades from the story of Siegfried as told in the *Nibelungenlied*. The remaining half of the work concerns itself with the murder of Siegfried by Hagen and the attempt of his widow Grimhild to avenge that death.

There can be no doubt that Brünnhilde is a major figure in the literature of both northern and southern Teutondom. There is, however, an odd and varied concept of her character, her duties and functions, and her relationships and associations in the writings of these two regions. There is no question, however, that Wagner turned to the Nordic myths for the essence of his Brünnhilde. She is the Valkyrie who was put into a deep sleep by the supreme god of Teutondom and who was awakened from that sleep by Siegfried, the man who knew no fear and the man to whom she then gives her divine wisdom. The Brünnhilde of the *Ring* is that Nordic figure who dies a self-death when her husband Siegfried is slain, a death by fire that will enable her to be with Siegfried forever in the afterlife.

A valid question arises immediately when the matter of Wagner's sources is laid beside the composer's stated objective in the composition of the *Ring* drama. Wagner stated that it was his desire to compose a truly national work of art, a drama that was thoroughly German in its entirety, a work that would develop the cultural facets of the German society, a work that would make known quite clearly the affirmative aspects of a proud German people. At the termination of the first *Ring* in Bayreuth in 1876,

Wagner made a stage appearance in his self-designed Festspielhaus, and at that time he reinforced what had been his earlier statements regarding a national work of art, that is, that he had now made his contribution to that end and what could the German society now do on its own behalf? The question that is now uppermost is, in effect, how Wagner could make such statements as he had when he had incorporated into his drama not the German version of the Siegfried legend, but rather the Nordic concepts, the Nordic figures, the Nordic actions. On the surface, it would seem that the only truly German aspects of his *Ring* are the names of the numerous players.

Wagner was very much aware of the internal as well as the external elements of his drama. If he had turned to the Nordic tales for the events, the situations, the various actions of his drama, it was because of the dramatic possibility that each of these tangible and outward elements offered. In each of these elements Wagner had found a quality that was important and needed when the matter of an argument for the stage was considered. What he had found in the wholly German work was something less tangible, less physical, less material, yet it was a quality that would make his work a truly German work. Wagner saw a reflection of the German people in *Nibelungenlied*. He saw the factors of honor and pride and dignity and moral strength. He saw valor and he saw loyalty. These were, in his mind, the elements that characterized the German people, and these would be the elements that he would include in his poem. These would be the elements that would make his work a national work of art. If Wagner went to northern Teutondom for the outward segments of his drama, it was in *Nibelungenlied* that he found the human substance that would broadcast to the world the fundamental structure of the German character.

See also: *Valkyries*

_____

BRÜNNHILDE (Name)

The early Germanic literature (Scandinavian and continental) contains several variations of this prominent name which, as is the case with numerous others of the *Ring*, is formed by the union of two separate words. The earliest of these names seems to be *Brynhild* or *Brynhilt* (bryn + hild). The prefix of this name, *bryn*, derives from ON *brynja* (OHG – *brunnia, brunia, brunna*; OE – *bryne*; Gothic – bruzjo; ME – *brynie, brinie*), which meant "corslet" or "mail-coat," a kind of armor that was made of connected metal links. (Some linguists attach the meaning of "shield" to this word, while others like to call it "breast plate.")

To some followers of the *Ring*, the word *hild* (see *Notes*) in the case of Brünnhilde, the Supreme God's favorite Valkyrie daughter, can only be translated as *Maiden*. However, both in the early literature and in Wagner's work she is very much a "warrior maid," hence a singular yet appropriate translation of this name is "Warrior Maid in Mail Coat."

BRÜNNHILDE'S ROCK

The setting for Act III of *Die Walküre*, as well as that of Act III, Scene 3 of *Siegfried* and that of the "Prelude" of *Götterdämmerung* is essentially one and the same. Wagner's directions call for "The Summit of a Rocky Mountain," surrounded by large rocks, and a forest to one side. The setting that the composer has designated for these several scenes is one that was considered by the early Germanic peoples to be a sacred part of nature, the kind of site that could, in some cases, be cause for veneration.

Large stones or rocks, especially those that were found on mountains and in forested regions, were often looked upon as objects that had a deep religious importance as well as significance. The hallowed attention that these peoples gave to large boulders was usually the result of a belief that a given site had some special or unique relationship with one of the gods. The people generally indicated the holiness of these rocks or boulders by giving each one the name of the god with whom it was associated. In later times, some of these boulders were named after the giants who had hurled them or who had lived upon them, after some divine or supernatural beings lesser than a god, after a hero, or even after another figure who had gained some prominence within the culture. These rocks did not have the sacredness or holiness of those that bore a god's name, but nevertheless they were physical manifestations of the respect, sometimes awe, in which the named figure was held.

There were two such rocks or boulders that are named in the Teutonic myths that have a relationship with matters that are found in Wagner's *Ring*. The first is called *Kriemhildenstein* or Grimhild's Rock. This boulder or huge stone was named after Grimhild (Kriemhild) who, in the southern or continental mythical version of the Siegfried story, is the wife of Siegfried, the woman who mourned the hero's death for many years and then sought revenge for his murder. (In the Nordic version of this tale, Grimhild is the mother of Gunther and Gutrune, and the latter is Siegfried's wife.) Wagner had no cause to consider this legendary rock and its name as part of his drama because he had placed the Grimhild of his *Ring* in a relationship different from that of wife of Siegfried, as was depicted in *Nibelungenlied*, the national epic poem of Germany. The Grimhild of the *Ring* is the mother of Gunther, Gutrune, and Hagen, but she is a figure who is named only and who has no role as part of the *dramatis personae*.

The second of this pair of boulders and the surrounding rocky area that bore a name and which was of interest to Wagner was that site on which Wotan (Odin) pricked Brünnhilde with a sleep-thorn, after which she fell into a deep sleep. This celebrated spot is known in the Teutonic myths as *Hindarfjoll* ("Mountain of the Red Deer"), and it is of such importance to Germanic mythical matters that the name of the forest in which it is located is also named, *Skatalund* ("Warriors' Wood").

The mountain site on which this mythical action took place was of much interest to Wagner because he was to include a similar if not identical action in his *Ring*. In his drama, the god Wotan was to kiss his daughter Brünnhilde into her deep sleep. Wagner was aware that the mythical site did not bear the Brünnhilde's name. Rather, it is named after animal of the forest. Wagner, however, was familiar enough with the myths of his culture to understand the importance of a name for this site, and he understood the process by which ancient names came into being. He also sensed that this site in his drama must have a name. Yet, a name like that found in the Eddic verses would be not only foreign to his drama, but it would also be very much a dramatic distraction in the development of his story. The composer followed his dramatic instincts and gave this site in nature not one, but two names.

The first of Wagner's two names for this setting in which Brünnhilde eventually is placed into her deep sleep is *Walkürenfelsen*, literally "Valkyrie Rock." Wagner's name is appropriate because the site first serves as the gathering place for the Valkyries as they rest on their return from the battlefield with their slain warriors, en route to their final destination, Valhalla. Later, when Wotan kisses his daughter into her sleep, and gently lays her down on that same rock, Wagner indicates that the rock is now *Brünnhildenstein*, or "Brünnhilde's Rock." It is here, to Brünnhilde's Rock that one day the fearless hero will come and awaken the former Valkyrie to mortal love.

Wagner's act of naming the rock in question is an action that follows Teutonic mythical practices. That he should devise a name other than that of the myths is a matter of dramatic adaptation. That he should give the same rock two of his own names is both dramatic adaptation and dramatic economy. His plan worked and mythology was no less the worse for that plan.

BRÜNNHILDE'S WISDOM

In the second scene of the "Prelude" of *Götterdämmerung*, Siegfried presents to Brünnhilde the ring that he had taken from the transformed Fafner. This ring, which was part of Alberich's treasure and which Siegfried took, along with the Tarnhelm, as reward for killing the dragon, is a pledge of his fidelity and an expression of his appreciation for the former Valkyrie's gift to him. That gift is, of course, the gift of her wisdom, that is, the wisdom with which she, as Wotan's favorite daughter, was divinely blessed. In his *Ring*, Wagner successfully conveys the idea that this *wisdom* is *divine knowledge*, that is, a knowledge that is derived from the holy runes of ancient Teutondom, a wisdom that is reserved for those of the divine world, and even there, only for certain of the divine beings. Yet, despite the importance of this wisdom, Wagner believed, and correctly so, that in his poem this wisdom must be essentially a generic wisdom because, as he reasoned, there was neither dramatic need nor emotional insistence that this wisdom receive a specific and detailed depiction.

Wagner, therefore, did not include in his *Ring* drama, either precisely or in any substantive way, the essence of Brünnhilde's wisdom. It remained merely *wisdom*, the light of Brünnhilde's love for Siegfried. Yet, it is most improbable that the composer was unaware of what that wisdom contained and of what it consisted. The total quality as well as the numerous elements of Brünnhilde's wisdom are laid out in the work that Wagner admitted was his primary source for both the story and the ambience of his drama *The Poetic Edda*. It was in that storehouse of Teutonic mythology that Wagner encountered a relatively short poem that obviously furnished him much of the framework for his final scene of *Siegfried*, and which also detailed the knowledge that is Brünnhilde's gift to the Volsung. This poem, which is untitled in the original manuscript, can rightfully be called "Ballad of Brünnhilde." There is in the Eddic work a prose introduction that tells of Siegfried's finding the sleeping maid on a fire-ringed mountain, his awakening her and, then, there follows in both prose and verse the story of her banishment by Wotan. After this segment of the tale, the former Valkyrie then brings to Siegfried a special drink, a drink in which there are charms and healing signs, as well as good spells and the runes of gladness. The charms, healing signs, and good spells are not described, but there are several stanzas, each of which conveys a specific rune, a special kind of magic that grants the power necessary to realize some unique and special end. It is these runes, in their totality, that become in part the gift that Brünnhilde gives to Siegfried.

The runes that Brünnhilde delivers to Siegfried, in the order that they are presented in the *Edda*, are as follows:

1. *Victory-runes*: That knowledge which, when accompanied by an invocation to the god Tyr, brings victory in battle. These runes are to be inscribed on the warrior's sword.

2. *Ale-runes*: These are the wisdom that prevent a drink, received from a host's wife, from bewitching the recipient. These runes are to be written on the drinking horn and on the backside of the hands.

3. *Need-runes*: These runes satisfy the need of a given moment or situation. These runes are to be written on the fingernails. (The runes use the term *Naut*, that is *Nôt* as in *Notung*, and their explanation obviously served Wagner in his dramatization of Siegmund's finding the sword in the hour of his greatest need.)

4. *Birth-runes*: These are runes that will assist anyone who lends aid to a mother at birthtime, as well as to the child that is born. These runes are to be written on the palms of the hands and on the joints, and the fates (Norns) are to be implored.

5. *Wave-runes*: These runes permit one to steer to safety a ship that has been caught at sea in a storm. These runes are to be engraved in the steering apparatus and on the oars of that ship.

6. *Branch-runes*: Sometime called *life-runes*, these runes give one the power to cure illness and to heal wounds. They are to be scratched into the bark of trees whose boughs bend toward the east. (It was believed that when these runes were cut into the bark, the illness or wound was transferred to the tree.)

7. *Speech-runes*: These are runes that allowed a speaker to communicate in such a manner that an adversary (listener) would not become angry or enraged.

8. *Thought-runes*: These are runes which permit the user to be considered intelligent and keen-minded.

There is yet more to the heavenly wisdom of the Valkyrie. In the stanzas that follow those in which the gift of the runes is made, Brünnhilde presents Siegfried with a series of counsels that are distinct from the runes in the kind of knowledge that is proferred, but which, nevertheless, are a part of her wisdom. It is now advice that Brünnhilde gives to Siegfried, counsel that will render him a stronger and better individual, a greater hero. Brünnhilde says to the Volsung:

1. Be free of any guilt or hatred against your kinsmen.

2. Never think of vengeance against those who have harmed you.

3. Be true to any oath that is taken.

4. Avoid a verbal battle with those who are fools with words. However, to remain silent for too long a period of time leads others to believe that you are a coward. Fame, to be retained, requires continuous action, but if you are taunted falsely because of your silence, kill the one who has harmed you.

5. Mingle little with wily strangers who may be witches who can dull your sword and your courage.

6. Beware of the charms of pretty maidens.

7. Avoid the words and company of those who have drunk too much.

8. Fight in full battle rather than remain at home to burn to death.

9. Avoid evil.

10. Shun liars.

11. Do not violate a maiden or another man's wife.

12. Cleanse and bury any corpse that you find.

13. Do not trust the family of anyone whom you have slain.

14. Shun the wrath and treachery of false friends.

The runes and the counsels that are given over to Siegfried represent, in sum and substance, the aggregate of Brünnhilde's wisdom. Over the years, the argument has been advanced that the work that contains this knowledge and wisdom of the Valkyrie is not a separate, single poem. Rather, it is proposed that the thirty-seven stanzas of this poem were, at one time, part of another poem, and that some of the oldest manuscripts of that poem has been lost, and further, that the several manuscripts that are extant are at variance with that original.

In addition to the questions about the origin and format of this Eddic piece, there are other matters that generate still more hesitations and doubts concerning the work. As a poem in and of itself, this work contains some rather bewildering internal elements. There is some confusion of names in the poem as it is usually presented, and several of the runes and counsels that are stated in its verses appear in similar form in other poems, posing a question of the work's originality. Indeed, there are some scholars of the mythology of Teutondom who maintain that the poem is not a single, individual work that has been handed down through the ages, but rather that it is really a compilation of several poetic fragments, some gathered from other poetic works, to which numerous interpolations have been attached. Despite the rather convincing evidence of the relatively regrettable form and manner of the work, there is no other Eddic poem so complete and thorough for the purpose of ascertaining the divine knowledge and wisdom of Brünnhilde.

It is interesting to note that this wisdom and knowledge that was part and parcel of Brünnhilde's nature was of more than passing interest to its early audiences. The anonymous compiler of the *Volsungasaga*, for example, thought it significant enough to incorporate into two chapters of his celebrated saga.

See also: *Charms*

Runes, Supplement C, (Vol. I)

-C-

CALLS (Horn) See: *Horn Calls*

CHARMS

In the regions that were inhabited by the ancient Teutonic peoples, the equivalent of the term *charms* designated a kind of magic that was somewhat more forceful than the magic that was known as *good spells*, but not nearly so grand and much less powerful than that of the *runes*. These charms, which existed throughout all of Teutondom and which were a part of the thought of all the Germanic clans and tribes, were a kind of magic that was supposed to bring about something pleasant to behold or enjoy, something attractive to the eye, fascinating to behold, or worthy of possession. These charms were, 'exercised' or 'worked' by means of song or chant. In time, these chants were symbolized by some kind of trinket or small ornament, an amulet that could be worn as part of a bracelet or necklace. These small objects, which became a part of almost every person's dress, were almost sacred in the minds of the heathen Teutonic peoples who believed most sincerely that there was a supernatural being always in or around the charms, a spirit that was always available to bring about the good luck or success or freedom from evil that the holder wished.

The Teutonic charms, along with runes, were part of the wisdom that the Eddic Sigrdrifa (Brünnhilde) gave to the hero Siegfried who broke through the circle of fire that surrounded her on the mountain top and who awakened her from her sleep. The Germanic myths do not elaborate upon the matter of the charms in Brünnhilde's gift, at least not in the same manner as they treated the runes. Much is made also of the gift of wisdom that the Brünnhilde of the *Ring* gives to her awakener, yet in this situation little specific is known about this gift because Wagner offers no details, not even a referral to the magic runes. Wagner's 'divine wisdom' is really generic wisdom. However, Wagner has demonstrated frequently his keen knowledge of the Teutonic myths, a knowledge that is supported by a deep understanding of the societal concepts that were part of that early culture, and it seems apparent that charms were part of that generic gift.

Fortunately, the myths are more specific in the matter of charms, at least when the principal figure is Wotan. An Eddic myth states that Wotan knew eighteen charms, all of which were sung or chanted. The myths do not reveal any of the songs, but the specific result of each charm is always offered. If the appropriate charm were sung correctly, for example, the supreme god would always have a calm sea for his boat, or the curse of a dead woman could not do him harm, or wit and words were always his when he needed them.

The matter of lack of charms in the *Ring* is of no significant concern, either thematically or dramatically. These bits of mythical lore do not constitute an important segment of the divine wisdom of the gods of Wagner's drama, and they were but a lesser aspect of the mythical Brünnhilde's gift to the Volsung. These charms are, nevertheless, a part of that mythical divine wisdom, and the song or chant that causes them to be operative and the result that was realized are integral to the totality of early Teutonic thought. Indeed, Wagner omitted them from his drama, but his omission was intentional, and obviously correct in that the magic of the charms was slight and somewhat superficial, whereas the magic that he was to bring into the *Ring* was to be of cosmic proportions, a magic that would even allow the possessor of a ring to govern the entire world.

See also: *Brünnhilde's Wisdom*

CLOAK (Wotan's)

The mythical Wotan was known not only for the numerous journeys that he made about the universe, but also the manner in which he disguised himself to avoid recognition while on these journeys. To complement his distinct guises and to conceal even more his identity, the god often took on a byname that described or depicted in some manner an aspect of his disguise. One such byname of the god was *Baleyg*, which translates as "The Flaming Eyed" and which makes reference to the god's remaining eye. Wotan had given his other eye to Mimir, the guardian of the Spring of Wisdom for a drink of those celebrated waters. Another of Wotan's many bynames was *Harbard* or "Greybeard," which of course referred to the grey hairs of the beard that the god had grown. A third descriptive name of the god was *Sidhott*, which means "Broad Hat," a term that refers to the broad-brimmed hat that Wotan frequently wore as he wandered about the universe, a hat that he tilted downward in order to hide his missing eye.

Wagner was obviously attracted to the mythical concept of the frequent travel of Teutondom's major deity. It seemed to be a mythical factor that he could bring into his *Ring* drama, provided, of course, that it enhanced the argument, and that it caused no distraction from other, more important thematic matters. Wagner found that scene of his drama in which he could bring his Wotan down from his celestial heights, down to earth, and then cause the action that he would write into his poem to be of a consequential nature. The scene in which Wagner made his dramatic move in the direction of a disguised Supreme God came in the first act of *Siegfried*, when the god enters Mime's cave, in which he soon engages the Nibelung dwarf in a contest of questions in which the one who cannot respond correctly to the other's questions loses his head. In this scene Wagner called his god *Wanderer*, and his stage instructions tell that Wanderer should be dressed in a *dark-blue* cloak and that he should wear a broad-brimmed hat that dropped downward over one eye.

Wagner used no less than two of his mythical sources as a guide in the matter of name and dress for this segment of his Wotan. There is an Eddic poem that tells of a situation in which all are to be aware of a stranger who possesses great magic and who can easily bewitch anyone he desires. The people are told that they will know this stranger because no dog will bark at him. In due time a stranger arrives upon the scene. The dogs do not attack, and they do not bark as the man makes his way. All say that this stranger wears a *dark-blue* cloak and that he calls himself *Grimnir* ("The Hooded One"). The stranger is, of course, Wotan.

There is a second source for Wagner's treatment of a disguise for the Allfather of the ancient Teutonic world. This incident is found in *Volsungasaga* (*Saga of the Volsungs*), a work that Wagner cited as one of his primary sources for his dramatic argument of the *Ring*. The opening chapters of this saga tell of a sword that a stranger has buried in the trunk of a tree and which cannot be withdrawn by any of those who wish make it one of their possessions. Then Siegmund (Sigmund) is able to withdraw the sword, which he then claims as his. One of those who tried to withdraw the sword and failed was King Lyngvi, the son of King Hunding. King Lyngvi is envious of Siegmund because the latter has won the coveted sword, and when Siegmund then woos the beautiful Hjordis away from him, he becomes quite angry. The pair then do combat, and as they are fighting, a stranger appears. He is dressed in a *blue cloak* and wears a slouched hat! The stranger has but one eye, and he carries a billhook in one hand. The stranger approaches Siegmund and Lyngvi as they fight. Siegmund raises his sword, to strike his foe. However, the stranger (Wotan) intercedes with his bill and Siegmund's sword strikes the staff and then "breaks asunder in the midst." Lyngvi then thrusts his sword into Siegmund and the latter dies. (In a later chapter the tale reveals that Siegmund's sword was broken into two pieces.)

Followers of the *Ring* will quickly recognize the scene depicted in *Volsungasaga* as the obvious source for parts of two scenes in *Die Walküre*, which, it must be recalled, was written after Wagner had composed his poem *Siegfried*. One scene occurs in the second act, when Hunding and Siegmund fight. Wotan intercedes in that struggle. The god interposes his spear into the fray. Siegmund's sword, poised on high to be brought down of the Neiding, strikes Wotan's spear and breaks into two pieces. Hunding then slays the defenseless Volsung. There is much of the *Volsungasaga* scene that Wagner brought to this *Ring* scene. The other scene in *Die Walküre* that recalls some of the saga's tale is that of the first act in which Sieglinde tells of the stranger who came to Hunding's dwelling on the day of her forced wedding with Hunding, and who thrust the sword to its hilt in the trunk of the tree that grew there in the house. Until this day, none has been able to withdraw that sword, but Sieglinde is now certain that the lost person who has straggled into her home is the person who can at last succeed where all others have failed. As Sieglinde tells her story of how the sword came to be in the tree, she relates that the stranger who came into the house wore a *blue* mantle, and on his head he wore a hat that was pulled down over one eye!

(It is curious to note that most German language editions of *Die Walküre* contain the word *blauem* ("blue") as the word that Sieglinde speaks when she refers to the color of the cloak that the stranger wore when he entered Hunding's dwelling. There is at least one edition, however, that substitutes *grauen* ("grey") in place of *blauem*, a change that obviously causes Wagner's intent to be at odds with the mythical source. When the extension and profundity of the composer's dependency on mythical fact, that of major and substantive concept as well as that of minor or less important belief, as the primary source and inspiration for his drama is taken into consideration, there can be no doubt that Wagner's original word was *blauem*, the color that is very much a part of the Teutonic myths. It would violate all logic to assume that Wagner had used the word "grey" in the aforementioned scenes. He used the mythically correct word "blue" in the scene in which Wanderer enters Mime's cave, and there are those numerous editions of the *Ring* that include the mythically correct word, "blue," when it is a matter of the disguised Wotan and his entrance into Hunding's dwelling. To surmise as to how, or when, or why the word "grey" came into the drama, or even to speculate by whom the word was introduced into the *Ring* would be folly.)

Critics and reviewers of the *Ring* through the ages have mentioned, mostly in a rather passive manner, that Wagner 'based' his drama on this or that work of Teutonic mythology! What seldom occurs to many of these writers is the fact that Wagner did not really *base* his drama on the mythology, rather he made his work mythology itself. Indeed, this rather insignificant episode of Wotan's blue cloak, its mythical existence and its later appearance in the *Ring*, is but one of an almost continuous series of similar matters of a mythical nature that Wagner somehow made a part of his drama. These same scenes also substantiate beyond any doubt that there was no factor of Teutonic mythical thought that Wagner considered to be of such little worth that it merited exclusion from his work. Indeed, in many ways Wagner's *Ring* is truly a mythical work!

CLOD (of earth)

A stage instruction that Wagner included in the first scene of the last act of *Götterdämmerung* directs Siegfried to pick up a clod of earth (*Erdscholle*) and, as he utters the words that are his, that he is to throw the clod backwards, over his head. The scene in which this apparently minor piece of action occurs is that in which Siegfried has been confronted by the trio of Rhine maidens who warn the Volsung that he is fated to die if he does not return the ring to them. Siegfried is unmoved by the words of the nixies, and he informs them that the Dragon that he slew also warned him of this death-curse. The hero then adds that his sword Notung has already splintered a spear, and with that sword he will sever any strand of a death-curse that the Norns have woven for him. (Siegfried has not encountered Alberich, and he is unaware that it was the Nibelung dwarf rather than the Norns who placed the death-curse on the ring.) Then, to illustrate what little value are his life and limbs, Siegfried leans over, takes a bit of earth in his hand, and throws it into the air.

Curiously, it seems that there is only a very small minority of the serious followers of Wagner's *Ring* who are aware of the true significance of this bit of stage action that is carried out by the hero. Neither do many of these followers realize that this act, which requires but a few seconds to complete, is a most exemplary indication of Wagner's careful attention to Germanic beliefs and practices, and also one of the numerous ways in which he intensifies the ambience of authentic Teutondom that he sought for his drama.

The source for Siegfried's action in this scene is to be found in an habitual and repeated practice of the Germanic peoples. This practice, which may be seen even today, originated, however, as a matter that was very much of a mythical nature.

In the early Teutonic culture, the earth was revered, not so much as a divine or even a holy object, but rather as the nurturer of all living things. This attachment to the earth was unbroken by time, continuous in that it was handed down from generation to generation. This concept of the earth as the source of all living matter eventually was converted into a view of the earth as *Mother Earth*.

The affinity that the Germanic peoples had for the earth is evidenced by numerous societal practices, each somehow associated with the earth and its soil, that the people of that early culture carried out. Each of these practices included the handling of soil in one fashion or another, and each practice in its own way revealed a certain popular attitude or belief regarding the earth. It was common practice, for example, for an individual who had sworn an oath to retrieve a piece of the earth on which he had stood when he made his pledge. This action was thought to indicate that since the earth was the source of all life, to which all must pay due homage, so too was an oath sacred in the same way. The handling of the soil allowed the earth and its vibrant energies and the oath to become one. (In early Teutondom the breaking of an oath was one of only two actions for which the offender could be put to death. The second offense was *murder*.) A second societal practice included the retrieval of a handful of soil from under one's foot as a petition to the earth as the universal mother and source of life itself, to heal a grave wound or to cure one of some illness. This same action could also become a petition to the earth for shelter and protection from the harmful effects of nature. On other occasions, when some object of value had been found on or in the earth, some of that very soil was picked up and rubbed on the object to ward off any danger that the object might contain and to insure that the earth itself would not object if the finder took permanent possession of the new-found treasure.

There is in each of the gestures or actions that has just been depicted a clear and evident demonstration of the particular significance that the earth had for the early Germanic peoples. The specific practice that Wagner demands of his Siegfried, that of picking up the soil and almost carelessly tossing it over his head, is yet another bit of cultural evidence of that significance. However, this particular cultural action, unlike most of the others, can be traced backward in time to that point where the matter is no longer simply cultural, but also mythical, that is, it becomes a practice that can be related to the religious beliefs of the heathen Teutonic society.

In the time prior to the acceptance of Christianity (about 800 A.D. in continental Teutonic Europe and about 1200 A.D. in the Scandinavian countries), the Supreme God of all Teutondom was Wotan (called *Odin* in Scandinavia). Wotan was the god of many matters, but one of his major roles was that of God of War and *Heervater*, or God of Armies. One of the principal wishes of the warriors of the day was that if they were to die in battle that they could fight valiantly and die as brave and true warriors. The reward for such a death was, of course, transport to the celestial abode of chosen heroes, Valhalla, where each warrior would be *raised* and then allowed to serve in the army of the great god himself. This belief was perhaps the strongest and most universal concept held by the ancient Germanic peoples. (Soldiers who fought badly in combat or who proved to be cowardly in any way, and those men who died of a cause other than of battle wounds, as well as all women and children, were forced to an afterlife in the foggy, dark and dank netherworld called Hel.)

One of the customs that these earlier warriors practiced was that action which Wagner directed that the Siegfried of the *Ring* should do. It was common custom for soldiers, even the non-professional kind and especially farmers, who were about to enter combat, to pick up a clod of earth, hold it so that it might be seen by Wotan, then crumble it in their hand and toss it away, aimlessly. This act was to demonstrate to the Supreme God that these individuals were ready and prepared for battle and that they were unafraid to be taken in death, much as the wind had just taken the dust that they had made. It was a warrior's way to indicate his value of life and to show Wotan that he was ready to fight bravely and die for the god. This practice became almost second nature to soldiers and was a common practice by military men in Germany well into the sixteenth century. However, as Christianity made itself felt more and more in these lands, the act itself took on a new meaning. Now, instead of its being a religious act dedicated to the heathen god Wotan, it was merely a way to show gallantly all who might be interested that life was like the earth, that is, it could be crumbled and tossed to the wind, and then be completely forgotten. In its new form, the act of taking a piece of earth and throwing it over one's head no longer had its religious attachment and was now a means whereby the warrior could demonstrate only what little value life had for him.

The relationship between a specific practice of the people, rooted as it was in the mythical beliefs and concepts of another time, and Siegfried's act is obvious. The act, in and of itself, is of little if any import in the thematic development of the *Ring*. The stage direction that Wagner gave to Siegfried could easily be removed from the drama's argument and the resultant effect in no major way would alter the continuance of the plot and the drama's theme. Yet, Siegfried's act is representative of early Teutonic practices and, furthermore, the act has its roots in the ancient religious practices and beliefs of the Germanic peoples. In that light, Siegfried's act can only be viewed as another of many aspects of cultural and religious life that Wagner incorporated into his drama, and therefore one of the many ways in which he strove to saturate his work with the mythicalness of the early Germanic peoples.

See also: *Alberich's Curse*
         Elements

COMPASS POINTS

There are no less than ten references in the *Ring* to major points of the compass, and these directional references handily serve as an accurate mirror, not only of their frequency of their use in the myths of Teutondom, but also of their significance in the beliefs of the people of that day. Wagner included these directional terms in his drama, but he used them in such a way that there was little, if any, dramatic development that made them a high point of concern, or even interest. An understanding of their purpose and their impact within the drama, therefore, presupposes a familiarity with the role of these points of the compass in the heathen Germanic scheme of the universe.

The Eddic poetry clearly reveals that the ancient Teutonic mind was quite conscious of geographic locations. This literature also includes the terms that this culture used in order to depict the universe as it was viewed in those ancient times. This early society was apparently so concerned with the matter of 'direction' that it even applied respective terms to that which existed *before the physical creation of the world*. According to mythical beliefs, prior to the existence of men and gods and seas and sun and moon and other signs of tangible life, there was only a Great Void (Ginnungagap), a vast, endless expanse of inert matter. Yet, the people of the culture divided this compound of endless space into two separate and individual regions. They called one of the regions *North* and the other was *South*! The former was an expanse of foreboding darkness, fog, ice, and intense cold. The region called South was an area of sparks, flames, fire, and great heat. At some time in the distant past the two regions slowly began to move toward each other. In time, North and South met and the fire and heat of the South then began to melt the ice of the North. It was this meeting, this event that set in motion the movement necessary for the succeeding incidents which ultimately resulted in the creation of the Teutonic cosmos.

Nine distinct worlds eventually emerged from the meeting of the North and the South. Each of these worlds, in one way or another, was the creation of the gods. In the center of what had been the Great Void a large tree grew. This tree was Yggdrasil, more generally known as the World Ash Tree, which embraced all of the nine worlds. The myths infer that Niflhel ("Dark Hell"), the World of the Dead, apparently emerged out of what had been the North, and the expanse of emptiness that had been the South developed into Muspellsheim, the World of Fire, sometimes called the World of the Fire-Giants.

Centered among these several worlds was Midgard, literally "Middle Enclosure," which was the world in which mankind was to reside. The gods had fashioned this world from the body of a great giant, Ymir, who was the first living creature of the universe. The gods used the giant's brain to make the clouds that would be in the world of man. They would house those clouds in the dome of the giant's skull which became the firmament. At the base of the skull there were four dwarfs, each positioned in such a way that together they could hold the world of man firm and fast. As with all else that achieved an importance or significance in the heathen Teutonic world, each of these dwarfs had names. In the geographically conscious Germanic culture these dwarfs were called *Northri (North)*, *Suthri (South)*, *Austri (East)*, and *Vestri (West)*. In OHG these terms became, respectively, *Nord, Sund, Ostar, and Westar.* This work that the dwarfs performed was quite important in the early Germanic scheme of things and it became known as the "Burden of the Dwarfs."

Another of the nine worlds of the heathen Teutonic universe was *Jotunheim*, the *World of the Giants.* Wagner included this world in his *Ring* drama, although he was to give the name a translation into German, *Riesenheim.* In the early Germanic geography, Jotunheim lay in the *East*, that is, east of the World of Men, and it was to that *East* that Donner often traveled in order to do battle with the giants that resided there. It was also to that *East* that heroes journeyed as they sought to perform heroic deeds. Wagner does not indicate in his *Ring* a specific geographic location for his Riesenheim, but he acknowledges in that work the ancient mythical belief that it lay in the East. This acknowledgment is given by the means of the words of a Valkyrie who states that the giant Fafner, after he had slain his brother, took the Nibelung gold and fled to a cave that was *East* of Valkyrie Rock, the place where the Valkyries gather before they continue on to Valhalla with their human cargoes. This directional indication is repeated later in the *Ring*, when Mime says that the den of Fafner, who now has the form of a dragon, is to the *East* and, therefore, Siegfried, in his search to learn the meaning of fear, must travel to that *East* for his encounter with the Dragon. This Teutonic *east-west* geography, that is the location of the World of Giants lying east of the World of Men, surfaces again in Wagner's drama, this time in a rather subtle manner when Hunding informs Siegmund that his mortal kin and their lands are to be found *west* of his dwelling.

There was a belief that was part of the Germanic concepts regarding geographic location that *North* was an ominous, ill-omened region. Such a conviction obviously was a retention that was allied with the concept of the expanse that was north of the Great Void, before the gods had made the universe. The ice and cold that was natural to the North, its darkness and its overall forbidding nature made it a veiled, mysterious region, a region to be avoided. Yet, this North was a region whose enigmatic qualities also made it a region that demanded a certain deference, as well as a certain form of respect. Pagan practices among the early Teutonic peoples required that prayers be offered while facing North, and that sacrifices of animals should be carried out while facing in the same direction. Later, as Christianity forged its way into the Germanic culture, these beliefs remained so firm, so resolute, so unmoved by the new religion and its practitioners that ultimately the priests of Christian thought and belief looked upon the North as a zone of heathenism that was unacceptable to Christian tenets and ultimately they deemed it a region that God had left unblessed!

One of the most vigorous of the heathen Germanic beliefs was that which gave existence to The Furious Host (Das wütende Heer), that fearful army of ghostly spirits and specters that stormed through the night skies with Wotan at its head, its *Heervater*. This dreaded army, with its intense noise and its intent to do great harm to anything in its path, always came from the *North*! Wagner was no doubt aware of The Furious Host and its lack of thematic import to his drama of the *Ring*, but he knew of its unquestioned acceptance in the Germanic mind, and that knowledge included the potential of The Furious Host as theatrical action. Thus, with or without a dramatic reference or inference, Wagner felt compelled to include some aspect of The Furious Host in his drama. He found the proper place for such action in *Die Walküre*, in the opening scene of Act III, as the King of the Gods rushes at full speed in pursuit of the fleeing Brünnhilde, to avenge her disobedience of his command that Siegmund should not have her protection in his combat with Hunding. The Valkyrie sisters are alarmed and quite upset when they cry out that the darkness of night is overcoming day and from the *North* the angry and wrathful Wotan is descending upon them much like a raging storm! They seem to cringe and step backward in fear of the approaching Heervater.

The apprehensive concept of *North* that has been shown to be so apparent in the early Teutonic mind is reflected yet again in the Norn scene that opens the "Prelude" of the *Ring's* fourth drama. In this short but dramatic tableau, the three Norns weave the Cord of Destiny, that property that held the strands of life and death for all living things. As these mythical fates weave the threads of destiny for all the world, they tell of what once was, what now is, and what is yet to be. It is the Third Norn who reigns over the future, and when she speaks she tells her sisters that the forlorn Wotan sits on high, in Valhalla, there awaiting the doom that he knows is to come. As she concludes her dire words, she casts the Cord of Destiny to a sister, bidding her to catch it, adding, as she lets loose the end of the *Ring's* record of fate and destiny, that the Cord comes from the *North*. The Third Norn's prediction of the downfall of the gods, a prediction that is woven into the Cord of Destiny which comes from the North, uniquely reflects the presentiments that the term *North* regularly inspired in the ancient Teutonic mind. The sense of despair and futility prevails in this scene as the other Norns beg to know more of the future and as they toss the Cord among themselves. Finally, the Third Norn now wishes to cast the Cord *northward*, but it is too short and it does not stretch. The Cord then breaks, ending the eternal wisdom of the Teutondom's trio of fates, and dramatically inferring that the doom of the gods is near.

There can be no doubt that Wagner used the Norns and what is regularly called 'The Norn Scene' to interweave thematic details of his story and also to cause this first scene to establish a truly Teutonic mythical ambience which would then carry over into the remainder of that drama. Wagner's ideas, his concepts, and his presentations of this trio and their significance in early Teutonic life are most exact and the resultant scene and its dialogue are most persuasive. There is, however, one slight detail that Wagner includes in his scene which may go unnoticed because of its apparent insignificance, a detail that is, however, yet another example of the care and caution that the composer used in order that he could present as mythical a work as possible. Wagner included as part of his dramatization of the Norns a facet of the cultural attitude that was pervasive among the early peoples as well as present in the Eddic literature, but a matter that has never been discussed, either in brief or in detail, in the myths or in the studies of those myths. This aspect of the Norns is simply that two of these three sisters are promoters and promisers of good, while the third Norn, that is, the one who throws the Cord of Destiny from the *North* and later attempts to throw it *northward*, is the Norn who also casts or otherwise depicts an evil or untoward fate. This association of the Third Norn and a negative, adverse, or otherwise less than favorable destiny and the compass point of *North* cannot be dismissed as mere coincidence. There two factors seem to be inseparable elements in Teutonic mythical thought, and each equates and complements each other at one and the same time. Wagner sensed this concept and he brought it into his drama, delicately, subtly, but, nevertheless, with a deft and definite hand.

The mythical concept of the compass point *North* as a magnetic yet mysterious and powerful force was an extensive belief in heathen Germanic thought. It is presumably because of this power to fascinate and to attract that Wagner conceived another dramatic situation in which *North* is evident, a situation that seems to arouse a curiosity as to cultural meaning or interpretation. This situation is found in the fourth of the dramas, *Götterdämmerung*, when the drugged Siegfried, disguised by the Tarnhelm as Gunther, goes to Brünnhilde's Rock to win her as the Gibichung's bride. To accomplish this act, the Volsung finds it necessary to spend the night in Brünnhilde's cave. Later, when the question of Siegfried's fidelity in the matter is raised, the Volsung youth informs those concerned that he and Brünnhilde had lain together, in the cave, as *East* and *West*, with *North* between the two, together that is, so near to one another yet separated by an insuperable power. If there is in this scene a distinct yet understandable facet of the attitude that embraced the mythical *North*, there is still another segment of that concept that is revealed when Siegfried explains that the *North* that separated him and Brünnhilde while they spent the night together in a cave, was his special sword Notung, that sword that had been given to the Volsungs in order that their race could carry out specific and heroic deeds. Siegfried's words essentially equate *Notung* with *North*, a pairing that associates the awesomeness of *North* with the intrinsic powers that were inherent in the sword, a pairing which, when studied from somewhat afar and without too much attention given to detail, creates a kind of reverence, perhaps it is subliminal veneration, because of a force that cannot easily be countered by the minds of mortal men. (Wagner's seems to have been inspired in his Norn scene by a scene in the Eddic literature that deals with the popular Danish hero, Helgi. In those verses, the Norns are weaving a web of fate that will bring great fame to Helgi. The Norns weave the strands, and they lay one end of the cord in the East and the other in the West and all that would be in the middle would be Helgi's land. One of the Norns then throws a chain northward, and as she casts it she demands that it be held firm and fast.)

The compass points of East, West, and North figure prominently in the *Ring*, but the term *South*, or any reference to the word, is not to be found in the text of any of the four dramas. This exclusion of the fourth major directional word was probably intentional, and despite the occasional use of the word in early Germanic literature, Wagner's decision to omit the word *South* and any inferences of the cultural concepts associated with it was quite logical when studied from the level of theme and plot. The dramatic soundness of Wagner's reasoning in this matter becomes amply evident when certain details of the story of the end of the gods, as presented in the literature and as found in the *Ring*, are compared. In the mythical Teutonic mind, the universe of the gods was not infinite, that is, of unlimited time. If the duration of that world exceeded the life span of man, the finality of the gods was not only inevitable, it was unforeseen. Thus, the dusk of the Teutonic gods is not only a theme in the Eddic poetry, it is a matter that is poetized in some detail, and, in the ultimate consummation, *the* Eddic South and its related features are of primary significance.

The physical destruction of the gods occurs in what is generally called The Last Battle. This action begins when Surt, swathed in a ring of fire, leads an army of Fire-Giants from their home in Muspellsheim, one of the nine worlds of the Teutonic mythical universe, to do battle with the gods. This land, which also is the home of sparks and fire and flame, is located in the *South*, that same South that existed before the creation of the universe and which, in its own way paved the way for that creation. (During the struggle that ensues, as Surt and his followers slay the gods and in turn are slain, the fire that the Giants had brought with them burns the Rainbow Bridge and then engulfs and consumes the world.)

Wagner envisioned the doom of the gods in a manner different from that which the Eddic literature presented. If his universe of gods and men was to perish by fire, much like that universe of myth had perished, that fire would not be brought to the divine world by the Fire-Giants from the South! Rather, the fire that would scorch the heavens and the earth of his drama would have its stimulus within the confines of that drama, and, therefore, there would be no need to have Wotan enter into combat with a supernatural that had come from a world of fire. In his drama Wotan would be the prime mover of the finality of the world, the protagonist as it were whose acts betray the trust and fidelity of the gods. Wotan's greatest enemy would not be any of the other gods, or even a supernatural from any of the other worlds. Wotan himself would be an enemy to himself, and in that light he would bring destruction upon himself. Wagner understood quite clearly that his drama would have to project the matter of Wotan essentially condemning himself to extinction and, therefore, that drama would be seriously compromised if a dramatic stranger would enter to set the world afire, compromised if even there were the slightest hint that the fire-world would be a prime factor that was to be brought in from another world.

Thus we have the four cardinal points of the compass as developed and used both in the Teutonic mythical literature and in Wagner's *Ring*. Much like the literature, Wagner employed *East* and West and *North*, and he used them much in the way that they are depicted in the Eddic literature. But, there is no *South* in the *Ring*, and that lack certainly mirrors the use of that term in the *Eddas*, which at the most can be termed only sparingly. Again, as in so many other ways, even with the major points of the compass, Wagner is essentially thoroughly Teutonic and thoroughly mythical, an end that he sought so ardently.

See also: *The Furious Host*

_____

CONTEST (Question)

The term *contest*, as used here, refers to that series of questions that Mime and Wotan direct at each other during the first act of *Siegfried*.

See: *Question Contest*

CORD OF DESTINY

The Cord of Destiny that is so evident in the "Prelude" to the fourth of the *Ring's* dramas is a paramount mythical concept that Wagner extracted from Eddic poetry and then adapted to the thematic requirements of his work. The adjustments that Wagner made to the Germanic concept were minor, and his presentation of this important Cord is essentially an accurate and faithful duplication of the literary and cultural counterpart.

In the early times of Teutondom, the Cord of Destiny was fundamental in the determination of the ultimate destiny of all living things. The belief of the Teutonic system held that all that existed was predestined to perish, and that the time of that inescapable end, and often the manner, was preordained by the three Norns who wove their determinations into the Cord of Destiny. Once that fate had been incorporated into the Cord, no change could be made. The Cord of Destiny, when viewed in terms of the beginning and end of all matter, essentially shaped all life. The ordainments that the Norns made through the Cord were absolute, not subject to alteration, and, therefore, the Cord of Destiny and the Norns who controlled it exercised a power that was mightier than even that of the gods.

The Cord of Destiny that existed in heathen Teutonic thought was carefully woven by the Norns, who were viewed as spinners. They used a golden thread for each individual life and as each thread was intertwined with all the others, a pattern of societal life emerged for all concerned. The ends of the Cord were then cast into space, into the *East*, into the *West*, and into the *North*, after which the specific fate was then fastened forever in the sky.

Wagner's cord of fate, as it appears and functions in the Norn scene of *Götterdämmerung*, captures both the physical and conceptual symbolism of its mythical source. This cord, as the Norns of the *Ring* use it, permitted the composer a means by which he could dramatize his version of the final destiny of the gods and the world that they had created, and also the manner in which that world would meet its end. As Wagner's Norns spin and weave the Cord of Destiny, and then cast it skyward, their eternal wisdom is pronounced and the inevitable is declared.

Wagner's Cord of Destiny features one quality that uniquely differentiates it from the Cord of Destiny that is found in Eddic literature. This matter is an element that is at once specific to the web that is found in the *Ring*, and pertinent only to that Cord because the Wagner's story associates the Cord with vital elements of the drama's argument, a rather minor factor that becomes a truly significant contribution to both the dramaturgic and the mythological aspects of Wagner's story. As the Norns solemnly weave the fate of the gods into the Cord of Destiny, they speak of the curse that Alberich placed on the ring, the death-curse that the Nibelung pronounced after he had been stripped of the gold by Wotan. This curse, which the Rhinemaidens later identify as one of the strands of the Cord of Destiny, then begins to gnaw at the Cord, to erode it and to weaken it. As the First Norn inquires of the fate of the Nibelung dwarf, the Cord suddenly begins to untwine. Soon, the Norns are unable to control the Cord, and they can only watch it as it unravels, and then breaks. It is in that moment that the primal wisdom of the daughters of Erda is ended forever!

Into this brief instance of dramatic action Wagner incorporated a serious and final judgment, a sense that the predestined doom is not only near at hand, but also that even the Norns, the controllers of all destiny, are now themselves without power to exercise their call and thus they, along with all else in the universe, are fated to oblivion.

There was a second method that allowed the Teutonic Norns to record a destiny that they had declared to be in effect. This method, if less prominent in a cultural sense, and perhaps even less dramatic than that of spinners weaving a web or cord, was that of recording the matters of fate and destiny on runes and then carving those runes into the trunk of the World Ash Tree. This latter method is that which is depicted in the "Lays of the Gods," those poems in *The Poetic Edda* that focus on the activities of the Germanic deities, while the method that produced the Cord of Destiny occurs in the Helgi lays, that is those Eddic poems that focus on Helgi, the Danish hero.

See also: *Erda*
       Norns

CREATION

Since its first performance in Munich in 1869, the opening bars of *Das Rheingold* have prompted and stirred followers of many dramatic as well as musical persuasions to describe or otherwise depict the first 136 measures of that music-drama's prelude. Normally played while the theater remains in total darkness, the music tends to evoke inferences of a vast nothingness, a primordial presence perhaps, a cosmic essence that is primal in all its elements. Continuing in what can only be termed an almost unbroken, seamless sound, the E flat triad of double basses, bassoons, and horns swirls to a climax that opens onto a theatrical scene of rushing water, spray, and mist that is cloaked in greenish twilight. In its own way, this opening, the music as well as the theatrical setting, has been associated with the beginning of time, the initiation of a world fated for doom and destruction, the Creation.

Such a perception, that is, that the orchestral prelude of *Das Rheingold* sounds out the beginning of all matter, the beginning of all time, the beginning of all life, may not be a concept that is altogether too exaggerated. Few are those who would deny that the sound of the music itself, when offered as the initiation of a theatrical presentation, does much to transport the listener into a sense of timelessness, into a nebulous world of transformed sensitivities. That personal reaction, that personal comprehension, that personal experience, were precisely the matters that Wagner had in mind when the inspiration for that music came to him on the afternoon of September 3, 1853, in a less than first-class hotel in Spezia, Italy. As Wagner later wrote in his autobiography, he had been unable to sleep the night before because of the noise. He had taken a walk earlier in the day, and when he returned to the hotel, he lay down to rest. Then, as he dozed away, he suddenly felt that he was in the center of a great flood of water, sinking in the whirling waves.

> The swirl and rush of the water formed a musical sound in my brain. It was the E flat major chord. The broken chords became melodic passages that constantly increased in motion, although the triad of E flat major never changed. Its continuance seemed to impart infinite significance to the swirl in which I was sinking. I awakened from my nap, terrified, as if the waves were swirling about over my head. At once I recognized that the orchestral prelude to *Rheingold*, which must have been within me for some time although it has been unable to take definite form, had at last been revealed. I quickly realized my own nature, the flow of life in me was not to come from without, but from within myself.

The unusual experience that Wagner underwent as he conceived the prelude to *Das Rheingold* is not really unlike that which can result when the first words regarding what was to become the *Ring* are studied. In October, 1848, after some restless months of wandering within a creative vacuum, Wagner put on paper the initial words that would one day be expanded into the tetralogy. He called what he wrote "Der Nibelungen Mythus, als Entwurf zu einem Drama" ("The Nibelung Myth as Sketch for a Drama"). The opening lines of that Sketch are as follows:

> Out of the womb of night and death there sprang into being a race that dwelt in Nibelheim (Nebelheim, the place of mists), that is, in dim subterranean chasms and caves. These beings were called *Nibelungs*. Like worms in a dead body, they swarmed about the entrails of the earth with varying, restless activity.

The indescribable sensation that overcame Wagner in an Italian hotel and the haunting words that he had penned years earlier are both, in their own ways, somewhat equivalent to the emotional reactions that are evoked by certain verses that he once had read in *The Poetic Edda*. Those verses, like the scene depicted by the first words of his Sketch, like the feelings that are aroused by the initial sounds of his prelude, also had to do with a 'beginning,' and they too had a moving quality, an element of infinity that was yet to be stirred. The verses state that once there was no sea, no waves, no sand. The earth had not yet been formed, and there was no heaven to see. All that existed was a huge yawning gap (Ginnungagap), in which no grass grew. There was no sun, no moon, no stars, for these things had not yet found their ways through the universe. All was silent, and black, and cold. Then, at last, the gods of the universe assembled, to hold counsel, and they gave names to 'morning,' to 'noon,' to 'twilight,' to 'evening,' and they also gave years with which to call by number. Then, the gods made temples and tools, and they determined how the race of dwarves should be made. The gods came down to land, and soon, out of the body of Ymir, the giant, they had made the world and all that was to be in that world, and then the mortals who were to live in that world.

The mythical act of creation is developed further in the *Edda*. There are verses that tell how the mountains, the oceans, the clouds, the sky, and all else came into being. Wagner was well aware of the mythical act of creation, as the *Edda* had depicted, but as he wrote his Sketch and as he composed his prelude, it was that first movement, that first stirring, that first point of light within a dark nothingness that had interested him. It was those acts that had taken place prior to the opening of his drama that were of his concern. He understood that in a mythical sense the world had been formed before the time of *Das Rheingold*, but somehow, in some manner, he must put into sound that primordial quality of the Creation, the sense of all beginning, and still open his *Ring* onto a full and total universe. Indeed, as he recalled the concepts that he had placed in his Sketch, and as his mind carried him into the oblivion of rushing waters, he found his 'beginning,' he found his 'creation.' Like the Eddic verses that tell of the beginning of all things, so it is that Wagner's first music of the *Ring* thoughtfully and emotionally brings into focus the beginning of all things.

_____

CURSE

The laying or placement of a curse on a being, on an animal, or even on a material object, was not unknown in the cultural patterns and the mythical thought of the early Teutonic peoples. A death-curse, however, like the curse that Alberich utters in the final scene of *Das Rheingold*, is even more of a rare occurrence. The belief in curses existed, if not extensively, throughout the several regions of the Teutonic world. It was a belief, however, that was essentially particular to the Northern races, that is, among those peoples of the Scandinavian and Icelandic regions, and it did not appear in any substantial manner or number in the mythical thought of those peoples who would be known later as the Germans.

Wagner, however, accepted the mythical feature of the death-curse for one of his own thematic ends. Not only did he disregard the matter of its scant acceptance and rather limited popularity among the early heathen people of his native soil, but he seemed to move in the opposite direction as he expanded the concept into a continuous and inciting undercurrent that would run silently but steadily throughout the story that he developed in his *Ring*. The composer was supported in this dramatic action, at least indirectly, by the existence of another belief, one of rather secondary nature that was held by some of the people. The culture believed that the dwarfs of the Teutonic world, when forced to do so, were capable of putting a curse, though not necessarily a curse of death, on weapons which they, as the metalsmiths of the mythical world, had made. Certainly Wagner's gold ring is not a weapon in the usual sense of the word, but, nevertheless, it was fashioned from metal, and it was a dwarf that had brought it into existence. These two mythical features were, at least in Wagner's mind, sufficient justification for him to incorporate his death-curse into the *Ring*, and to cause it to originate with the principal dwarf of the mysterious netherworld.

There was, however, yet another type of curse that was very much a part of the early Teutonic peoples' beliefs, a curse that Wagner used with some success, albeit passive, in his *Ring*. This curse did not necessarily carry the threat of death, but it was, nevertheless, a curse whose powerful forces were very much feared.

The situation for the development of this curse unfolds in the second act of *Siegfried*, immediately after the Volsung hero has dealt a death-thrust of his sword into the Dragon's heart. Fafner realizes that he is about to die, and he asks the Volsung who it is who has killed him. The youth answers that he does not know who he is, and then even asks the Dragon to tell him who is his (Siegfried's) father!

The scene, as developed by Wagner, brings to a thematic climax the possibility, or perhaps it is a threat, of the laying of this ancient Teutonic curse. The specific belief held that if a being, either man or beast, who had been wounded in some form of combat and who was dying, could utter the name of his slayer, a great curse would fall upon the slayer. Such a curse was to be avoided at all costs because the mere pronouncement of the slayer's name would bring him much harm, and thus it was that warriors were reluctant to let their name be known to their foes, preferring rather to be known by some form of byname. Fafner and Siegfried are placed in that position of victim and victor, and Fafner weakly, but deftly, requests to know the name of his slayer! Siegfried, in the custom of the day, answers only that he does not know who he is, and thus avoids the dreaded curse of the one he has killed.

In the matter of such a curse, there was one appropriate time when the slayer could reveal himself. If he desired, the victor could give his name, but still void the possibility of the force of the curse if he revealed his name only when the victim was literally exhaling his final breath of life. Such is, of course, the situation when Siegfried responds to Fafner's request and at last calls out his name. Fafner is dying and has strength enough only to be able to repeat the Volsung's name as he dies. The curse of the dying victim has been avoided.

As with Alberich's curse of death, so too with the curse of a dying man, Wagner understood the Teutonic societal mind as he adhered to the fundamental aspects of the curse in that thought. Thus it is that as the drama of the *Ring* is played out, he was able to weave into the fabric of his story, if ever so delicately, another of the Germanic mythical matters that are so diffused throughout his drama.

See also: *Alberich's Curse*

-D-

DAY See: *Moon*
Sun

DEATH

The passing of a member of any society in any civilization has always required a final treatment of the corpse in a manner that is appropriate to that society's concepts and attitudes about death. The ancient Teutonic peoples were no exception to this practice.

Burial, that is interment as it is generally understood and practiced in the twentieth century, was seldom carried out by the vast majority of the heathen Teutonic peoples. Although there is evidence that some of these early tribes frequently condemned certain types of criminals to death by burial alive in the bogs of the region, placement of a corpse in the ground was not a regular part of the cultural order. Such interment was not practiced in order to avoid an invasion of the corpse by worms, which, according to beliefs, would prevent the deceased from journeying to the appropriate afterlife. Then, too, the worms that attacked cadavers were really maggots, which, in turn, were creatures that the gods had treated in a special manner. The gods had first encountered maggots as they fed on decayed flesh and as they made their way about beneath the surface of the earth. These deities saw a special usefulness in these creatures, and they then caused the maggots to have an abbreviated or miniature human form, after which they sent them to live deeper into the earth where they became the smiths of the universe, working in the ores and precious metals that surrounded them. In Teutonic beliefs, the maggots that had been transformed by the gods were the black dwarfs who lived in one of the nine worlds of the universe.

The ancient Germanic peoples regularly cremated the dead. The body was placed upon a pyre whose wood, ideally, was either ash or oak. The ash wood was symbolically linked with Yggdrasil, the World Ash Tree, the Teutonic peoples' Tree of Life, and the oak wood was symbolic of the strong oak tree that was associated with the popular god Donner (Thor). If death occurred at sea, the body was weighted and then dropped into the water.

The heathen Germanic beliefs also held that there were two special locations to which the dead were sent for an afterlife. The first of these places, and that site to which the great majority of the people journeyed after death, was known popularly as well as mythically as *Hel*, a dark, dank, gloomy region that was considered to be one of the nine worlds of the universe. The complete Old Norse name of this world was *Niflhel* ("Hell of Darkness"), which was located at the roots of the World Ash Tree. (On occasion, *Niflhel* was rendered as *Niflheim* and *Nebelheim*.)

The warder of the netherworld of the dead was also called *Hel*, a name that was often changed to *Hella*. Hel was one of the three monster offsprings of Loki (Loge) and the giantess Angrboda. The gods were well aware of the potential harm that each of this trio of supernatural creatures could wreak upon the world, and in an attempt to avoid such dangers, Wotan ordered that each be sent to some distant location, some place far from the worlds of gods and mortals. Hel was sent deep into the earth, down into the blackness of the lower world, where she remained as guardian of the dead. Hel's brother, Jormungandr, who became known as Midgardsorm ("World Serpent"), was sentenced to live in the oceans of the world where he grew in size until his body encircled the earth and he was able to bit his own tail. Hel's second brother, Fenrir the wolf, was condemned to chase the sun and the moon. Each of this trio would figure prominently in *ragnarök*, the doom, destruction, and downfall that was to be the fate of the gods. (Hel brings her army of the dead to do battle with the gods; Donner slays the World Serpent, but then drops dead from the poisoned slaver that the serpent drooled upon him; Fenrir swallows Wotan, but is then killed by one of the god's sons.)

Hel was not a supernatural that killed, and neither did she send for the souls of the dead. On occasion, Hel traveled to where death had already occurred, and then escorted the corpse to her underworld. There was no necessity, however, for Hel to accompany everyone in death. Some souls rode horses into Hel, some sailed in their boats, and some even walked to their afterlife. Hel was reserved for all women and children, and for those men who died of illness, accident, or old age, as well as those who had not died a glorious death in combat.

The second location in which the Germanic peoples believed that an afterlife was possible was the celebrated Valhalla, a name that is perhaps the best known and most readily recognized symbol of heathen Teutonic religious belief. An assignment after death to Valhalla was held to be the single most sought after honor that was available to the early Teutonic peoples. Of course, it was only men who could be given this honor, and to be selected by Wotan and then brought to Valhalla by a Valkyrie, one had to be a brave and courageous warrior who had fought valiantly and who was subsequently slain in combat. Once in Valhalla, the warrior was "raised" into an afterlife in which he practiced daily the skills of war with and against the others of Wotan's army which one day would be called upon to defend the gods against their enemies.

Wagner was well acquainted with the ideas, beliefs, and concepts that the ancient Teutonic peoples had for death and life after death. He wrote twelve deaths into his drama, excluding those that would come about as a result of destruction of the world with which he concludes his work. The giant Fasolt is murdered by his brother Fafner after an argument about the division of the Nibelungen gold. Two heroic warriors, Sintolt, the Hegeling and Wittig, the Irming, have been slain in combat and are being transported to Valhalla by Valkyries. Siegmund is slain in a struggle with Hunding who, in turn, dies at the magic wish of the King of the Gods. Sieglinde dies in childbirth. Mime, the dwarf, is killed by Siegfried who also slays Fafner, the Dragon. Hagen murders Siegfried and Gunther, and is then drawn to his death in the Rhine by the three Rhinemaidens. Brünnhilde, the last of the principals of the *Ring* to die, meets her death through self-immolation.

It is obvious that death, as viewed in that early Germanic mind was not understood in the same way as in later civilization. However, the plethora of deaths in the *Ring*, both the quantity as well as the manner, was not only a natural series of situations, but also an acceptable one, at least according to the heathen and primitive Teutonic scheme of things. Four of the deaths are those of warriors whose bravery and courage merit their admission into Valhalla. Siegfried, the hero, is cremated on a pyre. Sieglinde is denied an afterlife in the celestial fortress because she must "breathe the air of earth." (Of course, Sieglinde is also a woman, and thus an impossible candidate for membership in Wotan's heavenly army.) Hel, that is the place (Hella), is mentioned by name by Siegmund, who prefers it to Valhalla if he cannot have Sieglinde with him, and Hella, the guardian of the dead, is mentioned by Alberich, who says that with her army he will one day conquer Valhalla, and by Brünnhilde who wonders if the disguised Siegfried, who has come to take her as Gunther's wife, is one of Hella's army, that is a dead figure. Yet, as Wagner brought these varied and numerous deaths into his drama by means of the Teutonic thought and belief of an earlier day, as he gave them an acceptable mythical cause and then successfully enveloped them in a remarkably authentic heathen Teutonic ambience, there remains one aspect of the matter that some followers of the *Ring* have attacked, often quite severely. These interested parties assert that Wagner coded into his work a certain definite romantic, and therefore non-Teutonic, aspect that good and righteousness always conquer, or at least subdue, evil, and then, that the death of the righteous is in and of itself an heroic deed.

Individual philosophical attitudes regarding the matter of death in the *Ring* will vary. Regardless, however, of personal considerations it cannot be denied that there is in the drama a special ambience that is wholly reflective of early Teutonic beliefs regarding death, an ambience that is reinforced by certain dramatic as well as theatrical acts and actions. Wagner obviously understood that early thought, and he was uniquely able to bring to his work an accurate and authentic interpretation of those concepts that were so prevalent in the ancient era.

DESTINY See: *Cord of Destiny*

DONNER See: *Donner* (Vol. II)

See also: *Gods and Goddesses*

DONNER (Name)

The term *Donner* that Wagner applied as a name to one of his gods is the modern German word for "thunder," and was taken, of course, from the name of the early Germanic deity who was the God of Thunder and Lightning. There are several compound words in the language that use this word to denote aspects of this phenomenon of nature (e.g., *Donnerkeil, Donnerstrahl, Donnerwetter*).

The original Old Norse name of the god was *Thorr*, which today is spelled *Thor* in English as well as Scandinavian languages. The Nordic name evolved into *Thunrs* in Gothic, while in OHG it became *Thonar*. The initial sound of this word voiced in the southern Teutonic countries and the name thus became *Donar*, eventually developing into the modern *Donner*. (The English word *thunder* is also derived from the same original word, as evidenced by AS *Thunar* and *Thonar*, and ME – *Thoner*.) The god remains honored in German by the common word *Donnerstag* and in English by the equivalent *Thursday* (Thor's Day).

DOOM OF THE GODS

The fundamental doctrine of fatalism was universal in the world of the heathen Germanic tribes. From the remotest of times, these peoples held the belief that the universe and all that was in that universe was destined for total destruction. The idea of ultimate doom and death, the final end of all things, was not visualized simply in terms of the lesser beings of the world, but rather in terms of the gods who had created the world, the deities who ruled over it, and who governed all that they had placed in the world. The ancient phrase that designated this ultimate disaster was the compound term *ragnarök* ("doom of the gods") [*rök* – "fate" or "doom"; *ragna* – the genitive plural of "power," which was synonymous with "god"]. In time, the word *rök* became confused with a similar word, *rökkr*, which meant "dusk" or "darkness." Wagner drew much of his dramatic version of the ends of the gods from the *ragnarök* that is depicted in Eddic literature. From *ragnarökkr*, that is, "dusk" or "twilight of the gods," *Götterdämmerung* in German, he gained the title for the fourth and final part of his *Der Ring des Nibelungen*.

To understand the subtle complexities of *ragnarök*, one must consider the heathen Germanic beliefs from the ancient but unknown time of their inception. Teutonic belief held that the gods of Teutondom were a convivial group, at least at the time of the creation of the universe and for some time after its existence. These gods partook of games, they enjoyed banquets of fine food and drink, they mingled with each other, and they gathered in council each day to discuss matters of the world and to make decisions for that world, decisions that were beyond the scope of the forces and powers of mankind. Embedded in the matrix of these gods, however, was the seed of their destruction which, when it came to the gods, would also fall upon the world that they had created. According to mythical thought, the primary cause of all ills of the universe was to be found in Wotan (Odin), the King of the Gods, in whose blood there flowed a latent corruption that would one day erupt and leave havoc and ruin in its wake. The universe of the gods was, then, a precarious world, one that was to be plagued from its very beginning by terrible and powerful forces of decay and destruction.

Early on in the existence of the universe, the predestined malevolent forces began to appear and to make themselves felt. Dishonesty arose among the gods. Soon, these gods demonstrated a mutual distrust of each other. Lasciviousness became widespread. Incest and infidelity were often practiced by the gods, and fratricide was frequently carried out. In time, disagreement and dissension and animosities became rampant. Quarrels erupted, bitter hostilities, even enmities developed, and struggles, battles, and even wars became almost routine. These collective evils slowly eroded the inherently weak fiber of world structure, and eventual disintegration was inevitable.

Although the deities of Teutondom, as a race, were involved in one way or another in all these matters, there was one supernatural figure who, more than any other, was the major catalyst of evil. The central contributor to the decay that was to overwhelm the universe was the demigod Loge (Loki). The calculated activities of this cunning, wily, and usually shrewd being are ever-present in his movements among the gods. In addition to each and every one of his suspicious moves, Loge also had fathered, with the giantess Angrboda, ("Distrust-Bringer") the three most fearsome creatures of the universe. These monsters not only engendered fear and persistent wariness among the gods, they also would rise up at *ragnarök* to wreak harm and damage upon the world, and these three would also confront the gods in the final battle of the world. This trio of unsavory figures consisted of Midgardsorm, the World Serpent whose body circled the earth, Fenrir the monster wolf, and Hel, the ruler of the Otherworld and goddess of the dead.

The destruction of the world, *ragnarök*, is concisely but graphically depicted in "Voluspo" ("The Prophesy of the Prophetess"). This Eddic poem is one of the most important, and perhaps the most famous of the poems of mythical literature. Its stanzas were an inspiration for Wagner and, as will become quite obvious, those stanzas were also a rich thematic source for the argument of his *Ring*.

The Eddic verses signal the physical beginning of the end of the world with the death of Balder, the favorite son of Wotan and Fricka (Frigg). This god was the purest, wisest, and most merciful of the gods, and the most respected divine figure among the pantheon of Teutonic deities. Balder's death was orchestrated by the wily Loge, as was much else in heathen Teutonic mythical thought, and the death of this god caused such grief and sorrow in the divine world that Wotan begat a son who, on the day after his birth, attempted to avenge his half-brother's death. The disaster of Balder's death, coupled with the loss that this death meant to the gods, was to be the first of a series of actions and events from which the world would be unable to recover, and because of which, as the prophetess says, axe-time and sword-time would soon be at hand, brother would then fight brother, and no man would be spared.

There was uneasy movement in the universe after Balder's death. In the Land of the Giants, the river Slid ("Fearful") began to rise and pour out of its banks. The Dwarfs who lived deep within the earth became aroused. The dead in Hel's kingdom began to stir, and Nidhogg ("Dread-Biter"), the serpent that gnawed the roots of the World Ash Tree, sucked the blood of the slain.

The rumble of impending doom became more intense, and that hollow sound slowly spread throughout the universe. Nature erupted in one of its most violent forms, a period of three winters with no intervening summers. During Fimbulveter ("Terrible-Winter"), there were unending snows and great blizzards; there was frost and intense cold and biting winds. The sun was helpless to aid with its warmth because the wolf Skoll, an offspring of Fenrir and grandson of Loge, chased it, caught it, and then swallowed it. Hati, another of Fenrir's offspring, stole the moon from the heavens. Fenrir himself fed on the dead, and then smeared the home of the gods with their blood. Then, Fjalar, the guardian cock, crowed to awaken the Giants who long ago had become enemies of the gods. (The gods, by means of Loge's trickery, had cheated a giant out of a payment that would have been rightfully due him, and when the giant complained, Donner (Thor) killed him with his hammer.)

There was more to *ragnarök*. Garm, the dog that guarded the gates of Hel, howled mournfully, and a cock awakened the gods and the army of slain heroes who dwelled in Valhalla. The spirits of the waters began to writhe in the depths, and Yggdrasil, the World Ash Tree, shivered and shook. As the Giants groaned and the muffled movements of the Dwarfs became louder, the gods met in emergency council. Wotan, beset with anxiety, sought guidance from the severed head of Mimir, the wise spirit who had once been guardian of the Spring of Wisdom that flowed at the foot of the World Ash.

The end of the world was now eminent. Hrym, a giant, captains the ship Naglfar which had been made of the nails of dead men and which carries the Giants to battle. Hraesvelg, another giant that had taken the form of an eagle and had sat on the edge of heaven and created the winds of the world with his wings, begins to gnaw on screaming corpses. The monster World Serpent, Loge's offspring, twists and coils in the waters of the seas, and then emerges spewing venom all about. Another of Loge's offspring, Fenrir, advances, followed by wild men. The wolf's mouth is opened so wide that one jaw touches the sky and the other touches the earth. The dead of Hel sail out from the north on a ship that has Loge at the helm. Surt, the ruler of the Land of Fire that stretches out south of the Land of the Gods, leads his army of Fire-Giants across Bifrost, the Rainbow Bridge that serves as the entrance to the world of the gods. When Heimdall, the sentry of the gods, blows his trumpet Gjallarhorn ("Shrieking Horn"), to warn the deities, the divine ones immediately prepare themselves for battle. Then, with Wotan at their head, the gods of Teutondom and the great army of Valhalla make their way into what will be known as The Final Battle.

The fall of the gods takes place on the vast plain of Vigrid ("Field of Battle") that stretches out before Valhalla. There, the gods, the Fire-Giants, the Frost-Giants, the dead of the universe, and the monsters of the world come together and do battle. Wotan attacks the wolf Fenrir. The wolf kills the god, and then swallows him. Then, Vidar, a son of Wotan, avenges his father's death by killing Fenrir. Donner advances on the World Serpent, and slays him with his hammer. But, the god is overcome by the serpent's venom and, after walking nine steps, he falls dead. Froh (Freyr) attacks Surt, and the two slay each other as do Heimdall and Loge.

The gods of Teutondom fight and die in the violent combat. As they struggle, the sun turns black and the stars lose their light. The earth begins to tremble and shake, mountains crash, and the heavens are torn apart. The world is shattered as it then bursts into flame. The fires spread, and engulf the earth, and then the searing flames reach into the heavens. The waters of the oceans rise and flood the earth, which now sinks slowly into the watery depths amid a giant swirl of smoke and hissing steam. The end, *ragnarök*, is at hand. The doom and destruction of the gods is complete!

Wagner's story of the causes of the doom of the gods is one of his own creation. The details specific to his drama differ, often radically, from those of mythical beliefs. Yet, the causative essence of the downfall of the gods that Wagner embedded in his drama, as well as the explosive aspects of the dramatic cataclysmic event to which these causes lead, reflect a remarkably similar thematic parallel to those of the *ragnarök* of Teutondom. Wagner injected his own germ of corruption into his divine quintet, a seed that, for dramatic purposes, he causes to germinate and make itself known and felt through the King of the Gods. This seed of evil emerges early in the first of the *Ring's* four parts, quickly multiplies, and then spreads as Wotan leads the way into a moral pathway that ends, ultimately, in the fire and flood of annihilation.

There is a sense of apprehension throughout the *Ring*. That ambience intensifies as one after another of the major figures of the drama becomes ensnarled, in one way or another with each other, in a bind of deceit and suspicion. There is deception in Wotan's mind as he makes his initial agreement with Fasolt and Fafner. It is that pledge that Wotan gives to the Giants that allows the edgy, quarrelsome nature of the gods to be exposed. In turn, the giant brothers infer their mistrust of the King of the Gods and his divine cohorts, and then soon reveal not only a mutual distrust of each other, but a vicious personal greed that quickly ends in murder. There is a constant hostility and a profound hatred that exists between Alberich and Wotan, and a resultant persistent insecurity as each ponders the possible actions of the other. There is a disturbing and unsettled intranquillity between Fricka and her husband Wotan. A suspicious uneasiness dominates the relationship of Fricka and the primary Valkyrie Brünnhilde. A profound moral dishonesty shapes the plans that Mime contrives for Siegfried. There is an evil cunningness in the character of Hagen. And, there is even a personal but perhaps naive, if not innocent, lust that stimulates Gunther and his sister Gutrune. Indeed, the seed of decay and corruption that pervades the heathen Teutonic Eddic story of the gods and their world is easily recognized, despite its very distinct form, in Wagner's tale of the *Ring*.

As each of the actions and acts of Wagner's drama weaves its dramatic way through the total argument, it fuses with the others, and melds into a portrait of debasement and depravity. Total removal of the sources of this condition, that is, the elimination of the gods and the world of their making, becomes the only recourse, the only resolution. This end, this elimination, this removal, at least the physical aspects as Wagner dramatized them in this drama, begins when Brünnhilde sets the torch to Siegfried's pyre. As the banished daughter of Wotan lauds the slain hero, she cries out to the gods to look down at the earth in order that they can see what they have wrought, to see the injurious ravage that they have brought upon the world, to know the guilt that is theirs. The flames of the pyre burn high and then leap into the celestial heights, and there, those flames engulf the gods who sit in silence, observing all that transpires as they await their end. As the great fire subsides, and turns into smoke, the Rhine overflows its banks, and inundates the earth. All is ended, and the gods are no more!

The *ragnarök* of the Teutonic mythical world and the *twilight of the gods* in Wagner's *Ring*, with a similarity of cause and a likeness in physical realization, symbolize the end of a defiled world. If, however, the fire and flame and flood that enveloped the Eddic universe, and rendered all that it touched into a nothingness, those same violent forces of nature also brought about another event of monumental significance. As these natural powers overwhelmed and laid waste to the world that was, as they eliminated the impurities of that corrupt and evil world, as they cleansed the universe of the moral pollution that had stained all that existed, they were essentially making way for another world. This new world would be born in freshness and purity, and none of the evils of the past would exist in this new life.

It was the sibyl who had detailed the Eddic *ragnarök*, and it would be that same figure that would envision that universe that would rise to fill that great void. This 'wise woman,' the prophetess of Teutondom tells that this second world will begin anew with no reference to the world that has disappeared. The new world will be green, and fruit will grow. In this new world the sun will find its place in the heavens. Fish will swim in the waters, and birds will fly in the sky. The sibyl sees a large and radiant hall, roofed in shining gold, where the gods will dwell. These gods are righteous gods, who know only happiness. (Balder is one of the gods who is raised for life in the new world.) This new world is free of the ills and evils that plagued the past, and there are seeds of a new mortal life. From those seeds there will come a healthy, thriving race of man.

Wagner ended his *Ring* with the cataclysm of the gods. He chose not to include in his drama a dramatization of the birth of a new world. There is no doubt, however, that he was aware of the significance of that new world in early Teutonic belief, of the thought that the doom of the old and the appearance of the new were not separate and unrelated matters, but rather than the two events were part and parcel of a *single* belief. The *ragnarök* of old was necessary, inevitable, and it would occur because there would have to be room for a new world to emerge. Just as *ragnarök* was destined to disappear, so too was a new and fresh world destined to fill the void.

Wagner's interpretation of the prophetic genesis of the new world was not made by means of poetry and dramatic action, but rather by means of music. As Brünnhilde concludes her praise of the slain hero, and as the world is engulfed in flame and flood, there is interwoven into the music that signals Valhalla, the Rhinedaughters, the hero, and the end of the gods a musical motive of supernal tranquillity, a motive that projects infinite harmony and absolute peace. It is with this musical motive, which is often referred to as the motive of Redemption, that the composer ushers in the foundation of that pure and virginal world which is to be. It is with that music that Wagner introduces, but does not dramatize, the beautiful world that is destined to allow a second life for the gods as well as for man.

The follower of the *Ring* would do well to consult the *ragnarök* of Eddic literature. The resemblance of Wagner's dramatic finality of the world and that which was the mythical end in the distant past is remarkable. Yet, there is a unique originality in the last of the world that comes in the *Ring*, an end that conveys the infinite that is inborn in the mythical concept, and, at the same time, one that is sprinkled with a modernity that is immediately recognized and accepted by contemporary citizens of whatever culture. Indeed, Wagner had the Eddic literature as source and inspiration, but it was always his genius instinct that allowed him to blend and balance that which was the ancient with that which was of his own day, and to cause to result a work of intense universal aspects, a drama whose concepts are as valid today as they were in the composer's day and in that ancient, distant Teutonic past.

DRAGON

The huge, monster-like serpent known by the English word *dragon* is a mythical creature that breathed fire, had scaly skin, and had wings that allowed it to fly. The term by which this beast is known in English is derived through the Latin *draco* (AS – *draca*; OHG – *traccho*) from the Greek *drakon*. The equivalent word in Old Norse was *dreki*, which, however, was a little used term because the Nordic concept of this beast was that of an animal that had no wings and therefore did not fly. The Old Norse equivalent of a non-flying dragon was the word **Fafnir*. A popular phrase that was frequently used in Old Norse was *fafnis boeli*, which translates as "dragon's couch." The term "couch" in this phrase refers to a huge treasure of gold upon which it was commonly thought that dragons lay as guards. (The initial word in this phrase is in the genitive case and suggests that the nominative would be the term as shown.) It is not known when or how the common noun that was used in Old Norse to denote "dragon" became the proper noun that is found throughout the mythical stories as well as in the Eddic literature.

A second Nordic word that denoted a large, reptile creature, that is, a snake or serpent, was *ormr*, which became *wyrm* in Anglo-Saxon and *Wurm* in Old High German. The latter word, of course, was the English word *worm*, a term that took on a distinct meaning of its own.

The term *Fafnir* apparently became a proper noun early in the development of the Old Norse language because it does not figure in the semantic confusion that existed between the terms *dreki* and *ormr* in reference to the reptilian creature. This animal makes its appearance in numerous Germanic stories and tales and is called *dreki* in *The Prose Edda*, but only on one occasion. At all other times this beast is called *ormr*. In *Nibelungenlied* (*Song of the Nibelungs*), the poetic epic of the German people, the beast is known as *lintrache* and *lindrache*, while in *Siegfriedslied* (*Song of Siegfried*) the creature becomes a *lintwurm*. Wagner tends to restrict himself principally to the German *Wurm*, and to the more modern word *Schlange*.

The matter of a wingless dragon that lies guard over a great treasure of gold is one of the numerous fancies of imaginative thought that was prominent among the early Germanic peoples. This episode, in which the creature is eventually slain by the hero Siegfried, is one of the most popular and most enduring of the early Teutonic tales. This story is also recounted in several of the major works that Wagner consulted, and which he used to gather source material for that adventure that he was to retell in his *Ring* drama.

Wagner's rendition of this celebrated mythical episode is unique to his drama. Fafner and his brother Fasolt, the last of the Earth-Giants, quarrel about the manner in which they will divide between them the hoard of gold that Wotan has stacked before them. This gold, which the god essentially had stolen from the Nibelung dwarf Alberich, has been accepted by the giants in lieu of the goddess Freia, whom the god originally had promised as payment for their labors on the new celestial home of the gods, Valhalla.

Fafner then slays Fasolt, takes the entire treasure, and flees with it to Neidhöhle ("Hate Cavern"), where he transforms himself into a dragon, the better to guard his riches.

The details of this segment of the tale, as found in *The Poetic Edda*, are at some variance with those of Wagner's account. In the Eddic stanzas, Fafnir (sic), who is not identified as a giant, slays his father, steals his father's gold, and then flees to Gnitaheid (Gnita Forest) where he becomes a dragon in order to guard the treasure that he now calls his.

The question that regularly arises when either of these similar yet distinct stories is discussed is that which inquires of the means by which Fafnir (Fafner) effected his transformation into a dragon. In the Eddic version, Fafnir has a *fear-helm*, of which all living creatures are terrified, and therefore no one will attempt to steal the gold. This fear-helm, however, does not include the magic of transformation. Wagner's hoard includes the Tarnhelm which, if it did not frighten men, at least it gave its possessor certain magical powers, one of which was the power to change form at will. Some students of the *Ring* maintain that Wagner intended, and that once he even stated publicly, that he had hoped to infer that his Fafner had realized the physical change by means of the magic helm. There is, however, nothing specific in this regard in the drama, and the question remains essentially unanswered. There are also those followers of the Wagner drama, and likewise students of the Teutonic myths, who are quick to make reference to an ancient Germanic belief that held that those who practiced sorcery also had the magic to transform themselves into another form. Fafner's actions, that is those of the *Ring*, as well as those of Fafnir, his mythical counterpart, surely are not sorcery, at least if a rigid definition is suggested. Yet, the evil and maleficent nature that is characteristic of each of these figures prior to transformation is such that a more flexible definition of the word 'sorcery' might be enough to grant each of these figures the mythical magic to change form. In any event, the change is made, both in the *Ring* and in the *Edda*, as well as in other renditions of the tale, and it would seem that most mythologists tend to believe that the transformations were effected simply by the power that is possible through mythical beliefs.

In the *Ring*, it is Mime who leads the Volsung hero Siegfried to the cave in which Fafner, now a dragon, sleeps over the Nibelung hoard. In the Eddic tale it is Regin ("Counsel-Giver"), teacher and companion to Sigurd, the Nordic name of Siegfried, who serves as guide. Regin is an intelligent dwarf who is a brother to Fafnir. He had asked for his share of their father's gold, but when Fafnir refused to share the treasure and then fled with it, he told his tale to Siegfried, who then offered to help.

Wagner's Siegfried carries Notung, the sword that the youth had reforged. In the Eddic tale the name of the sword is Gram, and there are two mythical versions of its origin. One poem declares that Siegfried had forged the sword, for himself, specifically to venture to the forest to meet with the dragon. A second poem of the *Edda* states that Regin forged the sword, and then gave it to Siegfried. In any event, the Eddic sword is so sharp that when thrust into the Rhine and a strand of wool brushed against it, the strand was immediately cut into two pieces. Siegfried also used Gram to split Regin's anvil, on which it was forged. Wagner's Siegfried uses his Notung for a similar purpose in the *Ring* drama.

In time, Siegfried and the dragon meet. Wagner causes his hero to come face to face with the beast and then, after a series of sword thrusts, the fearless youth sends the weapon into the animal's heart. Wagner's hero later moves the dragon's body so that it blocks the entrance to the cave. In the mythical literature, Siegfried has dug a trench in which he places himself. When the dragon passes over the trench, on his way to the stream that is nearby, to drink, Siegfried kills the creature with a single sword thrust into the animal's underbelly. The mythical Siegfried makes no move whatsoever to disturb the beast after it has died. (It seems appropriate to note here that it is at this point in the German legends that Siegfried becomes invulnerable. The youth is crouched in the trench over which the dragon passes, and when he thrusts his sword into the underside of the beast, the rush of blood downward covers all of his body, all of his body except a spot on his back where the leaf of a linden tree had fallen and had stuck to his skin. From that point on, Siegfried's body is invulnerable to weapons, all his body, that is, except that small spot on his back where the leaf had been. Wagner did not use the dragon's blood to grant invulnerability to his hero. Rather, this aspect of the youth's being was bestowed upon him by the Valkyrie Brünnhilde, who used her divine magic to bless only the front of his body, knowing full-well that he was so brave that he would never turn his back to a foe.)

The matter of comprehension of the language of the birds, which is integral to this scene of Siegfried and the dragon, is also at variance in the *Ring* and in the mythical tales. The magic that permits Wagner's Volsung hero to understand the song of the birds is the dragon's blood that is on his sword and which ran down onto his fingers, which he then instinctively put into his mouth. In the Eddic verses Regin approaches the body of the dragon, cuts out its heart, which he then gives to Siegfried after he has drunk some of the dragon's blood. Siegfried puts Fafnir's heart on the fire, to cook it. Later, to test the meat, he presses it with a finger. The hot meat burns the youth, who immediately puts his finger to his mouth. It is then, when the blood from the dragon's heart touches the mouth of the hero, that he is able to understand "bird chatter." (Regin had drunk some of the dragon's blood when he cut out the beast's heart, but the magic to understand the language of the birds does not come down upon him.) Once Wagner's Siegfried is able to understand the song of the birds, he has but one encounter with one bird, Forest Bird. The Eddic verses show Siegfried in conversation with at least seven, and possibly as many as eleven, nuthatches, and the story, as told in *Volsungasaga*, reveals that the birds are woodpeckers, and that there are six of them.

Wagner continued to utilize the mythical tale of the dragon and Siegfried as source, and perhaps even inspiration, as he developed further his version of this aspect of the Siegfried legend. After the death of the dragon, the verses of *The Poetic Edda* depict the nuthatches as they warn Siegfried that Regin is about to betray the youth. Siegfried promptly cuts off Regin's head. Then, at the urging and instructions of the birds, Siegfried fills two chests with the dragon's treasure, loads those chests on to the back of his horse, Grani, and begins to make his way to a mountain that is ringed with fire and on which a beautiful maiden sleeps.

The death of the dragon as depicted in *Thidrekssaga*, also known as *The Wilkina Saga*, is quite different from that of either the Eddic version or that which is dramatized in the *Ring*. In the saga, Regin is the brother of Mimir, who is a companion to Siegfried. Regin was very skilled in magic, and also widely known for his evil deeds. Regin was changed into a dragon and lived in a forest where he killed anyone who came into the woods, all that is, except his brother Mimir. The young Siegfried was an unruly lad, and finally Mimir, wishing to be rid of him, sends the youth into the forest to burn charcoal, hoping that Regin the dragon will kill him. When the dragon set upon Siegfried, the youth grabbed a branch that was part of the fire that he was burning and hit the dragon repeatedly on the head, until the animal was dead. Siegfried then began to cook the meat of the dragon, and as he tested the flesh he was scalded on the hand by hot blood. He immediately put his fingers to his lips, and when he tasted the blood, its magic gave him the power to understand the language of the birds. Siegfried than cut off the dragon's head and took it with him to his home!

A short time before the dragon in Wagner's *Ring* dies from the sword thrust into the heart that Siegfried has dealt him, the composer inserts into the dialogue an enactment of a strongly held belief of the early Teutonic peoples. Fafner, the dragon, asks Siegfried who it is who has pierced his heart? When Siegfried answers the dragon, he does not give his name, but rather says that *he does not know who he is*! Wagner had found a similar situation in *The Poetic Edda* and in *Volsungasaga*, and in the latter work Siegfried utters words that may well have been the direct inspiration for those words that Wagner wrote for his Siegfried. The substance of each of the episodes is that Siegfried laments that his family is unknown to men, and that he is without father or mother. This apparent lack of knowledge of self is not a statement of fact, as it may seem to be to some readers. Rather, in the *Edda* and in the saga, as well as in the *Ring*, the refusal of Siegfried to give his name in response to the dying foe's wish to know who it is who has slain him is quite intentional. By not revealing his name in this situation, Siegfried avoids the possibility of a powerful curse being placed upon him. The heathen Germanic people believed most strongly that if a dying person could call out the name of his slayer, such action would place a curse on the foe. It was only when the dying person was drawing his last breath, literally, that a victor could reveal himself to his victim.

It is obvious that the appearance of the dragon in Wagner's *Ring* has as its sources the mythical tales of the ancient Teutonic peoples. (The fact that Siegfried has slain a mighty dragon is acknowledged in *Nibelungenlied*, the German epic, although neither the act itself, nor the dragon, appear in the poem.) It is essentially only minor details that vary, not only as the *Ring* deviates from the tales as Wagner found them, but also as the several versions of the story differ one from another. What is unique to Wagner's drama, in addition to the dramaticality of the scene itself, is the underlying purpose that the dragon fulfills in the composer's version of the Siegfried legend. It is by means of the dragon that Wagner joins and binds theatrically and dramatically the two major aspects of his drama, that is, his story of the gods and his tale of Siegfried. If the mythicalness of the Teutonic gods existed in early culture, and if the substance of the Siegfried legend was vivid and vital in early German society, the two had no fundamental relationship. Each had its place and its import in the total culture, but neither was associated with the other. The two matters existed as wholly unrelated subjects. It was Wagner's insight and talent that welded the two into a unified argument that is completely awash with mythical ambience, and it is by means of the dragon that the youthful mortal hero Siegfried is lead into the realm of the divine where he meets his grandfather, Wotan, and then the supernatural Valkyrie Brünnhilde, now transformed into a mortal maiden. And, as the dragon and the Volsung hero separate, Wagner is able to have the scene reflect a cultural belief that was fundamental to the societal conduct of the people. The overall purpose of the appearance of Wagner's dragon and the dialogic detail that Wagner brought into the scene, when studied carefully, become ample evidence of the keen and astute Wagner's dramatic talent, as well as one of the stamps of his thoughts about musico-dramatic composition.

See also: *Fafner*

DWARFS

The *Ring* figures Alberich and Mime are Wagner's principal dramatizations of the mythical dwarfs who ranged so widely throughout ancient Teutonic thought, and who also made their way into the early literature of Teutondom. The history of these dwarfs is a long one, proceeding as it does from the mythical beginning of the universe and continuing through the ages, and remaining, if in a much diluted form, in relatively contemporary folklore. Some cognition of the original word used to designate these unique figures is necessary if they and their position and status in the Teutonic scheme of things are to be understood thoroughly. Such information can also allow for a greater appreciation of the significance of these supernatural beings as part of Wagner's drama.

The original Old Norse word that was used to refer to the dwarfs was *alfr*. This word, which gave *alfar* as one of its earliest derivatives, indicated any of several kinds of small creatures that populated the ancient universe, along with gods, giants, and mortals. This Nordic term developed into *Alp* in Old High German, as well as into a second less frequently used word, *Alb*. In the earliest of times, the words *Alp* and *Alb* were synonymous, and each designated a fairy-like, joyous spirit or figure that usually inhabited the subterranean regions of the earth. Over a period of many years, the concept of *Alp*, and to a lesser extent that of *Alb*, as a mischievous but charming creature changed radically. *Alp* became associated with *dwarf* (OE – *dweorh*), an atypically small creature in human form. This association, however, was not with just any small forms, but only with those dwarfs that possessed an evil, daemonic nature. By the time of the late eighteenth century and the early nineteenth, the distinction between the sinister and cunning *Alp* and its small, light-spirited counterpart had become so fixed that the German language contained no word for the latter, no term that conveyed the original meaning of *alfr/Alp*. The romantics of Germany, in their search for a single word for the blithe, little figures turned to English, more specifically to Shakespeare, and borrowed the English word *elf* which, like *Alp* and *Alb*, had developed from *alfr*, but without the intervening *Alp* and *Alb* and the concepts of *devilish* and *fiendish*. The German language then contained the two principal words *Alp* and *Elf*, each of which designated a specific kind of *alfr*. The two words continued in use, but in time, as the acceptance of the maleficent and untoward dwarfs decreased and then disappeared, *Alp* lost its previous meaning. The word remained, however, in modern German, but then as *bad spirit* or *nightmare* (incubus), that sinister spirit that troubles people in their sleep.

The later concepts of *Alp* and *Elf* developed from earlier mythical thought that recognized, if only in a superficial manner, three kinds of *alfr*. The Eddic literature refers to them as *ljosalfar*, *svartalfar*, and *dokkalfar*, literally *light, black,* and *dark*. The first group was once called *lichtalp* in German. These were the happy-natured beings, the gobblin-like figures who lived beneath the surface of the earth, the genial spirit that found great pleasure in jesting and joking with humans. The origin of these "light alfr," which centuries later became the *Elf* of the German language, has never been determined although their home, *Alfheim*, was one of the nine worlds of the Teutonic universe.

The second group, the *svartalfar*, referred to a small being who lived in the inner regions of the earth. The mythical name of the home of these creatures is not specificaly indicated in Eddic poetry, but it is assumed to be *Svartalfaheim*, which was another of the nine worlds that existed in ancient early Teutonic mind. This *alfr* was quite unlike the "light alfr," in appearance as well as in nature. It is believed that the descriptive name *svart* ("black"), was attached, originally at least, because of the blackness of the soil and dirt that covered the bodies of these creatures. At some early date, the *svartalfar* and the *dokkalfar*, a nondescript group of "dark" figures, became a single group, a hybrid clan of mythical beings whose physical features and negative nature were thought to be much like the attributes that had been associated with the "dwarf." It was the *alfr* who was to become the cunning *Alp*, the Black Dwarf of Teutondom. It was this dwarf that was to become so vital and so integral to Wagner and his *Ring* drama. It was this dwarf that he portrays so vividly through his Nibelung figures. It was this *Alp* of the Germanic world who is embodied in the name that Wagner took as the name of his principal dwarf, *Alberich*.

From the unknown time of his origin, the *svartalfar* was destined to be a figure of daemonic nature. This fate was not ordained by the Norns, those mythical figures who regularly determined the patterns of life and death for living things. Rather, the fate that was attached to these small creatures was closely related to the manner in which they had been created which, in turn, was a creation that exemplified the dark and forbidding concepts of dwarfs that later became so fixed in Germanic thought. *The Prose Edda* states that at the beginning of the universe the gods gathered in council, and they recalled that there were small creatures that had flourished beneath the surface of the earth. They remembered that these creatures had come into life out of the flesh of the body of the giant Ymir. And the gods also remembered that at that time these creatures were called *maggots*! Then, the gods decreed that these maggots were to have human form and human understanding.

The version of the origin of the black dwarfs differs in *The Poetic Edda*. This story is less graphic and less macabre then that found in the prose accounts of mythical matters. This version does infer, however, some of the grimness that is associated with these beings. According to these versified myths the gods met in council, to determine who should "raise" the dwarfs that were to be created out of the blood of the giant Brimir and the legs of another giant Blain. One dwarf was created out of this blood and flesh, and then a second, and then there follows in the poetry the names of seventy-two dwarfs that were brought into existence. Andvari, the prototype of Wagner's Alberich, is one of those named in this group. If these small creatures were to have human form and human understanding, it is important to note that no version of the origin of these creatures, neither that in prose nor that in verse, gives to them the attributes that the gods bestow upon mortals at the time of their creation, namely *spirit, sense, heat,* and *goodly hue*!

The mythical dwarfs of Teutondom were a community or a race unto themselves. These creatures lived deep in the earth, although it was an easy matter for them to make their way to the surface through the cracks and crevices of the soil. The dwarfs came to the surface of the earth, however, only during the dark of night because if the rays of the daytime sun fell upon them, they were immediately turned into stone. Wagner was well aware of these mythical concepts that surrounded the dwarfs of Teutondom, and he skillfully wove them into the fabric of his *Ring* argument. He called his dwarfs *Nibelung* ("Child of Fog and Darkness"), and he gave them a home deep in the bowels of the earth, a home that he called *Nibelheim* ("Land of Fog and Darkness"). And he dramatized the actions of his dwarfs around an axis of *night*. It is Wotan who says that *night* gave birth to Alberich. It is Alberich himself who gloats over the powers of the ring that he has made and warns the King of the Gods to beware the armies of the *night* that will rise from silent darkness to confront the gods. Then, later, as Alberich speaks with his son Hagen, the Nibelung dwarf says that the struggle with the gods will take place at *night*.

The dwarfs of Teutondom had certain unique physical characteristics that rendered them unlike any other supernatural beings of the universe. As the giants were larger than mortals, the dwarfs were smaller. According to Germanic beliefs, the dwarfs reached their full growth at the age of three years. At that time, the growth equaled that of a human child of four years of age. By the age of seven, the male dwarfs had long grey beards. The dwarfs were ugly creatures. They had large heads, their backs were humped or otherwise misshapen, their bodies were covered with shaggy hair, and occasionally their feet were shaped like those of a goat or a goose. The life of the dwarfs deep within the earth, away from the sun, gave them a complexion that was ghostly grey.

Wagner was careful to make his presentation of Alberich and Mime duplicate the physical qualities that ancient Teutonic thought had associated with the dwarf. That presentation comes early in the *Ring* drama, in the opening scene of *Das Rheingold*. As the three Rhinemaidens tease and taunt the lustful Alberich, they call him filthy and foul. They say that he is a hairy, sulfurous, humpbacked *Alp*. These three nixies make reference to Alberich's scrubby, bristly beard, to his pricking, piercing glance, to his body that is shaped like a toad, and a voice to match. Later, in the third of the four dramas, it is Mime who is depicted through the words of his pupil, Siegfried. The hero calls Mime a grotesque wretch, a mangy, loathsome *Alp* who slinks about clumsily, hobbling and toddering as does a small child.

It was with stage directions as well as with dialogue that Wagner strove to convey the abhorrent physical aspects of his Nibelung dwarfs. The most illustrative example of Wagner's attention to this matter, and one that capsules his intent, is to be found in a stage direction that precedes the opening scene of *Siegfried*. Regarding Mime's appearance, he wrote:

> He is small and bent, somewhat deformed and hobbling. His head is abnormally large, his face is a dark ashen color, and wrinkled. His eyes [are] small and piercing, with red rims, his grey beard [is] long and scrubby, his head [is] bald and covered with a red cap. He wears a dark grey smock with a broad belt around his loins. His feet are bare, with thick, coarse soles underneath. There must be nothing approaching caricature in all of this. His aspect, when he is quiet, must be simply eerie. It is only in moments of extreme excitement that he becomes exteriorly ludicrous, but never too uncouth. His voice is husky and harsh, but again this ought of itself never to provoke the listener to laughter.

The dwarfs of the early Teutonic world were the smiths and the artisans for the universe. In their subterranean home, these small creatures collected the metals and ores of the earth and forged weapons and crafted great treasures with them. It was because of this kind of work that the dwarfs often had dealings with the gods. Although the dwarfs were never the equals of the deities, the gods considered the dwarfs to be necessary because of the valued possessions that they had made for them. It was the dwarfs who had built Froh's ship that always gathered a breeze when its sail was unfolded. It was the dwarfs who had made Froh's boar, the golden animal that drew the god through air and over water faster than a horse. It was these same creatures who had forged Wotan's spear, a weapon that never missed its mark. It was the dwarfs who had forged Donner's mighty hammer, a weapon that would never break and which, when thrown, always returned to the god's hand. It was these dwarfs who had fashioned the gold ring Draupnir, which every ninth night dropped eight gold rings, and it was these small beings of the Teutonic world who had made for Donner's wife the gold hair that grew upon her head.

Wagner gave to his Nibelung dwarfs the skills that had been unique to the *alfr* of the Germanic mythical world. It is his Nibelung dwarfs who gather the metallic wealth of the earth from the myriad of shafts and runs in Nibelheim. It is Alberich and Mime who are the craftsmen of the drama, the pair that forges two of the most significant property items of the *Ring* poem. It is Alberich who forges the coveted ring from the gold that he took from the Rhinemaidens, the ring that can grant its possessor mastery of the world, and it is Mime who physically fashions the Tarnhelm, the cap of change and invisibility from that same gold. Singular to Wagner's *Ring* argument, however, is a matter that essentially denies Mime the skill in metals that is a part of the character and nature that he gave to his dwarfs. Wagner causes his Mime to be unable to reforge the two pieces of the shattered sword Notung. Wagner's deviation in this instance from the norm of talents of Teutondom's dwarfs is not deviation for its own sake. Rather, by allowing Siegfried to remake his father's weapon and then to slay the Dragon with it, the dramatist subtly infuses into his work an indication of the natural superiority of the hero, as well as an added glorification of the Volsung mortal. Then, too, it should be noted that Wagner's Mime is truly lacking in those skills in metalcraft that are so characteristic of the dwarfs of Teutonic myths. It is true that it is Mime who forges the Tarnhelm that becomes so principal to the argument of the *Ring*. Yet, a careful review of the scene in *Das Rheingold* in which Alberich and Mime are in their Nibelheim home reveals that Mime in fact performed the physical tasks necessary to accomplish the Tarnhelm, but that he was really incapable of performing the work alone. The Tarnhelm was not only an idea that originated with Alberich, but it was also he who supplied the rather untalented Mime with all the details and instructions and overall know-how that allowed this valuable property and its magic to come into existence. (In one of the Eddic poems it is Siegfried who forges this sword, yet another poem states that it is Siegfried's dwarf companion who does the forging.)

There was a perceptible restless and disconsolate spirit in the Germanic mythical race of dwarfs. This spirit was coincidental with their singular physical appearance and their skill as craftsmen. This uneasiness of character is amply evident in the relationship that these supernaturals had with humans, to whom they were inferior both physically and mentally. To say the least, that relationship was tenuous, and it was only through necessity that the dwarfs of Teutondom had dealing with mortals. So strained were the associations of these two groups that there was an undercurrent of mutual distrust, and it was only when the dwarfs were left to themselves, in their own world, that there was any peace between the two races. And then, that peace was quite fragile! As the dwarfs did all possible to remain away from mortals, so too did humans show a wariness of dwarfs. Germanic beliefs held that the dwarfs were a thievish race, that a dwarf would make off with any unguarded item. This mythical thought also held that the dwarf was gifted with a certain form of divination, that the dwarf had the power to cast spells, that the dwarf knew of certain occult powers that were to be found in nature and that the dwarf was the only being who could master those powers. These beliefs also held that the dwarfs could make themselves invisible, that their possessions were cursed, that there was an evil fate in their glance, and that their touch and their breath brought illness, even death. If humans looked upon the dwarfs as *black* because of the soot and pitch that was all about them in their home, so too did mortals view them as having a dark and forbidding character, as possessing an evil spirit that rendered them inhospitable, a *black* nature. These dwarfs of Teutonic thought were, in all ways, *Black Dwarfs*.

Wagner's dramatization of the Black Dwarfs, at once an accurate portrayal of their physical qualities as well as of their status in the early Teutonic society, is also an equally substantial image of their mythical inherence. This complete depiction is uniquely significant because if Wagner was naturally concerned with the thematic aspects of his argument, he was also desirous of creating a total ambience and atmosphere that reflected the pervading thought in the heathen world. His success in the realization of this end is quite evident and cannot be discounted, and in large measure his dramatic picture of the Black Dwarfs contributed greatly to this effort. The composer used the figures of Alberich and Mime for his own thematic means, but with dialogue and stage directions he wove into this pair of dwarfs an innate and evil vileness. He made their intent suspicious. He made each one cunning and devious in his own way. He made Alberich and Mime dark figures, seething caldrons of perpetual hostility. Wagner made his Nibelung figures into *Black Dwarfs* in every sense of the words. Thus, when Wagner causes the King of the Gods to call the maker of the ring *Black Alberich*, and when he has the god speak of the dwarfs as *Schwarzalben* ("Black Alps"), he refers to more than physical blackness. Through his supreme god, Wagner is really referring to the essence of the total character of the dwarfs of ancient Teutondom.

See also: *Alberich*
              Mime

DWELLINGS

There is a unique difference between the concept of a single dwelling that Wagner gave to the gods in his *Ring* drama and that of the several abodes that these same gods inhabited in the Teutonic myths. In the drama of the *Ring* it is Valhalla ("Hall of the Chosen Slain") that is the home of the gods and the place from which Wotan can look down upon the earth, to observe all that was happening. In mythical thought, however, Valhalla was the celestial home of warriors who had fought bravely in battle and who had died in combat. These men were carefully selected by Wotan, and then brought from the battlefield by Valkyries. Once in Valhalla, these slain warriors were 'raised' and made members of Wotan's army. Each day they trained to improve their skills at fighting. Those who were wounded or slain in the daily combats were healed or 'raised' at the end of the day, at which time they all feasted upon pork meat and mead. The training and practice of these warriors were to prepare them for the fated day that they would have to defend the gods against their numerous enemies. If Wagner preserved this mythical concept of the purpose of Valhalla, that is, as the home of selected warriors, he also enlarged upon it by making it the home, the dwelling, of the five gods that are so prominent in his *Ring* drama.

Four of the five gods that Wagner brought into his drama from the Germanic mythical past possessed magnificent homes of their own. Donner's dwelling had 540 rooms, and was the largest house known to mortals. This home was called *Bilskirnir* ("Strong"), and it was located in *Thrudvangar* ("Field of Power"). Freia's dwelling was located in *Folkvangar* ("Field of the Folk") and it was known as *Sessrumnir* ("Rich in Seats"). Fricka's home, which is succinctly described as "most magnificent," was named *Fensalir* ("Sea Halls").

The most celebrated of the mythical homes of the gods was that which belonged to Wotan. This god's dwelling was called *Valaskjolf* ("Shelf of the Slain"). This home had been constructed for him by the gods, on a site that the god himself had chosen. The most outstanding feature of the dwelling was its roof of pure silver. There was, however, a special tower at one end of the building, a tower whose name was *Hlidskjolf* ("Top Shelf"). It was from this tower that Wotan looked down upon the earth each day, to learn what had occurred in the world that the gods had created, and what had transpired among the mortals that those same gods had placed there.

Froh is the only god in Wagner's drama who does not possess a specific mythical home or dwelling. Although the myths speak of Froh as the "foremost of gods," and even though he became the supreme god among the early people who lived in what is now Sweden, these tales do not include details that refer to a dwelling for the god, and there is not to be found any reason why Froh has no separate and individual home of his own.

Wagner placed two additional gods in the *dramatis personae* of his *Ring* drama. One of these deities was Loge, whom he called God of Fire, and the other was Erda, who became his Goddess of the Earth. Neither of these two figures was a god within the mythical order of the early Teutonic peoples. Loge was a cunning schemer, liar, and troublemaker who, according to the myths, lived in Asgard (Land of the Gods), but who apparently had no specific dwelling of his own. Wagner's Erda does not exist in the Germanic mythical thought. He created this figure specifically for his drama, although it is obvious to one familiar with the ancient myths that he patterned his Erda after the *volva* ("prophetess"), one of the special seers who is to be found quite frequently in the mythical tales.

See also: *Valhalla* (Vol. I)

-E-

EAGLE

There is reference in the *Ring*, if ever so brief, to an eagle. The scene occurs in the final scene of the first act of the fourth drama, *Götterdämmerung*, when the drugged Siegfried, who has taken the form of Gunther, penetrates the fire-ringed mountain, and encounters there the frightened Brünnhilde. The Valkyrie, whose divinity has been taken away by the King of the Gods, screams in fear as she sees this figure, and then, trembling, she shouts that an eagle has flown to the mountain top to tear her to bits! Wagner's intensive efforts to convey a sense of antiquity throughout his drama is enhanced by this inclusion of the heathen Teutonic mythical eagle, a creature frequently mentioned in the Eddic tales. (An additional degree of that ambience is achieved in this case by the choice of words that Wagner used in this scene. He was not content to indicate the eagle in his *Ring* by means of the word that is regularly used in modern German, that is *Adler*. Rather, he sought an older term, a word out of the past, one whose antiquity and then disappearance from the modern tongue had rendered the term a bit more poetic. That word was *Aar*.

Despite the brevity of the Valkyrie's mention of an 'eagle,' Wagner's use of the name of that bird reflects his awareness of the significance of this creature in early Teutonic beliefs. The eagle was one of the animal figures that had an integral role in the thought and ways of the ancient Germanic peoples, but it was somewhat unique in that it was a creature that never ascended to a position of true mythical prominence as, for example, the wolf and the raven! Yet, it was very much a figure in the mythical world, and it was Wagner's thorough and equally extensive knowledge of that heathen Germanic mythical universe that caused him to realize that this bird, somehow, should become a part of his drama. If the reference that Wagner included in the drama is brief, so brief that it may go unnoticed, it subtly reflects, nevertheless, the concepts and attitudes about the eagle that are to be found in the mythical literature.

The eagle that lived in the early Teutonic mind was somewhat of a sacred creature that nevertheless instilled much fear into the people. This bird's sacredness was not that which prompted invocation or veneration. Rather, that sacredness was more a serious concern as well as regard for what the eagle could do to sustain and to protect itself, and for the ways by which it achieved those ends. It was that same respect that caused the people to avoid this bird in the wild, not only because of its predatory ways, but also because of its great strength. There was the belief that when the eagle flapped its huge wings, the winds of the world were born, and the angrier that the bird became, the greater the intensity and velocity of those winds. It was because of the eagle's strength and power, as well as some of its ways, that the bird was often associated with the supreme god, Wotan. Once, when the Allfather stole the mead that conferred on him the gift of poetry, he transformed himself into a large eagle in order to have the power of his mighty wings to escape his pursuers. This association of the eagle and the King of the Gods is evidenced again in the myths that treat of Valhalla, the dwelling for slain heroes over which the god reigned supreme. According to mythical belief, the imposing figure of an eagle was carved over the western door of this hallowed building.

The strength that was natural to the eagle was a foundation for much of its fierceness. It was also because of that fierceness that the people avoided the creature. The beliefs held that this strength and this ferocity were cause to look upon the eagle as representative of an evil or sinister destiny. Part of that belief was another societal reason for the eagle to be avoided. The belief maintained that when the eagle fed upon the cadavers of animals and other birds, as it often did, it retained some of the blood of these bodies in its beak and then, when the bird flew through the sky, it sprinkled that blood upon those who were fated to suffer an unpleasant, even injurious, misfortune.

The eagle was such a commanding figure that it was associated with the Germanic tree of life, Yggdrasil, or World Ash Tree. (It was this tree that held within its branches and at its roots the nine worlds of the heathen Teutonic universe.) This eagle roosted in the branches of the World Ash, on that limb that grew far out from the world of mortals and stretched to the edge of heaven. This spot where the eagle resided was called "Eagle's Hill," and from there the eagle could look down into Hel, the World of the Dead.

The beliefs of the people also held that an eagle would have a role, albeit a minor one, at the time of *ragnarök*, the fated time of the downfall of the gods and the destruction of the world. As a prophetess envisions, at such time as The Final Battle of the world is being waged, a giant will take the form of an eagle. This bird will be called Hraesvelg ("Corpse-Eater"), and it will fly down to the field of battle, and there it will tear and gnaw on the flesh of the bodies of the dead and those of the screaming warriors who have been injured in combat!

The early Teutonic mind had endowed the eagle with what it viewed as a penchant for savage, coarse animalistic brutality. Yet, despite this negative nature that they obviously had witnessed, those same minds closely associated this bird with the hero, the fearless and brave doer of deeds that perhaps were somewhat beyond the capacity or the daring of normal man, but which, nevertheless, always bordered on the fantastic. The people welcomed, for example, the piercing, shrill scream of the eagle, when it was heard outside the house of a woman who was about to give birth. That cry, at that time, was the portent that a hero would soon be born there. This eagle-hero relationship is also evidenced in an Eddic poem that recounts how Sigurd (Siegfried) does battle with Lyngvi, the slayer of his father, Siegmund. After the hero has killed Lyngvi, Regin the dwarf, advises the youth that now a blood-eagle with a biting sword should be carved on Lyngvi's back as a sign that Siegmund's avenger fought with the strength and fierceness of that bird.

Wagner did not disregard these characteristics of brute-force, savage ferocity, and wild vitality that the early Germanic peoples associated with the eagle. The composer took these qualities, adapted them to his needs, and then related them, if ever so subtly, with the hero (Siegfried) in that scene in which Brünnhilde screams her forceful words as the stranger appears. There is a show of power, and bravura, even a sense of animal fierceness in this figure who has penetrated the fire that surrounds the mountain top and who now confronts the former Valkyrie. This is a figure who obviously is determined to fulfill his mission. In this figure's relative silence, and Brünnhilde's few words, Wagner successfully presents a brief dramatical metaphor as well as a primary understanding of the mythical concept that the Teutonic peoples had of the eagle.

See also: *Animals*
        Nine Worlds

EARTH See: *Elements*
          Clod (of earth)
          Midgard

EAST See: *Compass Points*

ELEMENTS

It is not totally unreasonable to claim that Wagner's interest in Greek tragedy led him into other matters of a Grecian flavor. It is widely known that Wagner passionately advanced the framework of the Greek tragedies as a basis for a rebuilding of a German national art. His writings reveal that he felt that the Grecian artform allowed a much desired synthesis of the major artforms of the day: poetry, drama, art (stage settings), a chorus, dance, and music. Wagner sincerely believed that this amalgam of creative action, when properly ordered, prepared, and presented, would not only satisfy the people's artistic hunger, but would also permit the revelation of those characteristics that constituted the true nature and character of the German people. Wagner was guided in his work by such concepts, and there can be no doubt that he attempted to apply them as he went about the business of composition of his *Ring* drama. (The design of the theater in Bayreuth, the Festspielhaus, was essentially of Wagner's own creation and he relied heavily on the form and shape and contour of the Grecian theaters.)

There was, however, another Grecian matter that attracted the composer's creative sensibilities. Scholars of the Wagnerian art have offered rather copious studies of this matter which, if only of a secondary import in the total picture of things Wagnerian, should nevertheless be a part of any consideration of the man and his art.

It was an early Grecian concept that Wagner could not avoid, one that would change in time but which nevertheless had made a lasting imprint in considered thought. This idea had proposed the basic and fundamental properties that had allowed for formation of the universe. The ancient Greeks held that there were four elements that were the ingredients out of which the universe was created. Those elements were: air, earth, fire, and water. Some studies of the composer and the *Ring* promote the idea that this drama is replete with the presentation of these elements, sufficient in number to prevent any distraction from the theory, and sufficient in number to substantiate the belief that Wagner purposefully included them in his work as a means of acknowledging either his awareness of their significance, or his acceptance of that significance, or possibly both factors.

The first of these elements, air, is a constituent that is heard and felt, but cannot be seen. It is very evident in the first and second scenes of Act III of *Die Walküre*. It is in these scenes that Wotan, in his rage and fury, pursues his daughter Brünnhilde who flees her father's anger because she has disobeyed his command. The supreme god had ordered that Siegmund die in his struggle with Hunding, but the Valkyrie had become so filled with compassion for the Volsung and his sister, Sieglinde, that she attempted to use her magic to rescue him from death on Hunding's spear. When Wotan interrupts this combat to establish his authority over the matter, and allows Hunding to slay Siegmund, Brünnhilde quickly gathers up the two pieces of Siegmund's shattered sword and beckons Sieglinde to flee with her. The two ride to Valkyrie Rock where Brünnhilde pleads with her eight sisters to aid her. It is then that the Valkyries begin to hear the rush of air that comes from the North. The sound of the air becomes louder, and louder still, and then, they see the supreme god in the distance, riding his steed furiously, in all his anger. Needless to say, Wagner made much of this scene musically. The action of this scene, which takes place almost entirely off-stage, is indeed a unique representation of Wotan as "Das wütende Heer," 'The Furious Host' of numerous religious beliefs.

The second element of the Grecian concept of the constituents of creation is *fire*. There are, of course, the fires that burn in Nibelheim and which are seen when Wotan and Loge descend to the home of the dwarfs in an effort to take over Alberich's treasure of gold. There is also the occasion when Donner calls forth his lightning to clear the air of clouds. And, there are other scenes in which fire in the form of lightning is a factor in the drama. There is also a hearth in Hunding's dwelling, a hearth whose flames warm the exhausted Siegmund as he seeks refuge from the storm outside. There are, however, two other scenes in the *Ring* that exploit fire as a component of all life, scenes that become most dramatic because of their fire. The first of this fire is generally known as the "Magic Fire," the great ring of fire that Wotan summons to surround the mountain top on which he has condemned Brünnhilde to a lengthy sleep because she disobeyed one of his orders. Wagner understood the theatricality of the fire of this scene, and he developed the fire and flames as a major component in the drama itself. He causes the god to summon the *Ring's* God of Fire who appears in the form of a small flame. As Wotan uses his spear to point out the circle that the fire should form, the flames grow in form as well as in intensity. Slowly, the fire takes its shape and flames become ever higher and more powerful. In time, the fire blazes at full force and the entire setting is aflame. Wotan's eyes are fixed on the flames that now hide his favorite daughter from view. He turns, and slowly exits the scene as Wagner's fire music brings the drama to one of the most striking conclusions in all of the musical and dramatic repertory.

The "Magic Fire" of *Die Walküre* does not disappear with the curtain on the last act of this second part of the *Ring*. Wagner brings those flames back on two more occasions, once in *Siegfried* as the Volsung hero climbs the mountain to penetrate the ring in order to awaken the sleeping maid, and then again in *Götterdämmerung*, as background for the three Norns who weave the Cord of Destiny and also for the second scene of that "Prelude," when once again the setting is that of the mountain where Brünnhilde slept and now awaits the return of Siegfried. Needless to say, the "Magic Fire" of these second and third appearances is neither of the same intensity nor of the same scope as the original, and in these scenes fire does not command the thematic attention that was evident when Wotan brought it into existence. Yet, the concept of fire is undeniably present.

There is yet another evidence of fire that lends its ambience to Wagner's *Ring*. This fire, of course, is that flame that begins with a torch that Brünnhilde tosses on the pyre on which the slain Siegfried has been placed, and which then grows in intensity, scope, and even grandeur until it has enveloped and destroyed the corrupt world and the gods who created that world. As with the earlier "Magic Fire," so too with the fire of the final scene of the four-part drama does the composer make capital use of fire and flame as a theatrical property. The fire is a single property that occupies the full setting for considerable time as the music that denotes that fire resounds. At the same time, all of this use of fire becomes a unique reminder of the importance that Wagner gave to fire, and equally so, a reminder of the importance of fire in ancient Teutonic thought, and possibly also, a reminder that fire was very much on the minds of the Greeks of another era.

The third element of the Grecian concept of the fundamental constituents of creation is water. This basic element of the Grecian idea is generously provided in Wagner's *Ring*, and not merely once. The first offering is evident at the rise of the first curtain, in the initial scene of *Das Rheingold* whose setting is the bottom of the Rhine River! It is this Rhine that steadily makes its own way through the lengthy drama and is regularly sensed as being almost ever-present by means of the numerous references to it by the players, and as evidenced in the final of the four dramas by its proximity to the great Gibichung hall that is located on its banks. Of course, the Rhine and its waters become a primary factor in the last moments of the *Ring*, primary in the sense that it is the Rhine that overflows its banks and floods the world, extinguishing the conflagration that has brought defeat and destruction to the gods. There can be no suggestion that the element of water is lacking in the *Ring*.

The fourth of the elements that the ancient Greeks believed was at the basis of all creation was earth, that is, soil. There are in the *Ring* numerous references to the flower and branch of the ancient world of Siegfried and his colleagues, the direct results of earth and its reproductive qualities. Linden trees, and fir and ash trees essentially abound throughout the work as forests are used as settings as well as inanimate properties to support the dialogue. Then, there is the character of Erda, the 'earth mother,' the all-wise, the Ur-Wala, as she is called by Wotan. Yet, if these several kinds of 'earth' are not so readily acceptable to one aspect of the Wagner audience, even then it cannot be said that the composer left any detail to chance, even in the matter of *earth*. In the last of the dramas of the tetralogy of the *Ring* Wagner includes a specific and definite bit of action that represents this theme of 'earth' and its significance. The scene is that of Siegfried and the three Rhine daughters. These nixies have pleaded with the youth that he return to them the ring of gold that he had taken from the Nibelung treasure after he had slain Fafner the Dragon. Siegfried is reluctant, and when the Rhine daughters tell him that he will die if he does not return the ring, he rebuffs them by picking up a bit of earth which he then tosses behind him, announcing that he is unconcerned about their prediction and that he values his life as much as he values the clod of earth. Again, as before numerous times, Wagner involves some bit of ancient thought into the web of his argument, some feature from the past that will add its color and tone to the total ambience of his drama.

The foregoing actions and dialogue extracted from throughout Wagner's *Der Ring des Nibelungen* are, in and of themselves, quantity and quality enough to demonstrate where and how the composer was able to involve in his gigantic work the four elements that ancient Grecian thought considered as the fundamental elements in the creation of the universe. Yet, if what he had done was on somewhat of a scattered basis, that is, separate incidents at relatively unrelated spots in his work, he was to crown this matter of the four elements with a single scene that not only boasts the appearance each of these basic constituents of the composite universe, but also shows them all as integral one to the other, and also to the more significant matter at hand.

The scene that includes all four of the elements that Grecian thought had proposed as fundamental to creation of the world is found in the first act of *Siegfried*, in that scene that concludes that act. Although Wagner did not offer titles for individual scenes of his work, over time some titles have arisen and persisted, and that title that has remained with the action of the one in question here is "Forging Scene." It is in this climactic scene that Wagner brings together the elements of water, fire, air, and earth as separate entities, and then fuses them as parts of a greater whole!

The "Forging Scene" includes a disturbed Siegfried, disturbed because the dwarf Mime has not forged a sword for him. It is Siegfried's intent to use the sword to face the dragon and thereby learn the meaning of fear. At the same time, the Volsung youth realizes that Mime is incapable of reforging the sword that had been that of his father, and he takes matters into his own hands and reforges the sword himself.

It is now, in the Forging Scene, that the four elements come into their own. Primary to the dramatic action is the forge itself, the place where the fire is held and upon which the entire action is based. However, crucial to the fire, at least to its intensity, is the bellows that is part of the forge and with which air is fed to the fire, to nourish the flames and to increase their effectiveness. As Siegfried works at the process of remaking the Notung of his father, he pours the liquid metal into a mold, and then quickly thrusts that mold into the water that is in a barrel at the side of the forge, to cool and to solidify the metal. The first three of the four elements of Greek thought are obviously an integral part of this scene. However, there is one more element that is important to the Grecian quartet and which remains yet unnamed, and, on the surface at least, absent from the scene. That fourth quality is *earth*, which the knowledgeable Wagner subtly provides in the form of the charcoal that fuels this important fire! As if the use of the charcoal as a symbol for the earth is not satisfactory enough to serve as the 'earth' in this situation, the composer draws specific attention to this fuel, thereby making it primary, by causing it to be made from the wood of an ash tree that grew in the forest, the very kind of tree that was so important to the early culture of Teutondom.

It is indeed speculative as to the manner, if any, that Wagner considered the four elements of Grecian thought significant. There is no doubt that he included them in his drama, and it is apparent that he made the four a part of a single scene. Yet, Wagner apparently never spoke specifically to this matter. It is not doubtful, however, that Wagner laid great faith on the matter of Greek tragedy, its format, its players, its properties, its setting, and above all, the mental and emotional reaction that it stimulated. With such fact as background, it is not unique, then, to allow for his dramatic association with another facet of Greek thought, that idea about the fundamental elements that were a part of creation. If such matters are not crucial to the intellectual universality of the *Ring*, they were crucial to the Greeks, and if nothing more can be said, perhaps Wagner is applauding the Greeks in the most appropriate manner at his disposal.

See also: *Clod (of earth)*
              The Furious Host

ERDA

Erda, as the name of a supernatural figure, is not to be found in the myths of ancient Teutondom. The term was not used as a name, and therefore there was no such being who figured among the Germanic divine hierarchy and with whom the early Teutonic peoples had some mythical familiarity. Rather, the name *Erda* is a name that Wagner created for his *Ring* drama, a name which, in his insistent desire to convey a sense of Germanic antiquity throughout his drama, came to him from the Old High German *Erada* and *Erda*, words that survive in modern German as *Erde*, all of which have meanings of *soil, dirt, clay,* and *earth*.

Wagner designated the Erda of his *Ring* as *Goddess of the Earth*, a name and a function that obviously served the purposes that he had envisioned for this supernatural being in the argument of his lengthy drama. Although the figure of Erda in the *Ring* is a product of Wagner's dramatic mind, he did draw on a relative minor figure that is found in the mythical literature and one about whom reference in Eddic poetry is frequently made. This figure is Jorth (pronounced *Yorth*), which meant "Earth." (The word is frequently spelled *Iord* in modern English.) In a number of the early Teutonic tales Jorth is depicted as both the wife and daughter of Wotan (Odin), and the mother of Donner (Thor). Presumably because of Jorth's name and its meaning, she was also "Earth Mother," although her role in this capacity never emerged as a lasting facet of Germanic belief, and no cult for her ever developed.

In addition to the matter of Jorth and her function and position within the world of the Teutonic gods, Wagner was also able to ponder certain of the societal and cultural attitudes that readily lend themselves to his development of the figure Erda. It would be these quasi-religious beliefs of the ancient Germanics, bolstered by the concept of the figure Jorth, that would ultimately confirm the dramatic decisions that Wagner had made regarding his Goddess of the Earth.

In the early times of the Teutonic peoples, there was a reverence for the earth. This reverence at times has been called 'worship,' yet if in fact earth had that type of following, it was not the worship of earth as a god, or the worship of the earth itself. Rather, such religious devotion for the earth was as *the mother of all things*, the factor in life that gives birth to all things in the natural world, and the nurturer of that nature. This concept of earth as "mother" has developed and persisted in numerous cultures and is still found today in several contemporary societies. (In most languages that have gender as a part of their grammatical foundation, *earth* is usually of the feminine gender.)

Relative to this concept of earth as a female being is that ancient and very ingrained Germanic belief in the divine capacities of women. These early tribes and clans believed that women were more gifted than men in this matter of divination, that in fact it was seldom that men were able to practice this magic. This reverence, which has also been termed 'worship,' caused decrees of prophesy to take on a special sacredness when uttered by a woman, and such decrees could include knowledge of the past as well as of the present. Thus it was that a kind of cult evolved around these female prophets, and that cult existed quite early in that ancient era of the Germanic people. Such women became the *all-wise*, the *all-knowing*. The beliefs of these people also held that these gifted women possessed the wisdom of the world, and that they were the figures to whom one turned for aid in the matters of fate and destiny. The belief in these women not only continued throughout the decades of the Teutonic world, but it intensified, and over a period of time the societal belief became so strong that these women were looked upon not only as the true revealers of destiny to mankind, but they were also counsels to the divine hierarchy of Teutondom. Possessed of such singular and unique magic, these women enjoyed an elevated status within society, and they were viewed as having an authority greater than that of other mortals, but somewhat less than that of gods.

The Old Norse word that denoted a female being who possessed the gift of divination and prophesy was *volva*. The magic that these persons possessed obviously served a need in the ancient culture, and as belief and faith in the pronouncements of the *volva* continued, their position within the culture became more exalted. The *volva* soon became so potent a power within the culture, and their authority became so commanding that the word *volva* ceased to be a generic term, that is, denoting one of many, and became personalized and acquired the meaning of a specific and particular figure, *the* Volva. In the Teutonic mind of that day the Volva became a special being who took on a divine quality, a special being whose aid and counsel was regularly sought because she was the only being who lived among the mortals who could 'see all over the world,' the one figure who knew all things of the past and the present, and the counsel who knew what was yet to come. Such is the Volva who appears in the Eddic tales.

It is to this Volva that Wagner turned as model, as well as inspiration and stimulus for the creation of his Erda. It is from this mythical figure who appears in *The Poetic Edda* that he gathered attributes for his prophetess. It is from this 'all-wise' being that he took certain qualities which he then adapted to the argument that he gave his *Ring* drama and which he included as part of his figure Erda, Goddess of the Earth.

There are two poems in *The Poetic Edda* in which Volva is a prominent figure: "Baldrs Draumar" ("Balder's Dreams") and "Voluspo"

("The Lay of the Volva" or "The Lay of the Wise One" or "The Wise Woman's Prophesy"). The Volva in each of these lays is the same figure, and her function in each of the myths is essentially the same. It is, however, in the second of the two poems cited that her stature as a revealer of all the periods of time is dramatically exhibited. It is most natural that Wotan also is a figure in each of the two poems as he attempts to gain more knowledge from the *all-wise* of the Teutonic world. The god uses his magic and his divine powers to force the Volva "to rise" and then to counsel him with her wisdom and to relate to him all that she knows. In "Balder's Dreams," Volva tells of the tragic death of the god Balder, the favorite son of Wotan and his wife Fricka. The prophetess then relates what will result from the incident of Balder's death, and who will be involved. In "Voluspo," the longer of the two poems, Volva answers Wotan's questions regarding the universe. She tells the god of the creation of the world, of Yggdrasil, the World Ash Tree, of the Dwarfs, of the Norns, and of the first war of the universe. Then, she tells the Allfather of the ultimate fate of the world, of the final battle in which Wotan, Donner, Froh, and Loge, will die. The Volva then reveals that fire and flood will destroy the earth and the remaining gods in their celestial heaven. As the final part of the Volva's revelation of the fate of the world and its gods, she states that the world will ultimately enjoy a rebirth, a rebirth that the myths claim will be a pure and sinless world with uncorrupted gods. (Balder will be one of the gods who is raised and will live in that new world.) In each of these lays, when Volva concludes her revelations, she "sinks" back into the earth.

There are several aspects of the Eddic poetry in which the figure of the Volva is present which are quite similar to details of the argument that Wagner devised for his *Ring* drama. This is especially true when one looks at "Voluspo" and Wagner's poem. It is also evident that the composer relied heavily on these lays for the fundamental nature and character of his Erda. It was in fact this figure, the Volva, or Wala as she is also called in the Eddic poetry and in the *Ring*, who became Wagner's Erda.

Wagner's turn to the mythical Volva for the nature and function of his Erda did not, however, result in a mirror-like copy. There are certain distinctions between the two figures, dramatic adaptations that Wagner applied to his figure as he viewed his prophetess in the thematic context of his tetralogy. In an overall view, Wagner's Erda successfully reflects more of the form and the aura of a divine being than does the Volva. Erda is a figure of non-earthly character, one closely related to the world of gods and the celestial activities. In the myths of the Teutonic peoples, however, Volva is at once a mortal woman who has died and now resides in Niflheim, the Land of the Dead and one of the nine worlds of the Germanic mythical universe. It is Wotan who, by means of his divine magic, causes her to rise from her grave, to seek the surface of the earth, and to speak to him in death, after which she "sinks" again into her grave. Wagner does not assign his Erda to a specific world although he does create the allusion that she is neither of the world of man nor the world of the gods. She is, rather, of her own world, a world to which only she has entrance. Erda's wisdom alone is reason enough for that singular existence. Wagner's Erda is obviously not a mortal being. In the composer's words, Erda "rises" and she "sinks," she becomes "visible" and she "disappears." When she rises, it is out of slumber rather than out of death, and as Volva returns to her grave, Erda returns to her unearthly sleep from which she gains her wisdom.

Wagner involved his Erda in two relationships for which there are no equivalents in the Eddic literature. It is evident that he included these relationships as a means of effecting a more unified drama, a more compactly interwoven argument which he obviously achieved because few of today's *Ring* audience question these arrangements in any way. The first of these thematic devices is that of Erda as mother of the three Norns. This type of mother-daughter relationship involving the Volva and the Norns does not exist in the myths of ancient Teutondom. The Norns of the Germanic past exist, that is, they *are*, without present and without past, and they will so exist for eternity. There is no doubt, however, that the Norns reflect a veil of the Volva's essence. They too are concerned with the fate and destiny of living things, each representing a segment of time as Past, Present, and Future. Each of the Norns also displays some facet of the greater Volva, in a distinctive manner perhaps, but nevertheless with that same haunting quality that is so much a part of the prophetess of old. It is obvious to the follower of Wagner's *Ring* that both Erda and the Norns project an unquestioned ambience of mythicalness, a dramatic portrait of the supernaturals of another day. The composer's created relationship of mother and three daughters, as arranged and presented in the *Ring*, is, then, very much within the realm of mythical credibility. His arrangement of this matter not only serves well as a dramatic grouping, it is also such that it becomes a most convincing interrelationship to those who are unaware of the mythical beliefs as they once held sway in the several regions of Teutondom.

The second of the relationships that Wagner created for his Erda is another which, like the first, can be readily accepted, especially when the essence of the mythicalness of the participants is considered. The myths of the Germanic peoples depict the god Wotan as a wanderer, a god who takes on numerous guises and constantly travels the universe searching for knowledge and for wisdom. He has drunk from the Spring of Wisdom that flows at the base of the World Ash Tree, a drink that gave him much wisdom but whose payment to the keeper of the spring was one of his eyes. The god also went to elaborate lengths to steal the Mead of Inspiration which gave him the gift of poetry. And, of course, Wotan seeks out the Volva, ever hopeful of learning of her art and the wisdom that her art provides. Wagner's Wotan, like the god of the myths, is also a wanderer, and he too travels abroad to gain as well as to dispense his wisdom. Wagner makes Wotan's visit to Mime in the cave of the dwarf and the contest of wits that is so familiar in the Teutonic myths into a very intense scene. Wagner did not include the Volva in his drama, but he had the Erda that he had created, and it is to her that the Wotan of the *Ring* turns when he is in need of counsel and guidance.

As Wagner brought these two characters of Erda and Wotan into his poem, he intuitively saw a dramatically beneficial relationship between the two, a relationship of the supreme god and the essentially divine, or at least supernatural, Erda. For specific purposes of his drama, he would bring these two together into a union that would produce the nine Valkyries that are part of the *dramatis personae*. It is thematic fact that Wagner causes his Erda to attempt to resist Wotan, but she is powerless when confronted by the divine forces of the Supreme God. (That Wagner made his Wotan the seducer of

Erda is quite consistent with the character and the activities of the Allfather god as accepted in the Germanic beliefs.)

Erda appears but twice in Wagner's *Ring*. Those two scenes in which the 'earth mother' is a figure focus essentially on her. She is the holiest and wisest of the *volvas*. She is the *all-knowing*, the *all-seeing*, she is the great prophetess, the mother of wisdom, the prime mother of the universe. As such, she is Wotan's wisdom and his knowledge, wisdom and knowledge that, unfortunately, the great god chooses not to use and, as a result, brings devastation to the universe. As in the myths of the Teutonic peoples, so too in Wagner's *Ring* does the aura of primitive wisdom finds its niche in a female spirit, the Volva of old and the Erda of Wagner's poem.

See also: *Ur-Wala*

ERDA (Name)

Wagner called this figure of his *Ring* drama "Goddess of the Earth," akin, at least in name, to the English "Mother Earth." This character, her godhood, and her name were not a part of Teutonic mythology, but were, rather, a creation of Wagner himself.

Wagner took the name of this goddess from the Old High German *Erda* [*Erada*], (Mod.G – *Erde*; ON – *jorth*; OE – *eorthe*; ME – *erthe*; Goth – *airtha*) which means "earth" in the sense of "world." The composer's mythical inspiration for this name probably stemmed from the name of the Teutonic goddess *Iord* (pronounced 'Yorth'), which translates into English as "earth." This mythological figure is frequently identified as the mother of Donner, and in some myths she is the wife of Wotan. The celebrated mythologist Jakob Grimm believed that Iord was also the mother of Wotan. In *The Prose Edda* Iord is depicted as the "daughter of Night."

EYE (Wotan's)

Throughout all of the Germanic mythical literature, as well as in the *Ring* drama, Wotan, the King of the Gods, has but one good eye. The literature reveals, if succinctly, how the god lost one of his eyes, but, curiously, Wagner includes in his argument two separate and distinct acts that occasioned that loss. One of these actions mirrors the account in the mythical literature, the second was a dramatic device created by Wagner himself.

The mythical act that deprived the supreme god of Teutondom of an eye is depicted in *The Poetic Edda* as well as in *The Prose Edda*. One of the prominent characteristics of the great god Wotan was his desire for wisdom and knowledge. The god was forever searching for greater understanding of all things in the universe. He traveled frequently, to all parts of the universe, ever alert for additional knowledge that he could acquire. On one of his trips, he journeyed to the Spring of Wisdom that flowed at the base of the World Ash Tree and which was tended by the wise water spirit, Mimir. Wotan drank from the Spring of Wisdom, and as payment for that drink, the god yielded one of his eyes. It was this mythical action and the resultant loss that Wagner carried over into his *Ring* drama, into the "Prelude" of the fourth drama. In that scene the composer causes the First Norn to tell how the god once came to the spring and took a drink of the waters of wisdom, a drink whose price was one of the god's eyes. (Wagner makes no reference in this scene to Mimir, the guardian of the spring, because it is from another mythical figure named *Mimir* that he found his inspiration not only for the name, but for the character of his *Mime*.)

It was during the composition of the poem *Das Rheingold* that Wagner brought into his tale the second of the causes of Wotan's loss of an eye. (Wagner wrote the four dramas of his *Ring* in the reverse order of intended presentation.) In this latter scene, Wotan is talking with his wife, Fricka. The Supreme God tells Fricka that he values women most highly, and as proof of his words he reminds her that the price that he had to pay to win her was one of his eyes.

Wagner's inclusion of this second cause for Wotan's loss is puzzling. His reason for retention of the *two* causes is an enigma. It is a well known fact that Wagner was noted for his serious concern for mythical matters, and that he had a sincere desire to create a dramatic ambience in his drama that accurately reflected the essence of that early Germanic world as revealed through those myths. It was, then, not mere coincidence that he incorporated into his work a myriad of Teutonic mythical matters, and further it is evident that when he felt himself obliged to alter or to modify a mythical matter, or even when he sensed the need to create a mythical incident, the results were in themselves essentially mythical in nature. Why, then, are there in the drama of the *Ring* two separate and distinct explanations that purport to tell how and why the King of the Gods lost one of his eyes? And, further, of the two causes that Wagner gives for Wotan's loss of an eye, why is one an obvious creation, a creation that came into being after he had already included the correct mythical cause?

The question of why Wagner erred so obviously in the matter of the cause of Wotan's loss of an eye cannot really be answered. The composer devoted some twenty-six years to the composition of the *Ring*, first as a drama and then as music-drama. He returned again and again to this work. He made numerous changes, revisions, modifications, additions, and deletions. There can be no doubt that he was aware that he had included two distinct causes for the loss of Wotan's eye. Yet, despite the fact that each of these stated causes in essence contradicted the other, despite the fact that one cause was that taken from Teutonic mythical thought and the other was merely a dramatic element of his own creation, Wagner never spoke to the matter, and he made no reference to the subject in his extensive writings regarding the drama. Thus it is today, as it was at the time of the composition of the *Ring*, there are two explanations for Wotan's loss of an eye, one that is mythically correct, and one that is really spurious to the drama's argument.

See also: *Eyes*

EYES

The early Teutonic peoples held that the eyes, more than any other part of the body, had special qualities. This ancient culture did not give major or prominent significance to this aspect of their beliefs, but, nevertheless, there were several beliefs that pertained to eyes that became popular. In some of the Teutonic regions it was held that a blink of an eye was the measurement of the shortest interval of time. Another belief equated Wotan's eye with the sun, especially when this god was looked upon as the firmament of the world. In this latter context, the *eye* was occasionally referred to as *the star of the skull*. (It was the skull of the giant Ymir, held aloft by four dwarfs, one at each corner of the compass, that became the world that was inhabited by mortals.)

If there were these and other scattered and lesser concepts pertaining to *eyes*, there were also those that were of a broader scope and of more profound texture. An early Germanic belief held that some of the inhabitants of the nine worlds of the universe had eyes in which there was a certain magic power, a power that worked for good or for evil. A mere 'look' from one of these special beings could conjure a spirit, or it could enchant. A 'glance' could affect the thought or the acts of others. A 'glance' could also effect the wishes or desires of those who knew the *magic of the eyes*.

The power that was wielded through the eyes was a natural force rather than an acquired one. The resultant harm or benefit that was produced by that force was dependent upon the user's power or status within the Germanic scheme of things. One belief that was held extensively throughout the entire Germanic culture was that which accorded the *dwarf* (Alp) a 'look' that could bring evil or inflict harm upon mortals. Essentially, the dwarf had what may be called in more contemporary terms an 'evil eye.' His glance was to be avoided at whatever costs. Wagner could find no thematic value in the use of such a concept in the makeup of his principal Nibelung dwarfs, Alberich and Mime. He did, however, make indirect reference to this aspect of the eyes of the dwarf in the opening scene of his drama. As Alberich makes lustful advances at the three Rhinemaidens, the water spirits taunt and tease their ugly suitor. At one point, the nymphs speak of the physical traits of the Nibelung which repulse them, and one of these traits is his penetrating or piercing glance. Given the mass of Teutonic mythicalness that Wagner brought to the totality of his *Ring*, it is possible to conclude that there is in the Rhinemaidens' words an indication of the powers of wickedness that lies in Alberich's eyes.

At the opposite end of the spectrum of powers or forces that were available through the eyes lay the belief that *good* could result from certain 'looks' or 'glances.' This concept, at least in part, held that the eye was capable of dispelling cares and concerns by instilling an inner solace and comfort, a sense of calm that released the receiver from his woes. Wagner was careful in his adaptations of this cultural belief into his drama, this first time in the final scene of the first act of *Die Walküre*, that scene in which Siegmund and Sieglinde, each burdened with personal despair, discover their real identities, declare their love, and then flee in search of a new existence.

It is Siegmund who first infers this power of the eye. As he stands alone in the darkness of Hunding's dwelling, the fire suddenly brightens, and its light strikes the hilt of the sword that is embedded in the tree that rises in the room. In what is obviously a reference to the love that is blossoming within him, Siegmund says that the gleam that he sees is the 'glance' that Sieglinde left behind when she left the room. This remark is also an indication of the emotional release that has come to Siegmund, a release from the consternation that has so persistently plagued him in his lifetime.

Sieglinde, in her turn, also speaks of the eyes as the harborers of tenderness. As she relates the tale of the stranger who thrust the sword into the tree, she refers to his eye, and to the 'glance' that struck terror into those others upon whom it fell. Yet, for her this 'glance' dispelled her sorrow, and if it was a 'look' that others felt as great power and force, it was a 'look' that gave her solace and comfort.

Sieglinde then talks of Siegmund's eyes. She says that her heart gave way to him when first his eyes looked upon her. She states that when he looked at her, she knew about love, at last, and that she was his, that within her there was a peace that had come from the majestic brilliance of his eyes.

A similar yet expanded application of this quality of the eye also forms a part of the final scene of *Siegfried*. It is here that the role that the eyes play in the *Ring* is most prominent. The scene is that in which the love of Siegfried and Brünnhilde is sparked, and then unfolded with passionate intensity. During the first moments of this scene, before Brünnhilde is awakened, Siegfried gazes intently on her serene face which he compares to the sun. Slowly, there develops within him a desire to see her eyes. Yet, he wonders if their light will be so intense that he will be blinded. Later, after he has kissed the maid awake, she gives her first greeting to the sun and to the light of the world. Siegfried now yearns again to look upon those eyes that have cast a bliss and a blessing about him. As the brightness of the scene increases, and as the love that each feels for the other unfolds, Siegfried says that he can see the light, the radiance in Brünnhilde's eyes. This joy of first-love is momentarily interrupted when Brünnhilde begins to recall what once she was, the Valkyrie favorite of the King of the Gods, and what she now is, a mortal. Wagner uses *eyes* as a means to enhance the dark emotion that invades the maiden as she expresses her concern that the light is fading from her eyes, that her eyes are becoming dim as darkness surrounds her heart. It is at this place in the drama that Wagner places a relevant stage direction, one that translates the significance of the role that he has given to the eye into a physical gesture. As Brünnhilde speaks her words, she covers her eyes with both hands! Siegfried then slowly takes the maiden's hands and lowers them from her face, and tells her that when her eyes are free and uncovered, the gloom of night and darkness disappear. As the world of light and love returns, it is Brünnhilde who asks her awakener if the 'glance' of her eyes, that is, the brightness of her eyes, does not take away his sight.

The love between Siegfried and Brünnhilde has developed intensely from the moment when the pair first came together, and *eyes* have held a conspicuous place throughout that development. And so too in the final climactic moments of their passion do the eyes have their prominence. As the Volsung youth embraces the former Valkyrie, he cries out to her that they shall share a single breath, that they shall join their lips, that they shall join their glances, and that they shall then be as one, mouth to mouth, and eye to eye. At the moment of total surrender, Brünnhilde happily exclaims to Siegfried that she is now his. The youth responds saying that he is engulfed, that his blood is kindled as their burning glances meet and merge. It is total love, and from its inception through its flowering, the *eyes* have not only been prominent, but they also have been an integral factor in the origin and the fruition of that love.

Wagner's dramatic concern with *eyes* during the "Awakening Scene" of Siegfried is his most concentrated application in the *Ring* of the Germanic concepts and beliefs associated with those parts of the body. Yet, despite the frequency of references to *eyes*, and despite their relativeness to the thematic situation, individually they are never bold, and in their totality they remain secondary to the dominant theme of first-love and its development. The manner in which the composer made this dramatic arrangement attests to his awareness of the strength of the concept within the culture and, at the same time, recognition of its somewhat limited scope.

There is in Wagner's presentation, however, a contradiction, perhaps it is more of a reverse arrangement, of the early Teutonic thought. This rearrangement, nevertheless, will justify its existence when it is viewed in light of the composer's ultimate dramatic intent. Stated in the briefest of words, Wagner invests the magic powers of the eyes in Brünnhilde, rather than in Siegfried. In Wagner's tale Brünnhilde belongs to mythology, that is, as a Valkyrie she is a part of the mythical Germanic past. The hero Siegfried comes from legend. The matter of the eyes and their forces were a societal concept, rather than an aspect of divine action. The Germanic culture acknowledged that the gloriousness of the hero in its midst, his courage, his strength, and his fearlessness were exposed and to be seen by the world through the radiance and luster of his mortal eyes. Whatever the forces of the Valkyrie, and there were several, they were not to be accepted as realized through her eyes, but rather as stemming from the *divine scheme* of the universe as projected in heathen Germanic beliefs. It is true that when Brünnhilde awakens from her deep sleep, she awakens as a mortal woman. In this guise the 'magic' of her eyes may be included and be readily accepted as part of her new mode of life. Yet, it is for strong dramatic reasons that Wagner arranged his scene as it is known today, and, essentially, gave to the maid what was culturally exclusive to the hero. As he wrote his *Siegfried* scene, Wagner was aware of what were to be Brünnhilde's actions later in the fourth part of the drama, her act of world salvation which included her own destruction as well as that of the corrupt universe. His dramatic intuition sensed that this deed would be viewed as no less than a supreme effort to set right the wrong that the gods had committed upon the world, and thus, if Siegfried was designated as the "hero" of the *Ring*, it would be Brünnhilde who, through her act, was to be *symbolic of the heroic*. In anticipation of this dramatic situation, Wagner carefully prepared the psychological springboard by which the divine Valkyrie turned mortal could be brought into such a role. Eyes and their powers, as exemplified in the ancient Teutonic culture, became a part of that transition, and Wagner copied faithfully the concept. investing it, however, in a distinct figure.

See also: *Eye (Wotan's)*

-F-

FAFNER

Wagner found the source of his character Fafner, and the latter's role as a dragon, in Eddic literature, and more specifically in two poems that are part of the twenty-one poems that constitute the "Lays of the Heroes" in *The Poetic Edda*. The first of these two lays is titled "Reginsmol" ("The Ballad of Regin"), and the second usually carries the title "Fafnismol" ("The Ballad of Fafnir").

The verses that relate the tale of Regin essentially set the stage for the role that Fafner (Fafnir) will have in these Eddic stanzas. Regin, whose name can be rendered in English as "Counsel Giver," is a wise and shrewd dwarf, skilled in magic, who had undertaken the rearing, teaching and training of the young Siegfried. He is a brother to Otr and Fafner (Fafnir), and the trio are sons of Hreidmar. Otr, who was in the form of an otter and sitting on a bank eating a salmon, was killed by a stone that Loge (Loki) threw. Then, Loge and his traveling companions, Wotan (Odin) and the god Hoenir skinned Otr. (Early Teutonic beliefs held that anyone who could kill and then skin an otter would have good luck.) As payment for his son's death, Hreidmar demanded that the three supernaturals stand the skin of his son on its feet and then hide it from his view with as much gold as necessary. Wotan sent Loge to a waterfall in which the dwarf Andvari lived, disguised as a fish, and in which he kept a large hoard of gold. Loge captured Andvari and forced him to relinquish the gold, including a gold ring that Andvari tried to keep for himself. When Loge forced the ring from him, Andvari put a curse of death on it. The trio used the gold to hide Otr, and there was enough gold to cover all of Otr from view, all that is except a single whisker that his father could see. Wotan then placed the gold ring to hide the whisker, and the three then continued their journey.

Hreidmar took the hoard into his home. Regin and Fafner then asked their father for their share of the treasure. Hreidmar refused his sons, and then went into his room to sleep. Fafner was very angered by his father's refusal to divide the gold. Then, as his father slept, Fafner went into the room and killed his father with his sword and took all the gold for himself. Regin then asked his brother for his share of the gold, as his inheritance, but Fafner refused his brother's request.

Fafner then fled to Gnitaheid (Gnita Forest), taking with him all the gold as well as a fear-helm ("aegis-hjalmr") which all living creatures greatly feared. Once at Gnitaheid, Fafner took the form of a dragon in order to lie guard over the gold hoard. Regin now tells Siegfried what has happened, and requests that the Volsung help him. To that end, Regin forges a sword, Gram, which he gives to Siegfried and with which the Volsung can do battle with the dragon. The sword was so sharp that when Siegfried brought it down upon Regin's anvil, it split the mighty anvil in two.

The poem "Fafnismol" continues the tale of Regin, Fafner, and Siegfried. (In *Thidrekssaga*, a work that served Wagner as a secondary source for thematic material to be used in the story that he was to include in his *Ring*, *Regin* is the name of the dragon, and the brother to the beast is called *Mimir*.) Siegfried decides to lend aid to Regin and the two travel to Gnitaheid. Siegfried digs a trench across the path that the dragon regularly takes to go to the creek from which he drinks. When Fafner, the dragon, awakens, Regin flees to a safe distance from the beast. Fafner slowly makes his way to the creek, his nostrils spitting venom, some of which spills down on Siegfried who has taken a position in the trench. When Fafner crosses the trench above Siegfried, the youth thrusts his sword, to its hilt in the dragon's stomach, and into the dragon's heart. The dying dragon asks Siegfried his name. Siegfried refuses to reveal himself, believing that a dying man could put a curse if he can curse a foe by name.

Fafner, the dragon, then offers advice to his slayer. He warns the youth to leave the gold, not to take any of the treasure because it would ultimately bring him injury and death. The dragon also tells Siegfried that Regin is greedy for gold and will betray him. At that point, Regin returns to the scene just as the dragon dies and as Siegfried wipes the beast's blood from his sword. Regin cuts out Fafner's heart and drinks some of his brother's blood. Siegfried takes Fafner's heart from Regin and places it on a fire. In time, he wishes to test the heart for its doneness. He puts one of his fingers on the meat, and the hot blood burns the finger, so much that he instinctively puts the finger in his mouth. As he tastes the dragon's blood, he suddenly realizes that he can understand the nuthatches that are in the trees. Seven of these birds speak to him and they tell how Regin plans to betray him. Siegfried then uses his sword to cut off Regin's head, after which he eats Fafner's heart. A bird then tells the youth that there is a battle-maid who could be his bride. This maiden sleeps on a fire-girded mountain, pricked into her sleep by Wotan because she caused a warrior to die, a warrior that the god wished to be victorious. Siegfried, now totally victorious over Fafner, goes to the dragon's hoard and loads two chests of the treasure onto the back of his horse Grane (Grani). The youth also takes the fear-helm, a golden mail-coat, and a sword. Siegfried then mounts his horse and sets out for the fire-ringed mountain and the sleeping battle-maid.

(There is an Eddic poem that states that Gutrune also eats part of Fafner's heart and she, too, comes to understand the language of the birds. In *Volsungasaga*, a work that Wagner considered primary as a source for themes, relationships, and other matters that could have a place in his *Ring* poem, it is Siegfried who gives a part of Fafner's heart to Gutrune. It is also in that saga that it is not venom from Fafner's nostrils that flows down on Siegfried, but rather it is the animal's blood that pours from the fatal wound that the Volsung had dealt the animal. This same writing reveals that Siegfried had been quite preoccupied with such a possibility, that is, that of having the dragon's blood gush upon him after he had reached up from his trench to stab the dragon. Before he had dug the trench in which he would await Fafner, Siegfried had asked Regin what would happen if the dragon's blood were to overcome him. Then, shortly after Siegfried had dug the trench in which he would lie, awaiting the arrival of the dragon, an old man appeared, as if from nowhere, and advised him where and how to dig other trenches in such a way that the blood would be carried away from Fafner's slayer. That old man was Wotan.)

There seems to be no doubt as to the source, and one might even say the inspiration, of the Fafner that has a significant place among the *dramatis personae* of Wagner's *Ring* drama. The revelations of the two Eddic poems leave no question as to the origin of Wagner's figure, and those same verses furnish the composer much of the thematic line in which his giant-dragon is placed. The changes that Wagner made as he brought the *Fafnir* of Eddic verse over into the *Fafner* of his drama are slight, and of no serious consequence to the original character. Wagner makes his Fafner a giant. The Fafner of the *Edda* is not called a giant, but neither is he said to be a dwarf, a depiction that is specific, however, to his brother, Regin. Then, too, Wagner makes a second change when he causes his Fafner to be the brother of Fasolt (who is indeed a giant in German heroic literature), and, then, together these two become the last of the race of Earth Giants, another thematic elaboration that is wholly the product of Wagner's creative mind. However, Wagner does allow his two giants to be builders, which was the only kind of work that the dullard mythical giants were capable of realizing.

See also: *Dragon*
          Fasolt
          Giants

FAFNER (Name)

The word *Fafnir* seems to be derived from an Old Norse term that was a common noun that meant "dragon." Early Nordic thought frequently associated dragons and large serpents with great treasures, most often as guardians. An Old Norse phrase that was in common use was *orms bedr*, a phrase that translates as "worm's bed." A second Old Norse phrase that was perhaps more popular and more often used than the first was *Fafnis boeli*, or "dragon's couch." In the case of the latter phrase, the word *Fafnis* is the genitive case whose nominative form could very well have been *Fafnir* with the common noun meaning of "dragon." This Old Norse word was used so frequently that in time it became a personal noun, hence the name Fafnir.

Some semanticists have suggested that the word *Fafnir* may have been derived from an Indo-European prototype, **Fadmir* (*Fathmir*), a substantive that supported a translation of "one who embraces." The concept that fosters this possibility is that of a snake or serpent or dragon that twists and coils itself about its victim. In the main, however, this semantic idea is most theoretical and is pushed well into the background in light of the known and used Old Nordic term.

Wagner took the name that he gave to one of the two giants and the one who transforms himself into a dragon from *Fafnir*, a name that is found in several poems of *The Poetic Edda*. This Eddic figure, although not identified as a giant, murders in order to take possession of a hoard of gold, flees with the treasure to a cave, and there turns himself into a dragon to lie guard over his wealth. Ultimately, this Fafnir is slain by the hero Siegfried (Sigurd).

FAFNER'S CAVE

In the drama of Wagner's *Ring*, the giant Fafner slays his brother Fasolt and then flees with the Nibelung gold to a dark forest, and into a cave or cavern. There, he changes himself into a dragon in order to lie as guard over his hoard. Later, Siegfried, the Volsung, forges the two pieces of his father's sword, Notung, and then orders Mime to guide him to Fafner's lair where, at least according to Mime, the youth will learn the meaning of fear.

Wagner called the cave in which Fafner seeks refuge *Neidhöhle*, or "Cave of Envy." He drew the inspiration for this cave from the mythical literature of the Teutonic peoples, literature in which the cave that harbored Fafner was known as *Gnitaheid*. (In the Eddic verses Fafner (Fafnir) slays his father Hreidmar while the latter slept, takes his father's gold, and flees to the cave.)

In the *Ring*, Siegrune the Valkyrie locates the cave of Fafner the giant in the dark forest, *to the East*. Wagner was mythically correct in locating this cavern in such a manner. The mythical thought of the early Teutonic peoples held that the Land of the Giants, one of the nine worlds of the universe, was located *in the East*, and it was *to the East* that Donner frequently traveled in order that he could fight and kill these giants who were sworn enemies of the gods.

There is a curious but nevertheless interesting history that is associated with this mythical cave. It is, however, a history in which Wagner showed little dramatic concern. After Sigurd (Siegfried) slays Fafnir the Dragon near its home in Gnitaheid, the property goes to the youth as a prize of combat. Later, when Gotthorm, a Gjuking (Gibichung) kills the youth, the cavern then becomes the property of the Gibichungs. The Eddic literature infers that the Gjukungs then gave the cave to Atli (Attila) who had married the Gjukung Kriemhild (Grimhild). After the death of Atli's sister, Brünnhild, the warrior-leader offer to restore the property to Gunnar (Gunther).

The use of a name for this cave is considered to be a matter of Southern (German) rather than Northern (Nordic) tradition. Historians have even attempted to identify the location of this cave. It is generally agreed that the cave of Fafnir the Dragon was located somewhat south of the German city of Paderhorn, about half way between modern day Dortmund and Hannover in Germany.

See also: *Compass Points*
         Neidhöhle (Name)

FASOLT

The role of the giant Fasolt in Wagner's *Ring* is a relatively minor one, confined as it is to a minimal dialogue of less than 400 words in two of the four scenes of *Das Rheingold*. Yet the name is well known in German heroic literature, appearing as it does in two major Germanic works. The first of these early writings is *Das Eckenlied* and the second is *Thidrekssaga*.

Das Eckenlied (*The Song of Ecke*) is a celebrated German poem that focuses on the famed German hero Dietrich von Bern (Theodoric the Great) and his encounters with giants. The original version of this work was composed about 1250 in Middle High German and a fragment of the poem is found in the *Carmina Burana*. The authorship is unknown.

The poem takes its name from the character Ecke, a giant of rather coarse and unrefined ways. Ecke is transformed into a powerful and strong knight-giant who then sets out to challenge the hero-knight Dietrich. Clad in his armor of gold, Ecke must walk because he is too large and too heavy for any horse to carry. In time, Ecke encounters Dietrich in a forest. The latter is somewhat reluctant to do battle with Ecke, but ultimately the two fight. Dietrich defeats Ecke and then beheads him when the giant refuses to swear loyalty to him.

The poem then turns to Ecke's brother, Fasolt (Vasolt). Dietrich comes upon the giant who has extremely long hair when the latter is chasing a young maiden through a forest. (There is some speculation that Fasolt's name in some way stems from a word that makes reference to the giant's long and flowing hair.) Dietrich hurriedly takes the maiden into his protection. Vasolt is angered by what Dietrich has done and he threatens to put the two to death by hanging. Vasolt and Dietrich do hand-to-hand combat, and Vasolt is defeated, after which he swears loyalty to the knightly Dietrich. That loyalty is later broken when Vasolt learns that it was Dietrich who killed his brother Ecke. Vasolt attacks Dietrich and even brings on other of his giant kin to face the hero. Finally, Dietrich defeats and slays the giant Vasolt.

Fasolt (Fasold) is also a figure in *Thidrekssaga*, a work that first appeared in Norway about 1250 and which is a more extensive depiction of the adventures of Dietrich von Bern. In this saga Fasolt accuses the hero Thidrek (Dietrich) of killing his brother Ecke (Ekka). Thidrek quickly defeats Fasolt, who then swears loyalty to Thidrek and joins his army of warriors. Later, Fasolt marries and then is slain by a famed warrior of the court of King Etzel (Attila).

In light of the manner in which the character Fasolt is depicted in each of the two popular literary pieces, it is difficult to ascertain which was of more importance to Wagner as he composed his character of Fasolt. It would seem that he might have turned to *Das Eckenlied* because, if for no other reason, this poem was a wholly German work and it is indisputable that Wagner was intent on composing a music-drama that not only made use of fundamental German factors, but a work that also boasted of the nature and character of the German society and its people. Yet, Wagner never mentioned *The Song of Ecke* in his extensive writings, and he did state at one time that *Thidrekssaga*, also known as *The Wilkina Saga*, was one of the works that he consulted as a source for the argument of his *Ring* drama.

The question as to which of the works served the composer best in the development of his *Ring* is really of little consequence. Neither of the works is of a mythical nature. Neither of the literary pieces has a storyline or a theme that is pertinent, or even relative, to that which is the thematic line in the drama. Both of the works highlight the figure of Dietrich von Bern who, if indeed a great and stalwart hero in the eyes of the German people, is of no importance whatsoever in Wagner's tale of the gods of Teutondom and the legendary story of Siegfried, Brünnhilde, and the Nibelung gold. Then, too, the incidents in these two writings in which Fasolt is a player are of a heroic if not a romantic nature which are wholly unrelated to the objectives and purposes that Wagner intended for his *Ring*. In light of the overall inconsequence of these two early works of Germanic literature in relation to *Der Ring des Nibelungen*, it is most logical to conclude that Wagner's only concern in the matter at hand was that he found in these writings an authentic name for one of the figures that would function in his poem, Fasolt (Vasolt, Fasold), and that figure was indeed a giant! Wagner would turn to other tales and themes of the Germanic past, as well as to incidents that were of his own creative mind, to convert the name Fasolt into the figure that is found in the *Ring*.

See also: *Fafner*
              Giants

———————

FASOLT (Name)

The role that Wagner developed in his *Ring* drama for the giant Fasolt is one that he himself created. The name that he gave to his character, however, is that of a giant that is major figure in two important medieval Germanic works, *Das Eckenlied* (*The Song of Ecke*) and *Thidrekssaga* (*Saga of Dietrich*). It is not known if Wagner was familiar with the poetic work about the giant Ecke and his brother Fasolt (Vasolt), but he once included *Thidrekssaga* as one of a list of the literary sources that he had utilized in the composition of his tale of the gods of Teutondom and the mortal Siegfried.

If the source of the *Ring's* Fasolt is relatively unquestioned, a precise meaning of the name, if indeed there is one, is quite uncertain. In *Das Eckenlied*, Fasolt (Vasolt) is depicted as a giant with long hair that flew in puffs as he traveled about the country. There are those scholars who would associate that aspect of Fasolt's figure with his name through the Old High German word *faso*, which meant "thread," and its modern German derivative *Faser* ("thread," "fiber," "filament"). If there is validity in that linguistic assumption, Fasolt's name, then, might be "Threading One," or possibly "Stringy One."

The name *Fasold*, as it appears in *Thidrekssaga*, suggests a semantic kinship with the modern German substantive *Fasel*. This word makes reference to a brood of young animals, and one of its compound forms is *Faselochs*, or "bull" [*bull-strength*]. This last mentioned word and the name *Fasolt* are similar in form and pronunciation and easily inspire a metaphorical analogy between "bull" or "bull-strength" and "giant" or "giant-strength." Perhaps any of those several words can serve as a name for this figure of mythical power and strength.

There is also the related verb form, *faseln*, which means "to talk foolishly" or "to talk drivel." It is this term that accounts for the compound *Faselhans*, which translates as "driveling fool," "muddler" or "scatterbrain." It is entirely possible that Wagner intended that these basic meanings also be incorporated into the name of his self-acknowledged awkward and slowwitted giant.

There is yet another possible association which relates, however slightly, the name *Fasolt* with such other words as words *Fastolf, Fastburg*, and *Fastmund*, names in which the prefix is somehow associated with "fast" in the sense of "firm." This latter suggestion seems to be but a remote possibility, given the sluggish and slow character which is mythically associated with the Germanic giants.

There is a final possibility regarding the meaning, or at least a relationship, of the name Fasolt. There seems to be some possible substance to the theory that Fasolt, the Teutonic giant, was at some time in the distant past related with weather and climate, that is a kind of weather spirit, and more specifically, an evil weather creature who dealt in violent storms, both on land and at sea. This seemingly remote suggestion does not openly offer a specific name.

Any of the several possibilities presented in the foregoing paragraphs may or may not have a germ of semantic validity when the question is that of the meaning of the word *Fasolt*. Then again, there may be hidden somewhere in the nebulous Germanic linguistic past a single precise and forthright term, a word, or an expression, that someday will come to the fore and remove the need for the theorization that is only possible at the present time.

FEAR

One of the several dramatic factors that Wagner developed successfully, and in a major way, in his *Ring* drama was that of *fear*, or, more precisely, the concept of the emotional state that fear regularly and normally initiates. Wagner included this matter in his drama when he causes certain of his figures to speak of 'to know' the meaning of fear. It is in the final moments of *Die Walküre* that this dramatic matter makes its initial appearance. Wotan is about to punish Brünnhilde because she disobeyed his command that she not aid Siegmund in his impending confrontation with Hunding. Wotan has said that he will put his daughter into a deep sleep, and that whatever man that shall awaken her will have her as wife. The Valkyrie pleads with her father, asking that if she must be punished as Wotan has indicated, that at least he make certain that her awakener will be a man of valor, that this man not be a coward. Wotan refuses Brünnhilde's wish, at first that is, saying that he cannot choose for her. After Brünnhilde voices additional pleas, the god gives in to his favorite daughter and tells her that he will surround the rock on which she will sleep with flames of fire, flames so intense that a coward will be immediately frightened away. The weak will flee, he tells her as he adds that only a free man will awaken her. The father and daughter embrace, and Wotan then places the kiss of sleep on Brünnhilde's brow. After the god has carefully placed his sleeping daughter on the rock, he calls to Loge, the God of Fire, and in time the rock is entirely girded by swirling, leaping flames of fire.

The matter of a mortal who does not know the meaning of fear is continued throughout the third of the *Ring's* four dramas, *Siegfried*. There is what can be called "Question Contest" in the first act of this work, and the final question that Wanderer asks Mime is who will it be who reforges the pieces of Siegmund's sword, the sword that was broken during his struggle with Hunding? When Mime cannot answer the question, the disguised Wotan reveals that he who has never known the meaning of fear will reforge the weapon. After the god has left Mime's cave, the Nibelung dwarf begins to realize that he has tried to teach love to the youth, Siegfried, whom he has reared, but he never taught him the meaning of fear. It is Siegfried who will reforge the sword! The cunning dwarf ponders the matter and concludes that he must teach the son of Siegmund what fear is. Siegfried returns to the cave and Mime then focuses on the concept of fear, describing to Siegfried some situations in which he should show fear. Siegfried seems to smirk at what Mime is saying. The dwarf then asks if Siegfried would be afraid of a dragon that kills and then eats his victims. Siegfried not only rejects the idea of fear, he eagerly seeks to confront the monster, even asking Mime to take him to the dragon's lair. Siegfried then says that he will reforge his father's sword for this adventure that he anticipates so eagerly. It is then that Mime discusses with himself the scheme that has been developing within him. The dwarf reasons that Siegfried, who knows no fear, will reforge the sword, an act that he has been unable to accomplish because he has known fear. Then he will lead the fearless Siegfried far into the forest, to Fafner's den. The youth will slay the dragon with the reforged sword, after which Mime will give the exhausted Siegfried a poisoned drink that will kill the youth. With Fafner and Siegfried both dead, there will be nothing to stop him from becoming owner of the treasure, including the magic ring and the marvelous Tarnhelm!

The second act of *Siegfried* continues to develop the matter of fear. The Volsung youth eventually confronts Fafner the dragon, with the reforged sword, Notung. One of the thrusts of the sword reaches the monster's heart. As Fafner breathes his last breaths, he tells the youth that he has been very brave to face him, a great giant. Fafner dies, and Siegfried soon learns to understand the language of the birds and also to understand what Mime is thinking. In this way, Siegfried becomes aware of Mime's sinister plan. To be free of the dwarf's scheme, Siegfried slays him. It is then that Forest Bird informs the youth that it knows where the youth can acquire a wonderful wife. After hearing Forest Bird's words, Siegfried becomes aware of a strange sensation that fills his breast. Forest Bird then tells Siegfried that whoever awakens the maid will be a fearless man, one who has never shown cowardice. Siegfried tells the bird that he is that person!

Siegfried sets out to seek the fire-girded mountain on which the maid Brünnhilde sleeps. He is guided by Forest Bird, who becomes frightened and flies away when the pair encounters Wotan. In time, fearless Siegfried shatters Wotan's spear when the god tries to prevent the youth from continuing on his way.

Siegfried finds his way to the mountain that is surrounded by fire. Fearlessly, he penetrates the flames and then spies the figure that sleeps peacefully on a rock. Thinking that the figure is a man, the youth removes his helm and breastplate, and when he sees the maid's face, he realizes that it is not a man. This is the first woman that Siegfried has ever seen, and strange sensations begin to develop within him. He feels a burning in his chest, and his eyes seem to be aflame. Siegfried sees himself in a situation that he has never known before. His thoughts are jumbled as they turn about in his mind. He does not know what to do, and there is no one who can respond to a call for help. He cries out to his mother as he speaks of his heart that trembles. Siegfried now realizes that he is afraid, that at long last he has come to know the meaning of fear, and as he cries out to his mother once again, he asks himself if what is happening to him is really fear. Then he admits to himself that a maid, asleep and resting quietly, has taught him the meaning of fear.

Wagner's use of the motive of fear and his development of that motive within his *Ring* is crucial to the dramatic action of his drama. The matter plays well as part of the argument, it adds much to the characterization of the hero Siegfried, and it also is a theme that can be easily understood and accepted by an audience. Gifted, however, as Wagner was in the determination of theatrical matters, the theme of the meaning of fear did not originate with him, but rather it was an idea that he had gained from his study of the Teutonic myths.

There are two poems in *The Poetic Edda* that focus on Brünnhilde's punishment by Wotan and to the matter of a possible rescue by a fearless hero, which, of course, is to be Siegfried. The resemblance between these Eddic scenes, both as to manner of development as well as content, and the final moments of Wagner's *Die Walküre* are quite obvious. The first of these poetic works is titled "Ballad of the Bringer of Victory" ("Sigrdrifumol"). In these verses Sigrdrifa (Brünnhilde), a Valkyrie, but who is not Wotan's daughter, slew a warrior to whom the god had promised victory in battle. Wotan then punished her with a sleep-thorn, telling her that she now would no longer be a Valkyrie, that she would fall into a long sleep, and that she would become the wife of the mortal man who awakened her. Brünnhilde then informs the god that she had made a vow that she would never marry the man who knew the meaning of fear! (The word *Sigrdrifa* means "Bringer of Victory," and is used in these verses as a epithet for *Brünnhilde*.)

The second of the two poems which served as source material for the matters of Brünnhilde's punishment and the fear-motive is titled "Helreid Brynhildar" ("Brünnhilde's Ride into Hell"). (The word *reid* in *Helreid*, which became *Ritt* in German, meant *ride* in the sense of a journey made on horse.

Wagner employed the term when he composed his *Walkürenritt,* or *Ride of the Valkyries.*) In these verses Brünnhilde recalls the action that led to her banishment. She states that she let a warrior die in battle, and gave victory to another, which angered Wotan greatly. Such action merited only punishment. Brünnhilde then adds that she was taken to Skatalund ("Warriors' Grove"), where she was surrounded by a ring of overlapping red and white shields. Wotan put her into a deep sleep, ordaining that her sleep would be broken only by a mortal who had never known the meaning of fear. Wotan then surrounds the ring of shields with a great wall of fire.

Most students of the *Ring* and of the myths and legends that served as that drama's sources are not unduly concerned about Wagner's slightly altered duplication of the mythical matter of the fear motive and its appearance in the Brünnhilde-Wotan scene. There are, of course, those who protest what the composer has done, both here, and frequently elsewhere in his lengthy drama. However, if Wagner borrowed closely and frequently from the tales that are found in both southern (German) and northern (Nordic) myths and legends, and if in turn he modified those sources to realize his own argument about the gods and the Volsung clan, it cannot be said that he ever violated the fundamental and basic mythical integrity of those stories, nor did he refashion or attempt to refashion in any major way the beliefs and concepts that the early Germanic peoples held. Neither did he lessen in any manner the significance of the cultural and societal way of life that those beliefs and concepts allowed. Wagner was ever-loyal to his sources, keenly aware that he was dealing with a spirited and energetic past that for centuries had held sway in much of modern Europe, including his own continental Germany. Wagner's mythical essence is the Germanic mythical essence. It is only in detail that Wagner deviated from time to time, a matter that can easily be determined in the case at hand by means of a dual reading of each of these scenes that include the element of fear.

See also: *Kiss*
      Question Contest
      Ride
      Siegfried (The Hero)

FIRE See: *Elements*

FLOSSHILDE See: *Rhinemaidens*

FLOSSHILDE (Name)

The prefix of this compound name *Floss* (ON – *flot*; OHG – *floz*; MLG – *viote*; OE – *flote, flot*; ME – *flote*) denotes at once a "float" or "raft" and the word also serves as a reference to "flowing water." (Old English *fleotan* meant "to float.")

The suffix *hilde* of this name of one of the daughters of the Rhine translates as "maiden," (see *Notes*). Together, the two words of Flosshilde's name in English become "Maiden of the Flowing Water."

FLUTE (*Reed*) See: Pipe (Reed)

FOREST

With few exceptions, most of the thirty-six scenes that comprise Wagner's *Der Ring des Nibelungen* are set in one way or another in or near a forest. In *Das Rheingold* the composer specifies "a mountain top, with valley below" for two of the four scenes of that drama. In *Die Walküre* the setting of the scenes of Act I is in Hunding's dwelling, which is deep within a forest. All the scenes of the second act are in "a wild craggy place," and those of the final act are "on the summit of a rocky mountain." In the first act of *Siegfried*, the three scenes take place in the cave in which Mime and the Volsung live and whose stage direction locates it in "A Forest." The scenes of the second act are set "In the depths of a forest" and the three scenes of the final act take place on "A wild place at the foot of a rocky mountain." The 'forest' does not have so major a role in the last of the four music-dramas, *Götterdämmerung*, as it had in the earlier works, although one stage setting is given as "On the Summit of a Rocky Mountain," and another is "A Wild, Wooded and Rocky Valley on the Rhine."

It is logical to assume that the stage settings for the numerous scenes in such a work as Wagner's *Ring* must emit essentially an aura of primordial nature. The types of figures and many of the actions that are found in the drama make such a demand. It was not, therefore, a matter of necessary judgment and decision for Wagner as he went about the business of composition of the poems. The settings of the acts and their scenes came about naturally. There is, therefore, a factor of mythical reality within Wagner's work, a reality that permits the overall setting of his work to reflect a societal concept that existed as part of ancient Germanic thought.

The early Teutonic culture was a *forest* culture. History has demonstrated this matter most conclusively over the ages. Yet, if the matter of that history were insufficient to support the idea that this was just such a culture, the Eddic literature would make it undeniable. The verses of *The Poetic Edda*, that singular repository for the mythical thought of the Teutonic peoples, project most convincingly the 'forest' or 'woods' setting as the several numerous and varied tales are developed. To lend additional support to the concept of a 'forest' society, the *Edda* calls no less than seven of these forests by name!

Three of these forests were of no dramatic interest to Wagner other than in the fact that they contributed to the intensity of the concept of the mythical forest orientation of the people. These woods deal with Helgi, the hero who is to the Danes as Siegfried is to the Germans. The first of these woods is called Bragalund ("Leafy Woods"), and it is here that Helgi hunted and captured bears. The second of these Eddic forests is Gnipalund ("Craggy Woods"). This wooded area is near a large body of water for it is that region that Sigrun, wife of Helgi, visits in order to give aid to stricken sailors. It is also at Gnipalund that this same Sigrun rescues her husband's ship from the claws of the evil Ron, wife of Aegir, the God of the Sea. This is the same Aegir who once invited Wotan (Odin), Fricka (Frigge), Froh (Frey), and Freia (Freyja) to a grand feast. The third of the forests that pertains to Helgi is Fjoturlund ("Fetter Woods"), the forest where the celebrated Helgi dies.

The remaining four named Eddic forests are all part of the Siegfried legend. One is called Barri ("Leafy Woods"). It is to this forest that Gerd, the maiden with whom Froh has fallen in love, will come at the end of nine nights, "there to grant pleasure." A second Siegfried forest is called Skatalund ("Warriors' Wood"). This famed woods is where Wotan put Brünnhilde to sleep and where Siegfried (Sigurd) awakened her. That specific spot, which is really a wooded mountain within the forest, was called Hindarfjoll ("Mountain of the Red Deer"). The sixth of the named forests that is associated with the tale of Siegfried is named Myrkwood, which is the forest that separates the realm of Attila (Atli) from that of the Gibichungs (Gjukungs). The last of the famed mythical forests of the Germanic peoples is named Glasirslund (Glasir's Woods"). This forest, which is described as "the fairest wood among the gods," rises majestically in front of Wotan's hall. Unfortunately, the myths do not indicate if this "hall" is Wotan's personal residence, Valaskjolf ("Hall of the Slain"), or the god's battle hall, Valhalla ("Home of the Chosen Slain").

Wagner was very much aware of the mythical forests and their importance, and perhaps more importantly their significance, within the myths and legends of the Teutonic culture. It is in one sense these woods and forests that serve as the primary background in and around which he developed the basic theme of the *Ring*. Although Wagner chose not to use the names of any of these mythical woods and forests in his drama, he does make reference to at least two of these celebrated spots, and gives them names of his own. The first of these *Ring* locations is what Wagner called "Valkyrie Rock," and which in the myths is Myrkwood, that dark, magic forest through which Valkyries flew as they made their way to Valhalla. Wagner's second reference to a mythical forest region is what he called "Brünnhilde's Rock" which, of course, is his naming of Hindarfjoll, the mythical mountain on which Brünnhilde takes her celebrated sleep. Curiously, some followers of Wagner's drama often identify, and with some validity, Valkyrie Rock and Brünnhilde's Rock as one and the same place. The matter is of little significance when the larger concern, that is the adaptation of the mythical ideas, is considered. What remains foremost is that the composer knew and understood what the world of his ancestors was like, what those people thought and believed, and what they recognized as primary. It was to these matters that Wagner always turned for his sources and his inspiration. And, in its own way, the adaptation of the mythical forests to his poems is an example of that dramatical practice at work.

FOREST BIRD (Waldvogel) See: *Woodbird*

FREIA See: *Freia* (Vol. II)
　　　　See also: *Gods and Goddesses*

FREIA (Name)

The original Old Norse name of this deity, whom Wagner includes in his drama as Goddess of the Golden Apples, was *Freyja* (the *j* was pronounced somewhat like English *y*). It was a simple matter for *Freyja* to Germanize into *Freia*.

This name means "lady" in the sense of a woman of noble bearing, possibly even a "lady of royalty." The name developed from the OHG *frouwa*, becoming ultimately the modern German word *Frau* ("woman," "wife," "lady," "Mrs.").

Like Donner, Freia the "Lady," is remembered in contemporary German by the word *Freitag*, and in English by the equivalent *Friday*, both of which evolved from the ON *Friadagr*. (Some scholars claim that this day of the week is named after Fricka [Frigge].)

FRICKA See: *Fricka* (Vol. II)

See also: *Gods and Goddesses*

FRICKA (Name)

The Old Norse name for this goddess, who was the wife of Wotan and who is the Goddess of Marriage in the *Ring* drama, was *Frigg* (*Frigge*). In AS her name became *Fricq*, while in ME the word was *Friggen* and in Mod E it became *Frigg*. In OHG there were several variations, including *Fricc, Frikk, Frikka,* and *Frikkia*. Any one of the latter words can account for Wagner's modern German version of the name.

The original ON name, and each of the subsequent developments within several languages, is a doublet of *Frico*. This latter term evolved from the Indo-European prototype *prij** which had a meaning of "love," but in a generic sense. For reasons of linguistic courtesy and because of her relationship with marriage, we can consider the name *Frigge* to mean "Love." In more prosaic terms, however, this root word was a coarse reference to male genitalia. Remnants of words and the various meanings that they acquired remain in modern German and in modern English slang (*v. tr.* "to frig"; *adj.* "frigging").

On occasion, this name is mistakenly taken as an associate of *Friko*, a Frisian word meaning "Peace Ruler" and rendered in English as *Frederick* and in German as *Fritz*. On yet other occasions further confusion is generated when Fricka's name is associated with *Frick* or *Friche*, both of which refer to a bold, brave man as well as to a man from Frick, Switzerland.

FROH See: *Froh* (Vol. II)

See also: *Gods and Goddesses*

FROH (Name)

Wagner's God of the Fields was known in the myths as *Freyr*. He was called *Frauja* in Gothic and in AS his name was *Frea* which became *Frey* in modern English.

The original name meant "Lord," in the sense of a "high" or "royal gentleman" and was the masculine counterpart to his sister's name, *Freyja*, which meant "Lady."

In Sweden and Denmark, this god was called *Fro*, a word that was very much a part of OHG. (Mythologists are aware of the early god with the name of Fro, but many believe that he was a deity unrelated to Freyr). However, a related word, *frono*, allowed for the development of modern German *froh*, which means "glad" or "happy." (The English word "frolic" is a development from this early Germanic term.) Wagner resorted to the mythical *Fro* and the German *frono* to derive the name *Froh*. Presumably the composer viewed his Froh as a spirited and colorful god.

FURIOUS HOST, THE

The Wotan of Wagner's *Ring* is addressed or referred to by several names in the course of the drama, not the least of which is *Heervater* ("Father of the Host" or "Father of Armies"). Some linguistic variations of this mythical word, which is first used by Brünnhilde and later by her Valkyrie sisters, are: *Heerfater, Heerfader,* and *Herfader*. (Other names by which Wotan is called in the *Ring* are *Walvater* ("Father of War"), *Streitvater*

("Father of Disputes"), *Lichtsohn* ("Son of Light"), and *Herrscher der Wal* ("Lord of the Chosen").

The prefix of the word *Heervater* is a substantive term with at least two primary meanings. The word *Heer* can mean "army" or "troops," while a second meaning is that of "multitude" or "many." The English equivalent of the German term is primarily "Host" in the sense of "many," as in a "Host of Angels," but it is also a term that is related to such words as "hostile" and "hostage." This English equivalent was derived from Latin *hostis*, which can be translated as "enemy."

Early in the days of the ancient Teutonic peoples the word *Heer* was joined with the name of the Supreme God of the Germanic clans, Wotan (Wuotan). The phrase then in use was *Wuotes Heer*, or "Wotan's Host," in the sense of "Wotan's Army." The name *Wuotes* was a variation of *Wuotan* which was one of several variations of the god's name, all of which had been derived from the Old Norse *vada*, which meant "fury" or "rage." The variation *Wuotan* went on to become *watan* and then *wüten*, both of which are associated with the concept of "fury" in the German language. Thus, *Wuotes Heer* eventually became *wütende Heer*, meaning *furious Host*, and then the popular "Das wilde wütende Heer" or simply "The Furious Host" in English.

The Furious Host, that is "Das wütende Heer" with Wotan as the "Heervater," was very much a factor in the lives of the heathen Teutonic peoples. (The concept of this Host actually became so strong within the minds of the people that it also extended well into the Christian era, especially in the Teutonic regions of continental Europe.) The initial concept came into existence through the belief that the Supreme God Wotan would ride through the skies at the head of a vast multitude of followers. When the god carried out this role, he always wore a long cloak and a broad-brimmed hat. Those who followed the divine leader, occasionally referred to as an 'army,' consisted of many types. This Host that Wotan guided could include spirits, specters or phantoms of any kind. This special army could include the souls of dead children as its warriors, or the souls of those who were about to die, or those who had gone mad, those who were berserk, and even assorted types of warriors and hunters. One of the followers was known as "The Wild Hunter" a figure that always rode a headless horse. On occasion, the people accepted Wotan himself as "The Wild Hunter." (Some tales include the spirit Holda, one of the names that Wagner attached to his goddess Freia, as a member of The Furious Host.)

It was not only the matter of the specific constituency of Wotan's Army that concerned the early Germanic society, but also how that vast multitude made itself known, and what it could do to the unwary. The Furious Host usually made itself known during the dark of night. The distant sound of rattling of warriors' arms or the noise of horses' hoofs were considered as signals that Wotan's Host was there, somewhere in the black of night, about to strike. The sudden uproar of barking dogs, again in the darkness of night, was also a sign of an impending invasion by this army. It was also held that if one would look into the skies at the proper moment, Wotan's army could be seen as cloudy shapes that floated about in the dark skies. If one looked quite carefully, giant horses could be seen as they leaped across great spaces in the heavens. The most certain sign of The Furious Host, however, was that of a roaring, howling wind that would rise in the distance and rapidly make its way across the heavens, destroying much that lay on the ground and in its path. It was also believed in most quarters that this wind, which always swooped down out of the north, was capable of sucking a person into its dark center, and if not the person's body, then his soul, thereby condemning that individual to the worst of all sentences, a most tragic existence, a painful condition, or one that would never know peace. Such a curse could never be altered, and the condemnation by The Furious Host would extend throughout the rest of an individual's life. A second belief held that an entire community could be the victim of the Host in that the appearance of Wotan's Army was a foresign of a bloody and harmful war.

The belief in The Furious Host and the destructive results that it produced was extensive throughout Teutondom. It was a concept that caused much alarm and true fear among the people who did not wish to have the Host descend upon them. A definite concern, then, was any rise in the speed of the wind, which to the Germanic mind could be the warning, the announcement so to speak, of the impending arrival of The Furious Host. A rise in the speed of the wind would urge caution as well as preparations to meet that more raging wind that perhaps would follow. A rise in the speed of the wind was an ominous sign, a threat that great destruction and misfortune were about to befall the unlucky ones, an indication that perhaps that harm was about to fall upon the people at hand. The early Germanics held that this warning wind was a sign that the Supreme God of Teutondom, Wotan, had become angered in some way, that his wrath and ire were so stirred that he was about to strike those who had angered him. There was but a single action that could lessen the great forces that The Furious Host could bring down from the heavens, or indeed to prevent those forces from making another unwanted appearance at some future time. The single remedy that would detour The Furious Host or deny that Host the need for a future invasion was the placation of the great god. By any means, by all means, Wotan's anger was to be soothed, which meant removal of whatever the factor that had stirred him into one of the early Teutonic peoples' most feared actions.

The use of the term *Heervater* by Brünnhilde and then by her eight sisters to address Wotan is a most definite indication that Wagner is utilizing the mythical concept of *Das wütende Heer* to convey the fact that his Wotan, like the god of myth, is the leader of that multitude of raging quasi-supernatural spirits. Yet, Wagner goes beyond the simple matter of language to convey this concept, and he does so, in the same scene in which the nine Valkyries gather at Valkyrie Rock.

Earlier in the drama, Brünnhilde had attempted to give victory to Siegmund in his struggle with Hunding. This action by the Valkyrie was contrary to that which Wotan had ordered his favorite daughter to carry out. This act of disobedience infuriated Wotan who, as soon as he had caused th death of Hunding, set out in full pursuit to catch the fleeing Brünnhilde who had taken up the pieces of Siegmund's broken sword, and with Sieglinde had fled. The scene shifts to Valkyrie Rock, where the Valkyries are gathering to pause on their journey to Valhalla with their fallen heroes. Soon, an excited Brünnhilde arrives, bringing Sieglinde with her. Brünnhilde quickly asks her sisters for help as she tells them that Heervater is chasing her, that they should look to the north to see if he can be seen. Ortlinde looks northward, and then tells the Valkyries that a fierce storm is bearing down on them.

Waltraute says that she sees great clouds gathering in the north. They all agree that the clouds and the storm are the Heervater Wotan as he rides his holy steed at full speed. Brünnhilde asks for aid as she tells her sisters what she has done and then calls Wotan a wild pursuer who rides while in an intense rage. The Valkyries do not dare disobey their father as Waltraute informs all that night and its darkness is descending upon them from the north. The Valkyries seem to cringe and to step away in fear of the approaching Heervater. It is then Ortlinde who says that wild neighs are being made by Wotan's steed. Brünnhilde again pleads for help as she tells her sisters that woe be to her when Wotan arrives, threatening his powerful destruction. The sisters refuse Brünnhilde's request, stating that their steeds have never fled the Walvater. Ultimately, Brünnhilde sends Sieglinde into the forest, to take refuge in Fafner's cave, a place that Wotan has always avoided. Waltraute then informs the group that a very angered Wotan rides now to Valkyrie Rock. In turn, the Valkyries tell that the god comes in a great roar. At that point, Wagner gives directions that Wotan is to arrive on the scene in a great frenzy.

In a most unique manner Wagner has included in this scene the mythical details that signaled *Das wütende Heer* of another time. The Supreme god is addressed as Heervater, that is, Father of the Host. The Valkyries, learning that the god is pursuing Brünnhilde, look to the north, the direction from which 'Das wilde wütende Heer' of early times regularly came. The Valkyries see great clouds in the distance, a matter that replicates the ancient belief that the clouds formed the shapes of the Host. The Valkyries also tell how Wotan rides a holy steed, at full gallop, an action that broadcasts the gods' intense rage and anger. A Valkyrie announces that the darkness of night, the most propitious time for travel and arrival of The Furious Host, is descending upon them, and again, that it comes from the north. The Valkyries, sensing the anger of the god, cringe in fear, aware as they are of the powerful forces of destruction and ruin that he can bring to bear upon them. Then, in a final verbal manner, Wagner directs that an angered, frenzied Wotan appear upon the scene.

There can be no doubt that this Valkyrie scene represents Wagner's dramatic presentation of the fundamental mythical concept of *Das wilde wütende Heer, The Furious Host.* Such is the composer's talent that he presents this concept by means of dialogue that acts out its own unique but unrelated theme and action. Wagner's blend of his Valkyrie argument and the concept of *Das wütende Heer* is, in and of itself, dramatically complete. Each word is basic to the plot development as well as for dramatic enrichment. Yet, as the composer gives his words real and powerful meaning, he also resorts to sound to develop and to explain the entire matter of the scene. The music for this Valkyrie scene, which he had first composed as music for his Norns, amply complements the thought and action of the supernatural figures. It is a kind of cosmic sound that he creates for Wotan's daughters, a huge, symphonic fabric whose sound colors seem to dart about in the frenzied meaning that he wishes to communicate. Yet, there is no frenzy in Wagner's dramatic or musical thought. He knew what he was doing and he knew exactly what he wished to achieve. Thus it is that The Furious Host, in its own curious way, becomes a secondary partner to the monumental argument of the *Ring*.

See also: *Bear*
      Freia (Vol. II)
      Horses
      Wotan (Vol. II)

-G-

GASTRECHT See: *Guest Rights*

GERHILDE See: *Valkyries*

GERHILDE (Name)

The ancient prefix *ger* in this Valkyrie's name means "spear" ("javelin") and implies "linear," that is, "in a straight line." There are several words in modern German that utilize this term as a base word. Two such terms are: *gerade* ("straight," "direct"); *geradeous* ("straight ahead"). This word also is part of several popular names in English: *Gerald* and its feminine form, *Geraldine* ("Spear Dominance"); Gerard ("Strong with Spear"); Gertrude ("Spear Strength").

For the meaning of the suffix *hilde*, see *Notes*.

It would seem that the most appropriate translation of this Valkyrie's name is "Spear Warrior."

GIANTS

The giant of the ancient Teutonic world was a supernatural figure that belonged to a separate race of beings. The belief in these giants originated early, and it endured throughout the long history of that heathen culture. Likewise, the belief in these giant beings was to be found throughout the entire region of ancient Teutondom. Like the dwarf of Teutonic mythology, the giant of Teutondom was also very much involved in the events of the mythological universe as well as in the lives of all the beings who were part of that universe. And, curiously, so strong and so potent was the ancient belief in these beings that there are still vestiges of that belief apparent in some of the tales and stories that circulate throughout the Teutonic world of the twentieth century.

The early Teutonic mind held that in the beginning of the world the gods began to take a careful inventory of the universe. They saw but a single figure in that universe. This being was a giant, and his name was Ymir, and he had waxed from the venom that had come down from Elivagar ("Stormy Waves"). (Some students of Teutonic mythology claim that Elivagar was a river, while others maintain that Elivagar was *The Milky Way*, which later came to be known as *Wotan's Weg* or "Wotan's Way.") In time, Ymir began to perspire, and once he lay bathed in his own sweat, a male and a female figure emerged from his left armpit. Then, when the giant rubbed his feet together, a second male figure came into existence. These three beings were giants, the first of a race of supernaturals that would have great significance in the thought and belief of the ancient Teutonic culture. (Ymir is the same giant whose body parts the gods later used to create the Land of Mortals, and also out of whose flesh came the maggots that became the *Alp* or "dwarf" of ancient Teutondom.)

The race of giants flourished in the great universe. They became noted for the beautiful daughters that were born to them, and marriages of these offsprings to the gods were not unusual. Teutonic belief held that the first giants demonstrated great wisdom, for which they were very much respected. However, as time went on and the dealings between the giants and the gods became more numerous and more involved, the state of affairs between these two races of supernaturals became strained. An undercurrent of hostility began to develop. The situation ultimately became so serious that even the peace that had existed between them was threatened.

During the swell of resentment that was growing between the gods and the giants, the deities were also having other difficulties and problems throughout the vast universe that they had fashioned. One such problem was the relationship of the Aesir (Ases) gods, of whom Wotan, Donner, and

Fricka were the principal gods, with another race of gods, the Vanir (Wanes), which included among their number the brother and sister Froh and Freia. The matter finally resulted in a war between the two races of gods, the first war of the universe. (Some students of Teutonic mythology maintain that the Vanir, who developed in the Teutonic thought that was dominant among the sea-people of the Baltic region, was not a race of gods, but rather a group or clan of water-sprites.) This first war was a terrible war, but in time Wotan and his clan were victorious. As a part of the peace treaty that was to be concluded, Froh and Freia were to be accepted by the Aesir as hostages. (Ultimately, this pair was viewed as if they had been born into the Aesir clan.)

Shortly after the two races of gods had agreed to the peace treaty, an event occurred that was to climax the uneasy peace between Wotan and his gods and the giants. This would be an action that would produce the permanent enmity that the two races were to know from then on. Obviously, Wagner considered this event of such importance and significance that he not only adapted it to his *Ring* argument, but he also made it the thematic action that would initiate the series of events that ultimately would result in the doom and destruction of the universe.

The land of the Aesir deities, Asgard, had suffered much damage in that destructive first war that was waged by the two races of gods. Wotan and his clan were desirous to have their land repaired, and to achieve that end they contracted with a giant who was to build a great fortress for them. The agreement that was reached between the gods and the giant stated that the giant was to complete the work within a specified period of time, and if he complied with that part of the pact, he was to be rewarded with the sun, the moon, and the goddess Freia as wife. (This agreement was reached at such time as Freia was still considered to be simply a hostage that had been gained from the Vanir gods.)

The work on the fortress went well, in part because the giant was aided in his labors by his horse. Each night this animal brought the huge boulders that the giant would use the next day in the construction of the building. The two worked laboriously, and it soon seemed that the giant would finish his task within the deadline, and therefore comply with the terms of the agreement. The gods now began to have second thoughts about the agreement, and they began to show concern. When it became quite evident to them that the giant would definitely meet the deadline, the gods were most disturbed, even fearful. They did not want to give the giant the payment to which they had agreed. The deities quickly sought Loge (Loki), a shrewd and cunning spirit who lived in the land of the gods. They told Loge that although he had advised them against the arrangement with the giant, he must come to their aid, he must somehow cause the giant to exceed the deadline for completion of the work. Loge hesitated, but the gods threatened him. Loge feared the wrath of the gods, and that fear was made even greater because he easily recalled the numerous times in the past that he had been the nemesis of these deities. Loge knew that he must somehow give aid to the gods.

The resolution of the matter was most unique. Loge changed himself into a mare, and one night, as the giant's stallion was hauling boulders, Loge approached. When the stallion became aware of the nearby mare, his thoughts soon turned to matters other than the boulders, and he quickly chased after Loge, who ran into the forest. (As a result of this union between the giant's horse and Loge, there was born a colt that would grow up to be the greatest horse in the universe. This colt was given the name of Sleipnir. He had eight legs, and could run through the heavens faster than the wind. Sleipnir became the prized possession of the Allfather god, Wotan. According to some myths, in his maturity Sleipnir sired a son, a horse that would also know fame. Sleipnir's son was called *Grane*, the same horse that Wagner brings into the *Ring* as the horse of the Valkyrie Brünnhilde, and later the horse that Siegfried rides as he sets out in search of heroic adventures.)

The flight of the horse put the giant into a quandary. He did not know what to do. His horse had been lured from him and there was no one to haul the stones that he needed for his work. The deadline came, and the giant had not yet completed the work. The gods now claimed that he had not complied with the terms of the agreement and they refused to reward him for his labors. The giant was angry because the gods had used trickery in order to be freed of their obligations under the pact. As he pondered how the gods had gone back on their word, he became quite furious. The giant then threatened the gods, whereupon Donner came forth and killed him with his mighty hammer, Mjollnir.

When the giants of Teutondom learned of the gods' deception, the entire race rose in defiance. The giants now felt that they could no longer trust the gods, and they vowed to have as little as possible to do with them. The giants now viewed the gods as enemies, and from that time on the relationship between the two races was tenuous and fragile.

It is immediately obvious to the follower of the *Ring* that this mythical tale was not only a primary inspiration to Wagner's dramatic pen, but also the principal source for a basic initial activity that he brings to his drama, the pivotal activity, as it were, that allows Wotan's theft of the Nibelung gold to become, ultimately, a cause for the downfall of the gods and their world.

It is in *Das Rheingold* that Wagner places his giants and his gods in an agreement that is much like that of the myths. Fafner and Fasolt have made an agreement with Wotan that they will build the fortress Valhalla, and for their labors they are to be rewarded with the goddess Freia. As in the myths, so too in the *Ring*, the gods become quite concerned when the giants, their task completed, ask for the agreed reward. The gods refuse, the disgruntled and disturbed giants become quite angry, and at one point Donner threatens them with his mighty hammer. It is at this turn in the *Ring* story that Wagner ceases to tell the tale that he found in myths and now steeps it in a continuation that is of his own creation.

The giants of Teutondom, the mythical enemies of the gods, were like the other races of supernaturals, that is, the gods and the dwarfs, in that they were human in form and nature. However, in relation to humans, the giants were large, and they possessed strength in proportion to their size. There was also a wildness and a fierceness about them, qualities that in later Teutonic beliefs became associated with the more violent phenomena of nature, such phenomena as earthquakes, hurricanes, and mountain slides.

According to the early Teutonic beliefs, the giants of the universe usually traveled in pairs. They were easily provoked, and when so stirred they could be quite dangerous. These heathen Germanic beliefs also held that the weapons of the giants were large stones that their strength allowed them to hurl with ease. These giants were an energetic race, known for their stamina. The only skill that the giants possessed was that of builders, however, their buildings were so well constructed that they lasted forever.

It was stated earlier that the myths of Teutondom reveal that the early giants were much admired and respected for their wisdom. This concept underwent a radical change after the race became an enemy of the gods, a change that was to instill itself permanently in Germanic thought. In the later depiction of these beings, the giants were depicted as having a rough, coarse nature. They were haughty and insolent, and they could be quite overbearing in their actions. If once they had shown alertness through wisdom, there was now a dullness about them, a slowness of thought that ultimately was looked upon as stupidity, and they demonstrated an ineptness that stood out in sharp contrast with the common sense of mortals, and the shrewdness of another race of supernaturals, the dwarfs.

The giants, like the other races of the universe, lived in their own land, which was one of the nine worlds that made up the Teutonic mythological cosmos. Their home was called *Jotunheim*, which translates as "Home" or "Land of Giants," and which was a term that had developed from the Old Icelandic *Jotun-heimar*. Wagner rejected *Jotunheim* as the name for the home of the giants of his drama, probably because the term was not a true German name. He resorted to the popular word for "giant," that is *Riese*, and proceeded to devise his own original word that named the world in which the giants lived, *Riesenheim*.

The myths that reflect early Teutonic thought also reveal that the Land of Giants lay "to the East," to the East of the home of mortals, the "Land of Men," which in mythical terms was called *Midgard*. These same myths also contain numerous tales that tell of Donner and his frequent travels "to the East," where he stalked the giants in their own land, and then fought with them and killed them with his hammer. Wagner does not give a compass location to the Riesenheim of his *Ring*, that is, he does not state specifically where the Land of Giants lies. In his own manner, however, he acknowledges the ancient belief that this world was located in the East. This acknowledgment occurs in *Die Walküre*, when the composer causes a Valkyrie to state that the giant Fafner has taken the gold and has fled to a cave that is *to the East*. This bit of mythical ambience is reinforced later when Wagner makes a similar acknowledgment of the ancient belief, this time in *Siegfried*, when he causes Mime to say that the den of the transformed giant is *to the East*, and therefore the Volsung hero must travel *eastward* for his encounter with the Dragon. This concept that located the Land of Giants in the East and the Land of Men in the West is again made a part of the *Ring*, but now in a manner that is not only more subtle than the previous method, but one that is also presented in an indirect manner. Now, the word *East* is not a part of the dialogue. The incident occurs in *Die Walküre*, when Hunding informs Siegmund that his mortal kin and their lands are to be found *West* of his dwelling. This third example of East and of West, circumlocutory as it may be, joins with the previous ones to become mythical information that can be most helpful for a fuller and broader understanding of the giants in Wagner's *Ring*. These examples also become another demonstration of the mythical thoroughness that Wagner attempted to bring to his drama. Additionally, these examples also demonstrate that the mythicalness that he wrote into his *Ring* is, essentially, an accurate reflection of the thoughts and beliefs of a very ancient Teutonic culture.

Wagner's mythology conveys a rather definite idea about the land in which his giants Fafner and Fasolt live. By means of the stage directions and the dialogue, it is learned that the brothers live on a mountain, in a region that is separated from both the world of men and the world of the gods by a mountainous ridge. This home of the giants of the *Ring* is isolated, separated, apart in a most remote area. Wagner relates this distant home with the kind of giants that he calls his pair. Wagner's Fasolt and Fafner are *Earth-Giants*, a designation that reflects, at least in part, certain ancient Teutonic beliefs regarding giants. The early Teutonic peoples held that there were different kinds of giants, and they gave names to each of these distinct clans or groups. Those names always reflected some dominant characteristic of the nature or the geography of the region in which they lived. Such Germanic thought, as reveled in the myths, recognized *Water-Giants* and *Fire-Giants* and *Frost Giants* and *Hill Giants*. There were no "Earth-Giants" as such in Teutonic mythology, but Wagner's giants inhabited a place that is not unlike the earth, and, in addition, they wander the earth, coming down to the mountain top to deal with the gods. When Wagner called his giants *Earth-Giants*, he was simply attempting to adhere to the pattern of names that was accepted in the mythical tales. Certainly, he was successful in that attempt.

Wagner's Fasolt and Fafner are essentially accurate depictions of the early Germanic concepts of giants. By means of the dialogue of the drama, by means of the physical appearance of the pair, and further, by means of the pair's actions, it is obvious that Wagner's giants are a race unto themselves. They are presented as beings of unusual size and strength, and there is a very evident untamed fierceness about them, a ferocity that causes them to distrust the gods, even to confront them. Wagner's Fasolt and Fafner also show an aggressiveness toward dwarfs, and – in a sense – a similar attitude toward mortals. Wagner's giants live in their own world, to the East. They travel in pairs, they are builders for the gods, and in the *Ring* as in the myths they are to receive Freia as payment for their labors. By their own words, Wagner's giants show themselves to be coarse, clumsy dolts, and it is Fafner himself who admits that their slow intelligence and dull wits have prevented them from catching the slippery Alberich who – in turn – has done them much harm.

Wagner's giants are like the giants that are found in the ancient Germanic scheme of the universe, and all that is in that universe. The physical appearances of Fafner and Fasolt, the total nature of each one of this pair, their relationships with other figures of the *Ring*, all are remarkably faithful to the accounts of the numerous giants, their actions, and their world that are to be found in the myths. There are, however, two major aspects of Teutondom's giants that were of no concern to the dramatist as he went about the business of creating his *Ring* poem. In the first regard, there is no dramatization, indeed not even a reference, to the origin of Fafner and Fasolt. Such a matter, which is basic to the concept of the creation as the ancient Germanics envisioned the beginning of all things, is, however, of no real consequence in the drama, and with the exception of the origin of the Valkyries, Wagner devoted no dramatic time to this aspect of any of his supernatural beings. In the matter of the Valkyries, it became amply evident that their origin was to have a thematic role in the drama, and thus there was full justification that their origin be included. The same cannot be said of, or for the giants.

The second mythical matter pertinent to the giants of Teutondom that Wagner ignored as he brought these supernaturals into his drama was one of association. It is dramatic fact that Wagner did not cause his giants to be associated with some phenomenon of violent nature. Neither Fafner nor Fasolt is involved in any form of natural catastrophe, as might have been expected had the pair been figures conceived as mirror images of those that were developed in the ancient Teutonic mind. If such an association with violent nature somehow would have contributed to the dramatic effect, it must be assumed that Wagner would have found a thematic method to make it part of his argument. Wagner refrained, however, because he obviously sensed that such an association in the argument as he had developed it might have detracted from the force and might that the gods were required to show. It is also possible that Wagner believed that such a demonstration would occasion a clash of character with the gods, and rather than risk such dramatic damage to his tale, he chose to impart the might and powers of his giants through their actions as they sought to gain the rewards that had been promised them for their labors. Then, too, the composer may have considered the dramatic fact that he had made two of his gods absolute representatives of the natural world. There was Donner who was the God of Thunder and Lightning, and there was Froh who became the *Ring's* God of the Fields and Guardian of the Rainbow Bridge. With such natural forces as those represented by the deities, there was no dramatic or thematic need to augment those natural forces, and then place them without thematic cause or reason in the hands of the giants.

Wagner may have omitted two mythical elements from the characterization of his *Ring* giants, but he also created one of his own. This added factor in the total depiction of Fasolt and Fafner can only be described, it cannot really be explained, and therefore the incident remains yet today both an enigma and a curiosity. The matter becomes evident in *Siegfried*, during Fafner's last moments of life. The Volsung Siegfried has pierced the dragon's heart with his sword, and the transformed giant laments that he has been dealt such a blow by one so young and so unworldly. As

Fafner tells the hero how he killed his brother Fasolt to gain the gold of the Rhine for himself, he indirectly informs the youth that he and his brother were the *last* of their race, and that after Fasolt's death only he of the giants of the universe remained. In Wagnerian terms, then, with the death of Fafner, the race of Teutondom's giants also dies. The Germanic giants are no more! Wagner's unusual mythical creation is not all like anything that he had encountered in the myths themselves. In those myths, Fafner the Dragon dies, killed by Siegfried, much in the manner as in the *Ring*. That Eddic death, however, does not signify the last of the giants, or even the last of any of the mythical races. It is a matter of speculation as to where or in what manner Wagner came upon the idea to terminate entirely a recognized and flourishing race of mythical supernaturals. It is equally, if not more puzzling why he then proceeded to make that idea of Fafner and Fasolt as the last giants of the universe a part of his dramatization, and then to cause both of them to die while making their demise a matter of some dramatic significance. There is no thematic need in the drama for such an occurrence. The added element makes no dramaturgic contribution to the drama, and neither does the element offer any possibility for added theatricality. And, of course, the mythology of Teutondom sees the matter in a much different manner. Wagner never offered a comment or an explanation of the matter, and one can only propose that he felt that the situation somehow added to the nobility of Siegfried's character, that somehow the incident lauded even more the bravery of his Volsung hero. However, all is speculation, and the matter remains today unresolved, and must remain so.

Such are the giants of *Der Ring des Nibelungen*, and those of the mythology that served as the composer's inspiration, his source, and even his literary catharsis. There can be no doubt that Wagner was careful about the mythical qualities that were to be part of these figures, yet he was able to develop their character and mold their nature much in the pattern of what he had found in the mythical literature. Indeed, Wagner's giants are figures in his *Ring*, but they are also essentially the same giants that moved about in a vast and expansive universe that once existed in the collective mind of an ancient Teutonic culture.

See also: *Fafner*
Fasolt

GIBICHUNG

The German surname *Gibichung*, formed with the name *Gibich* and the suffix *ung*, is one of the prominent names of its time, and it vies for the honor of being one of the oldest, along with *Nibelung* and *Volsung*. The name is to be found throughout the Germanic myths, legends, and sagas of continental Teutondom, as well as in those of the Nordic or Northern (Scandinavian) region. In those numerous tales that held the attention of the southern Teutonic peoples, that is the clans of continental Europe, the most common early form of the prefix word was *Gibeche*, with such variations as *Gibika*, *Gifica*, *Gibicho*, and *Kipicha*. In the ancient literature of these peoples, *Gibeche*, which Wagner modernized into *Gibich*, was the founder of what was to become a famed and celebrated line of Burgundian kings, often known as just that, the "Burgundian Kings." In the Nordic region, the root word gave such variations as *Gjuki* and *Giuki*.

Wagner brought the mythical and legendary Gibichung clan into his *Ring* through the characters Gunther and Gutrune. This brother and sister are the children of King Gibich and Grimhild, neither of whom is part of the *dramatis personae* of the *Ring*. Gunther, the elder and first male child, rules the Gibichung kingdom on the Rhine. Their half brother is Hagen, whose mother is also Grimhild, but whose father is Alberich, the Nibelung dwarf. (The drama tells that Grimhild fell under the influence of Alberich's gold!)

Wagner drew heavily from the Eddic poems for his depiction in the *Ring* drama of the Gibichung family. In *The Poetic Edda* Gjuki (Gibich) and his wife Grimhild are the parents of three children: Gunnar (Gunther), Hogni (Hagen), and Guthrun (Gutrune). A fourth child, Gotthorm, is a half brother to the trio through his mother Grimhild. Gunnar rules his clan from his palatial home which, according to the Eddic verses, is located in "the hills of the Rhine."

There is usually some aspect of the Siegfried legend present in the Eddic poems that tell of the activities of the Gibich family. It is recounted, for example, that Siegfried (Sigurd) will slay a dragon, and that he will then remove all the treasure that the dragon was guarding and take the hoard to Gunnar. These verses also tell how Sigurd becomes the husband of Guthrun, and that it is the half brother Gotthorm who slays Sigurd at Brynhild's (Brünnhilde's) request.

The *Volsungasaga* records a familial relationship of the Gibich clan that essentially parallels that found in the *Edda*. In this celebrated saga, which in many ways paraphrases the Eddic themes, Giuki rules over a vast kingdom that is "south of the Rhine." His wife, Grimhild, is respected for her profound wisdom, but she is also feared as a "fierce-hearted woman." Giuki and Grimhild have three sons: Gunnar, Hogni, and Gotthorm, and one daughter, Gundrun, who is "the fairest of maidens." The anonymous compiler of this saga that focuses on the Volsung clan writes that these children of Giuki:

> ...were far above those of other kings, in all matters of strength, in goodness, and in growth, and Giuki's sons were always in combat and realized many famous deeds.

The *Nibelungenlied*, the famed epic of the German people, contains a similar, but nevertheless unique and distinct relationship of these celebrated figures. Gunther, Gernot, and Giselher are the three renowned Burgundian kings whose kingdom is located "on the Rhine" and whose capital is in the city of Worms. Their sister is Kriemhild (Grimhild), and all four are the children of Ute and Dankrat. (In this work, Hagen is a vassal of King Gunther.) Ute is the sister of Bishop Pilgrim of Passau. The daughter, Kriemhild, becomes the wife of Siegfried and later, after Siegfried is killed, she marries Etzel (Attila), the King of the Huns at whose court there is in attendance a wealthy and celebrated warrior, Prince Gibeche. It is Gibeche, a king in his own right, who rides out to greet Kriemhild as she arrives to become the bride of Etzel.

Wagner's arrangement of the relationships of the several figures associated with the Gibich clan is essentially his own. The relationship in the *Ring* of Gunther and Gutrune as brother and sister and children of Gibich

(Gjuki) is one that is found in many of the northern Germanic tales, while the southern versions most often make Grimhild the daughter and sister. Likewise, it is to a northern work, *Thidrekssaga*, to which Wagner resorts to gain his idea that Hagen can be a half brother through the mother of his Volsung pair. There is, however, no such relationship as Wagner has created in either mythical or legendary tales. Nevertheless, it is somewhat curious to note also that in this matter of the Gibichungs of his drama and their relationship one to another, Wagner was more swayed by the relationships that he had found in the Nordic literature (*The Poetic Edda, Volsungasaga,* and *Thidrekssaga*) than those that are part of the southern or German version (*Nibelungenlied*) of the tales. These relationships whose sources Wagner had found in his Nordic sources remained in his drama despite his statement, made on numerous occasions, that with his *Ring* he wanted only to create a German national work of art!

GIBICHUNG (Name)

This family name of Gunther and his sister Gutrune is the modernized form of a surname that is quite prominent in early Teutonic mythical and legendary literature, both Scandinavian and German. In the Nordic tales, the name is *Gjuki* (pronounced *Gyuki*). The southern version of this name, as found in *Nibelungenlied*, is *Gibeche*, and in other stories there are such variations as *Gibika* and *Kipicha*. Wagner preferred the variation *Gibich*, and when the suffix *ung* (See *Notes*) is attached, the word means "Child" or "Offspring of Gibich."

The famed mythologist Jakob Grimm states that the root-word, that is *Gibich*, meant "giver of good things," and, then, when the name is combined with the suffix *ung*, the word means "Child of the Giver of Good Things."

There is no reason to doubt the scholarship of so eminent a student of things Germanic as Grimm. In that light, then, both Gunther and Gutrune are "children of the Giver of Good Things," and when the storyline is part of a mythical or even legendary tale, the traits and characteristics of the parents are regularly found in the nature of their children. However, when the roles of the *Ring's* Gunther and Gutrune are examined with the family name of Gibich and its meaning firmly in place as a semantic backdrop, when the purposes of these roles, their function, and their nature, are carefully considered, there arises a certain semantic uneasiness, an instinctive wish, perhaps, to question the composer about the matter. Indeed, there seems to be little of the "giver of good things" that has come down to the brother and sister from their father. To the contrary, the character of each of this pair seems to reflect a modicum of personal greed which is deftly enclosed in a regal robe of naivete and simple innocence. Under such circumstances, it becomes apparent immediately that Gunther and Gutrune bear a name that is not truly exemplary of their natures, and it seems evident that, for whatever reason, in the case of this brother and sister, Wagner did not give to his characters a name that was expressive, if not pictorial, of the characters who bore that name. It can rightfully be said that this is the only major occurrence in the *Ring* in which Wagner deviated from his standard pattern of matching name and character carefully.

GNITAHEID See: *Fafner's Cave*

GOATS See: *Donner* (Vol. II)
               Sacrifice (Animal)

GODS AND GODDESSES

The ancient Teutonic peoples, those who existed throughout the several regions of the early Germanic world, did not believe in a single, supreme being. From the earliest of times in that world, the worship of these people was rendered to a famed and holy race of deities that included numerous and varied gods and whose principal figure was Wotan, or Odin as he was called in the Nordic regions of Teutondom. There is evidence that prior to the cult of Wotan and his pantheon of divine beings there had been worship of other, older gods, especially one known as Tyr (Tiw), but by the end of the first century the gods that were to appear in Wagner's *Ring* were well established in the ancient Teutonic world and accepted as a religious hierarchy. This order of gods continued its religious domination throughout all of Teutondom for some 800 years, at which time Christianity then became the accepted religious thought for most of western Europe. However, it would be another three hundred years before Christianity could replace Wotan and his cult in the Nordic or Scandinavian area of Teutondom.

The gallery of primary and lesser divine beings that satisfied the religious, social, and cultural needs of the early Teutonic peoples, as well as the concepts regarding those divine figures that the culture had developed, was incorporated into the name by which the race of gods was known, the *Aesir*. The term *Aesir* was the Old Norse plural of *As*, a popular word that projected two distinct meanings. Firstly, the word denoted a heavy beam or a rafter in the ceiling of the heavens, to which, at least conceptually, the gods and their strength were equated. At the same time, the word meant the ridge or the top of a mountain on which the gods of the Teutonic peoples were believed to have their dwellings.

The religion, that is, the worship of the Aesir, was known as *Asatru*, which translates roughly as "Belief in the Aesir." The home or land of these Aesir gods was called *Asgard* ("Land of the Ases"), and this land was one of the nine worlds that constituted the heathen Germanic universe. This world, that is Asgard, had been fashioned and created by the Aesir gods who had placed it in the exact center of the universe. Because of the vast expanse of this universe, Wotan, the chief overseer and administrator who was also known as *Allmattki As*, ("Almighty God"), early on appointed other gods to overlook, and in a sense to supervise, the several and varied functions and activities of the other worlds, one of which was Midgard, the world that was to be inhabited by mortals.

The early Teutonic peoples did not waver in their beliefs concerning the Aesir divinities. However, in time, another religious matter began to make itself felt among the numerous groups and clans of Teutondom. The sea-people who inhabited the region that included the Baltic Sea slowly but most definitely were developing a cult for a second race of divine beings, figures who apparently met the unique divine requirements of this coastal way of life. This second race of religious supernaturals was known as the Vanir (Wanes). Little is known today of the Vanir, but it is very probable that these religious figures were not truly gods in a way that the Aesir were gods, but rather they were more like water spirits, or perhaps sprites. The cult that the people developed for these figures never gained a true cultural prominence, and they faded rather quickly from the Teutonic religious scene. These Vanir existed long enough in the Germanic societal thought, however, to become the cause of considerable conceptual commotion and confusion, sufficient enough at least to have a lasting effect on the religious beliefs of the Teutonic people. It seems that one element of the Vanir dogma opposed the worship of any older gods, that is, gods from a former era. Although the Vanir were looked upon more as 'neighbors' to the Aesir and did not oppose or necessarily compete in any way with those gods, this segment of Vanir thought prevented any worship of the god Tyr that was mentioned above, a god who was now rather impotent, in a divine sense, but who was nevertheless accepted as a member of the Aesir hierarchy. The fierce opposition of the Vanir to the concept of Tyr seriously riled the Aesir, and in time the two clans of divine supernaturals were at war with each other. This war, which became known as *The First War*, was a violent conflict, a deadly war in which neither side could conquer the other. Finally, after much carnage, a treaty between the two warring factions was arranged. The principal aspect of the treaty of peace required that each clan of gods exchange hostages, a factor that evidently would deter each side from attacking the other. The Aesir gods surrendered two of their clan. The first was Hoenir, a lesser god, but one of a trio of gods that had created first man and first woman. The second figure to be turned over to the Vanir was Mimir who, if not a true god, was nevertheless a supernatural who was the Guardian of the Spring of Wisdom that flowed at the base of the World Ash

Tree and from which Wotan had once drunk and as payment for that drink had given one of his eyes. The Vanir met their part of the agreement by surrendering Njorth and his two children Freyr and Freyja, who would become known in German as Freia and Fro, and in the *Ring* as Freia and Froh. This trio of Vanir gods not only was accepted as equals by the Aesir, but the offspring of Njorth would eventually become two of the most respected, revered, and powerful gods of Teutondom.

The exact number of Aesir gods that roamed the heathen Teutonic divine world is uncertain. The myths often refer to numerous beings as deities, but there are then other myths that contradict such statements. Occasionally, there is a single reference to a figure as a god, but little if any additional information is ever found in the tales and stories. At times, a figure who is obviously a lesser being, perhaps a servant or a messenger, is spoken of as a god, yet more specificity regarding that being is never forthcoming. Despite this lack of a clear and indisputable account of the order of the Teutonic gods, scholars of the mythology seem to agree that in addition to Wotan, there were twelve gods (Ases) and twelve goddesses (Asynjas). Unfortunately, when lists of these gods are compiled, the names usually vary, depending upon the mythical work consulted. There is, however, no doubt or dispute regarding the most prominent and most dominant of the Teutonic deities. Of these gods, there were three who would stand out from all the others, a trio that would become the most powerful of the gods, three deities that would be worshipped most intensely by the Teutonic peoples. These three gods, often referred to in mythical literature as the *Triad*, were Wotan (Odin), Donner (Thor), and Froh (Freyr). Among the Aesir goddesses there were two that were the most renowned and honored. One was Freia (Freyja), who was a goddess of great beauty, and the second of these goddesses was Fricka (Frigge), who was Wotan's wife and therefore looked upon as the "Mother of the Gods." It would be precisely these five divinities that Wagner would bring into his dramatic world.

The relative import of these deities within the Teutonic culture cannot be overstated, yet what must also be comprehended is the absolute significance that the related concepts that forged that importance had upon the continuing Germanic culture. Perhaps the most revelatory, and indeed the most indicative, demonstration of this cultural influence is evidenced by a single but ponderous matter of fact: There are four days of the Germanic week that the numerous Teutonic cultures have named after the principal gods of early Teutondom. In the English language these days bear the names *Tuesday*, after the god Tyr (Tiw, Tiu), *Wednesday*, after Wotan ("Woden's Day"), *Thursday*, after "Thor's Day," and *Friday*, after "Freia's Day." (There are some mythologists who maintain that Fricka is the goddess honored by the word *Friday*.) These names had become fixed in the culture by the fourth and fifth centuries, well after the Romans had accepted the seven-day week. Today, some 1500 years later, and in the face of the sweeping dominion of Christianity over the entire Teutonic territory, the equivalents of these names, with only minor changes, persist, not only in the English language, but also in Afrikanns, Danish, Dutch, Flemish, Faeroese, Frisian, German, Icelandic, Norwegian, Swedish, and Yiddish. Perhaps it should also be noted that at one time the early Germans so revered the gods Wotan and Donner that the two days named in their honor were the two holy days of the week!

Richard Wagner not only selected the pre-eminent gods of the ancient Germanic world for his *Ring* drama, but he also endowed those figures with the major attributes and qualities that were associated with them as a race of divine beings, as well as those that each individual god had boasted in heathen thought.

Each of the deities of Teutondom had certain specified duties to perform and unique functions to carry out. These divine obligations essentially determined that god's rank as well as his limits of divine control. Wotan was the highest ranking god, the supreme deity, supreme in the sense that in addition to his own magical powers, and his special divine capabilities and functions, he could also perform any action that any other god could effect, and he also had the power to undue any action that had been taken by any other divine being. Wotan was the "King of the Gods," revered, honored and worshipped by all the Teutonic peoples. He was the most noble, the wisest of the gods, the final judge and decision-maker in all matters, the most powerful and the most influential of all the Teutonic deities. Wotan was also Teutondom's God of War.

A second prominent god of Teutondom was the much-venerated Donner. His dominion was that of God of Rain and Thunder (fertility), and he was the god who kept the giants in their subservient place. Donner was the second in rank to Wotan, the first to be invoked by the people if they felt that they had been treated improperly by Wotan. Donner actually became the principal god in some parts of what is today Norway.

The third ranking god among the peoples of the heathen Teutonic world was Froh. He was the God of Spring and Summer, and by means of one of his gifts, sunshine, he brought about an abundant fruitfulness through the fertility of nature. In some regions of what is now Sweden, Froh became the ranking god. (In the myths, Froh is not the Guardian of the Rainbow Bridge. That honor fell to Heimdall, another of the Aesir deities.)

Fricka was the wife of Wotan, and therefore ranked above all other goddesses. Fricka was often consulted by Wotan, although the pair often argued, and the myths frequently recount their domestic squabbles. It was regularly Fricka who ventured harsh and negative criticism about some action that her husband had taken, about something that he had done, or about some decision that he had made, and it would be this Fricka that Wagner would restructure for his drama. The mythical Fricka presided over marriages, and she had a special penchant for jewelry, especially that which was made of gold, divine qualities that Wagner would adapt to the Fricka of his *Ring*. Fricka was revered throughout Teutondom but, curiously, there was no cult for her godhood.

Freia was the second of the most revered, the most powerful, and the most renowned of the Teutonic goddesses. She was a beautiful figure who inspired love and whose blessings were sought by lovers, and she was frequently invoked and her blessings sought on marriages.

The Aesir gods of Teutondom were viewed, like the gods of many cultures, as human in form. Although Wagner gives no heed in his *Ring* drama to the origin of his gods and presents them in their maturity, the concepts of the early Teutonic peoples held that the deities were conceived and born, much as were mortals. The conception of these gods had taken place well before the existence of human life, and a major distinction between the gods and mortals was that the deities attained their full physical size and their mental faculties immediately after birth. Unlike the gods of other religious systems, particularly the Hindu and the Slavic, the Germanic gods were not deformed in that they had several heads or arms or legs. These gods did have, however, certain disabilities. The mythical Wotan had but one eye. Tyr, the god of old, had but one hand, the other had been bitten off by a wolf. The demonic Loge (Loke) walked with a limp. Wagner retained the matter of the Allfather god with but one eye, but he rejected the matter about Loge and a limp.

The gods of the *Ring*, like those of the Teutonic mythical past, met in council. The ancient gods traveled daily, to the World Ash Tree, which they reached by riding their horses across Bifrost, the Rainbow Bridge. There, by the great tree of the universe, the gods of Teutondom had constructed a special temple, Gladsheim ("Radiant Home"), which the myths describe as the largest building in Asgard and the one in which the gods gathered to hold their meetings and to make the judgments and decisions regarding all aspects of the mythical world. Wagner's gods also meet in council, much like those of the mythical past. The composer causes four of the *Ring* deities and Loge to gather and to discuss with some concern the plight of the goddess Freia who is being held by the giants as payment for their labors on Valhalla. They also exchange opinions that relate to the matter about Alberich's gold, if it should be made a factor in the situation, and if so, in what manner. (Wagner had made the Loge of his *Ring* a god, the God of Fire. In the myths Loge (Loki) is not a divine being, but rather a cunning and shrewd supernatural who is constantly at odds with the gods.) The scene of the gods and their meeting occurs early in the *Ring*, in the second scene of *Das Rheingold*. Wagner's gods do not have a special temple in which to meet, and neither do they cross the Rainbow Bridge to reach the World Ash Tree. The composer deemed these aspects of the Teutonic myths to have dramatic roles of much greater intensity elsewhere in his poem. Rather, the gods of the music-drama gather on a mountain top, a site that can be acceptable to mythical accounts and easily associated with the gods. In the myths the gods traditionally located their dwellings on the mountain heights and peaks that looked out over all the world.

In addition to a special building that the gods had constructed as a meeting place, each god of Teutondom, with few exceptions, had a separate, personal dwelling. The primary god had *Valaskjolf* ("Shelf of the Slain") and Donner's dwelling was called *Bilskirnir* ("Strong"). Freia's abode was known as *Sessrymnir* ("Rich in Seats") and Fricka lived in *Fensalir* ("Sea Halls"). Froh was one god who apparently did not have a personal dwelling, at least the Eddic literature does not make reference to such a place. However, it is mythical fact that this god often visited Wotan's abode in which he would sit and look down upon the activities of the other worlds. Neither does the mythical Loge have a specific dwelling. The myths state merely that he lived among the gods in Asgard.

As Wagner had rejected the mythical temple in which the gods met in council, so too did he reject the concept that the gods had individual dwellings. The exclusion from the *Ring* of the dwellings of the gods was occasioned, without doubt, because of the simple dramatic fact that such abodes obviously made no contribution to the argument, and indeed their inclusion would have been mere mythical coloration. At the same time, and unquestionably of more importance to the mythical ambience of the drama, was the concept of Teutondom's mighty *Valhalla* ("Hall of the Chosen Slain") that Wagner was to bring into his work and which he would project not only as the principal structure in his poem, but also as a significant and substantial, if static, player in the development of his argument. The composer had drawn Valhalla essentially intact from Teutonic mythical thought, but in addition to its primary mythical function, that of housing brave warriors who had died on the field of battle and who had then been selected to be a member of Wotan's army, Wagner reckoned that he could also use this imposing structure and its fundamental import in the totality of early Germanic beliefs to satisfy the mythical matter of the individual dwellings of the gods. Such an arrangement seemed to satisfy all the dramatic needs as he envisioned them, and, in addition, that arrangement brought the gods together as a single group and gave them the housing that is so much a part of the myths. Thus it is that Wagner's five gods (Loge excluded) are housed in the great Valhalla which, in the last scene of *Das Rheingold*, they enter so majestically, and where, in the final moments of the drama, they gather to look down upon the earth to observe the mortals that they had created and whose lives they governed, much as Wotan regularly had done in the myths of Teutondom.

The myths of the early Teutonic peoples depict the gods, as well as the supernatural Loge, as beings who traveled frequently and extensively about the universe. Although these journeys of the gods were occasionally made as groups, in the main the Teutonic gods traveled alone. Donner made frequent trips "to the East" where he fought and killed giants. Froh traveled extensively. These trips also allowed the deities to visit the vast expanse of the world that they had fashioned from the skull of a giant, to observe the actions of the mortals that they had brought to life in that world, and on occasion, to participate in some way in that life. In the myths, Loge was a frequent companion to Wotan as they journeyed about. Wagner's gods tend to emulate somewhat the travel of the mythical beings, especially the *Ring's* Guardian of Fire and its King of the Gods, Wotan. It is Loge, for example, in *Das Rheingold*, who advises the deities that he has traveled to the ends of the earth, over water and through the air as he sought from all the living things of the universe an answer to the question of what is valued more than a woman's love. It is in this same drama that Loge and Wotan travel from the mountain top down into the bowels of the earth, into deepest Nibelheim where they capture the dwarf Alberich by trickery and then bring him back to the mountain height. Then later, in *Die Walküre*, we sense the journey of Wotan, down to earth to control the matter of Hunding and Siegmund, and then shortly after the two are dead, to travel at full speed from the north on his valiant steed in order to confront Brünnhilde and to settle the matter of her disobedience of his command. Later, in *Siegfried*, the complete awareness of Wotan's lengthy journeys is made vivid as Wotan travels from the divine heights down to the earth, to Mime's cave in the forest, where he confronts the dwarf, and later, at the foot of Brünnhilde's Rock, where he meets Siegfried, the Volsung, who has been led there by Forest Bird. In Wagner's drama Wotan travels about the earth disguised in his blue cape and a wide brimmed hat that is pulled down over his missing eye, exactly as Wagner had found the god as he traveled about in the ancient Teutonic myths. In those ancient tales of the Teutonic peoples, they also believed that their god was very much an ardent traveler, and they gave him the name of *Gangleri*, a name that Wagner also gave to his god, a name that in German and English translates as "Wanderer." (This name of *Gangleri* is only one of three Old Norse names that mean "Wanderer" and which were associated with Wotan, and but one of the many names by which the god was known.)

Although Wagner was careful to make his *Ring* Wotan a traveler, much as the god was in the myths, the composer chose not to give his Wotan the magic of invisibility during his travels among the mortals, a magic that the Wotan of myths possessed. Wagner's rejection on this quality of the divine nature of the Allfather god, was prompted, without doubt, by the dramatic need for the power of invisibility to be an element of the magic of the Tarnhelm that he would bring into his argument, an element of magic that would be of vital significance as the story of the Nibelung gold unfolded.

In the *Ring* as in the myths the divine beings, including the gods, travel a great deal by horse. Each of the mythical gods possessed a horse. Each of the Valkyries moved from earth to Valhalla by means of a horse that could run through the air with great speed. (Brünnhilde's horse, Grane, is one of the great horses of the mythical past.) Wotan, too, traveled by horse, both in myths and in Wagner's drama. In the early Teutonic days it was held that Wotan rode a horse that was the fastest creature of the world, no doubt because it had eight legs. This concept of speed was such that when the god moved about, he moved so fast that a 'rush' or a 'din' was created as he traveled through the air. (Donner traveled so rapidly that he caused the clouds to split in two, and as the two sections rushed back together, they created a great noise that was called *thunder*.) Wagner retained this aspect of Wotan's divinity, not so much because it made a significant contribution to the argument of his *Ring* drama, but rather because this attribute of the god's total persona added to the mythical ambience that he wished to bring to his drama, and because the matter definitely added to the dramaturgical qualities that the drama offered. Wagner makes this facet of Wotan's figure known in *Die Walküre*, when the Valkyries have gathered at Valkyrie Rock and they acknowledge in words, as the composer does in music, that the angered god rides furiously from the north, as if he were a violent storm. In this instance, Wotan rides in wild pursuit of the fleeing Brünnhilde who has disobeyed her father's command that she withhold her protection from Siegmund during his battle with Hunding. In the myths, this 'din' that Wotan caused by racing about the universe at great speed was also caused by the *Heer* or *host*, another term for Wotan's army of raised warriors who inhabited Valhalla. Because Wotan was believed to be the "father of all things," he was also known as the "father of the army," that is, the "Father of the Host," or *heerfather* (*Heerfader, Heervater, Heerfater*), a term that greatly appealed to Wagner and one that he brought over into his *Ring*, as a means to augment the mythical ambience that enveloped this great god of Teutondom.

There were yet other matters that were attendant with the gods of Teutondom, one of which was their weapons. It is not too far amiss to state that the gods of ancient Teutondom were, in their own way, religious manifestations of the fundamental thoughts and beliefs of the society and culture that they served. In that light, the early Teutonic culture was very much oriented to war and conquest. The myths of that ancient past demonstrate quite clearly that violent combat was a natural matter with the people. History, particularly that of the Vikings, also makes this cultural statement, and later history of the Teutonic peoples has confirmed that cultural conclusion. Therefore, it is not unusual that weapons should play a major role within the Teutonic scheme of things, and also receive due attention in the myths that came into existence.

The revered gods of Teutondom, in the main, possessed individual weapons that usually were marvels in their own right, weapons that tended to manifest special, unique magic. Wagner's dramatic instincts caused him to retain some of these weapons and to put them to use at such time as they would add to the drama or the poetry of his *Ring*, or when they would make some contribution to the mythical ambience that he hoped would permeate his work. One such weapon was the mighty hammer that the mythical dwarfs had made for Donner, the unbreakable weapon with which the God of Thunder fought and killed giants. This was the hammer with which the great god also split the skies and caused the heavens to resound in what mortals called *thunder*. This was the weapon that spit great sparks when it was thrown against giant rocks, sparks that were called *lightning*. This was the weapon that always returned to the god's hand after he had thrown it. And, curiously, this was the instrument with which Donner, from time to time, blessed and made sacred the act of marriage! This was the weapon that the people had rewarded with its own name, Mjollnir. Wagner's Donner carries this hammer with him at all times. Although the god of the *Ring* is not able to put the unnamed hammer to all the uses that its mythical prototype served, Wagner's Donner does use it to threaten the giants Fasolt and Fafner, and in the final scene of *Das Rheingold*, as the gods prepare to enter Valhalla for the first time, he uses the hammer to clear the skies of the mist and fog that prevent a clear view of the fortress. Despite the relatively short time that Donner's hammer is a factor in the *Ring* drama, and despite the restricted use to which it is put, Wagner was able to project its mythical qualities of might and power, as well as its magical uniqueness. There is no doubt that the *Ring* hammer is the instrument of Teutonic myths, the instrument of violent nature, the weapon that slays giants, the weapon that brings a special mythical coloration to its owner, Donner, the God of Thunder.

There was yet another celebrated weapon of the gods that is found throughout the Teutonic myths and of which Wagner made dramatic use. That weapon was a spear, and it belonged to Wotan, and like Donner's hammer, the people revered it enough to give it a name, Gungnir. Like Donner's hammer, Wotan's spear had been made by the smiths of the Teutonic universe, the dwarfs. Its magic allowed the God of War to hit whatever mark at which he had thrown the weapon. The spear always dealt death to its victim, and thus it allowed the god to be victorious in each and every battle. It was this spear that Wotan had thrown at the enemy gods, the Vanir, in The First War, an action that gave the Aesir gods their great victory. (The Teutonic beliefs do not always present a complete, logical picture of the order of the universe, and the myths often offer accounts that conflict with each other. The beliefs regarding Wotan's spear are one such example. This weapon supposedly granted the god victory in battle, and the victory that the gods enjoyed in The First Battle exemplifies that belief. However, in The Final Battle of the universe, during *ragnarök*, the predicted downfall of the gods, Wotan, the other deities, and Wotan's army ride out from Valhalla, ready to do battle with the enemies. Wotan is astride his famed horse, is dressed in battle garb, and he proudly carries the great spear of victory, Gungnir. However, the spear is of little use in this last moment of the world because shortly after the battle begins, Froh and Donner die in combat and Wotan is killed and eaten by the World Wolf, the monster Fenrir!)

Wagner sensed the mythical authority of this spear, and he was able to envision the dramatic qualities that it could project. He used the weapon in his *Ring*, extensively and continuously, although he was to cause its origin to be that action with which Wotan tears a limb from the World Ash Tree, a limb which then becomes the great god's spear. The Wotan of the *Ring* carries the spear at all times, and on it are engraved the runes of his divine authority, the runes that give the god his supreme command. There is only one instance in the entire drama of the *Ring* when Wagner indicated that Wotan should lay down his spear. The scene in question occurs in *Die Walküre*, that scene in which Wotan becomes almost mortal-like with his feelings, the occasion when the god must punish his favorite daughter, Brünnhilde. Wagner actually directs that each party lay aside its weapons, apparently as a visible action that might allow the divinity of the two to be temporarily put aside, and that each may then become emotionally involved in the poignant scene of father and daughter.

Wagner utilized quite successfully, in a dramatic sense, those mythical weapons that are a part of the Teutonic myths and which are associated with the gods Wotan and Donner. Curiously, however, the composer does not bring into his *Ring* a third prominent weapon, a sword, a weapon that early Teutonic beliefs accorded the Froh of myth. Indeed, this sword is one of Teutondom's primary weapons, principally because it too, like Mjollnir and Gungnir, had its own special magic. There are numerous swords that find a niche in Teutonic myth, but of all those weapons early Germanic beliefs held that it was only Froh's sword which, when wielded by a valiant warrior, could fight and do battle by itself! (On occasion, there are those productions of the *Ring* in which the director or producer, familiar with the Teutonic myths, will provide the god Froh with a sword, and, in some productions even cause the god to deliver the weapon, in one way or another, to Wotan as the deities prepare to make their initial entrance into Valhalla.) Unlike Donner's hammer and Wotan's spear, however, the mythical sword of the god Froh is unnamed.

Wagner sensed dramatic ambience in the matter of his gods and the weapons associated with them. In that regard, Wotan's spear and Donner's hammer offered no untoward thematic or theatrical problems. To the contrary, each of those two weapons allowed for some most dramatic effects, theatrical as well as musical effects that Wagner would incorporate so successfully into his drama. However, he obviously envisioned serious thematic conflict if he gave his Froh the sword that belonged to the god of myth. The thematic conflict would be major in that it would defeat, or at least weaken, much of what he desired to bring into his drama in the form of a sword that a hero would wield and which he would use to slay a dragon. It would be Siegfried's sword that must have the prominence in the drama, not a sword that makes no contribution to the argument and which is visible and functional for only a few moments of stage time. Froh's mythical sword had to give way to the Volsung's weapon, to Notung, the single weapon of the *Ring* that bears a name.

Wagner's eager acceptance of the major gods of Teutondom and his generous dramatic adaptation of numerous of the principal divine attributes is uniquely matched by the attention that he also gave to lesser qualities that the ancient culture had attached to these deities. At times, the significance of these characteristics and activities are rather minor, at least as evidenced in the mythical literature, and on occasion, the presentation that Wagner gives to them in his drama may be somewhat at variance with mythical depiction. It remains fact, however, that Wagner was always essentially faithful to the beliefs that prevailed in the early Teutonic mind, regardless of the primacy of the matter.

Certain of the lesser of the divine qualities had much in common with mortal life. The deities of Teutondom slept, for example, as do the *Ring's* Wotan and Fricka on the mountain top, where they awaken to gaze for the first time on the fortress Valhalla that rises majestically in the distant heavens. The gods of Teutondom consumed food: salmon, ox, mead, honey, wine, ale, and apples. Wagner's gods also eat, although their fare is not so elaborate as that of their prototypes, really only mead and apples. Like mortals, the early Germanic gods married. Wotan had wooed and won Fricka as wife, much as Wagner was to depict their relationship in his drama. He felt, however, that he should ignore the other marriages among the gods, perhaps because additional marriages among his gods might detract from the primacy that he wished Wotan and Fricka to have, and therefore he gives no attention to Donner's wife, Sif, for whom the dwarfs had made a handsome gold wig. He made no mention either of the mythical fact that Froh had fallen in love and apparently had wed a giantess, Gerd. Neither did he give heed to Freia's husband who traveled about the universe a great deal and for whom, when he was away, the goddess in her loneliness cried tears of red gold. If Wagner retained only the relationship of husband and wife for his Wotan and Fricka, and ignored other mythical marriages, he obviously believed that some from of familial relationship should exist between his gods, that there should exist a blood-line that related the gods one to another. To that end, then, he resorted to the relatively simple plan of making Donner, Froh, and Freia brothers and sister to Fricka, and thus in-laws of Wotan.

Wagner was not lax in the application to the gods of his *Ring* of yet other of the lesser qualities of Teutondom's gods, qualities that resembled aspects of mortal life. The Teutonic gods regularly discussed matters of the world, they transacted affairs, and they concluded agreements. It would be these business-like actions that would assume a major significance in the *Ring* as Wagner's Wotan concludes an agreement with the giants regarding the work on Valhalla. (Wagner adapted this segment of his drama from a myth that relates a tale of a giant and the gods, and an agreement between the two regarding the construction of a building in the Land of the Gods.) The Germanic gods were also like mortals in that they experienced pain and suffering, and they felt passions, expressions that Wagner dramatized rather extensively. There is, for example, the serious personal concern that Donner, Fricka and Froh display when they learn that the King of the Gods has pledged Freia as payment to the giants for their work on Valhalla. There is the connubial resentment that Fricka displays when she recalls her husband's many travels away from her. There is also the deep mental and emotional despair, even distress, that pervade Wotan when he is forced to banish his favorite daughter, Brünnhilde, from the ranks of the divine. There is also a distinct despair that overcomes Wotan when he ultimately realizes that he is helpless in his resolution of the matter that he has brought upon himself, and then that he can only stand aside, to await the fated doom and destruction of his world.

Wagner had not yet concluded the matter of lesser divine qualities in the makeup of the early Teutonic deities and the nature of the gods of his drama. His keen knowledge of ancient Teutonic thought had shown him that the gods of the past were well versed in the matter of runes and the great powers that these singularly Germanic creations allowed. He brought the runes into his work, and he gave them an importance that they had once known in Teutonic history. Wagner caused runes to be engraved on Wotan's spear, one of the mythical places where runes could be found, and he made these runes those that gave the god his dominion as well as his powers in the matter of agreements and pacts! It was, indeed, the runes of Teutondom that also permitted Wotan to rule, to render divine administration of the universe.

Unique also to the divine ones of Teutondom was the prolongation of their lives by means of apples of red gold. Wagner brings these "golden apples" and their miraculous powers of eternal youth into his drama. He uses this fruit as an integral factor in the development of his argument when he causes the gods to become pallid and weak because they have lost access to these magic apples, a situation that they deem demands immediate attention. Of course Wagner associates the guardianship of these fruits with Freia, which allows him a thematic means to bring them to the forefront of his story although in this latter matter he has deviated from mythical beliefs. In the myths it is the goddess Idun, not Freia, who is charged with the cultivation and protection of these fruits and their magic powers.

There is yet another aspect of the *Ring* which, if not of primary importance, nevertheless has its own rightful place in the drama, much as it has in the Teutonic myths. Like the gods of Germanic antiquity, so too do the gods of the *Ring* receive the honor of animal sacrifice. This is an activity that Hagen initiates and which he wishes to make a part of the celebration of the wedding of Gunther and Brünnhilde. Hagen orders the vassals to slaughter oxen, sheep, a boar, and a goat as a sacrifice to Wotan, Fricka,

Froh, and Donner respectively. Although Wagner does not bring a simulated sacrifice to the stage, the mere reference to such action indicates his awareness of such ancient practices, and his call for animals to be dedicated to individual gods reveals a most extensive knowledge of the mythical beliefs. If Wagner's dialogue calls for animal sacrifices to each of several gods follows precisely the activities of the ancient people regarding those gods, so too is he mythically correct when he specifies that a specific kind of animal is to be sacrificed for each of the gods. The Wotan of myth was like the great bull-ox of mythical history and sheep drew the chariot of the goddess Fricka. Froh had a boar that the dwarfs had made of pure gold, an animal that the god rode through the air and over the water, and Donner's chariot was drawn by two goats! (It should be noted that Wagner's sacrificial animals, like those of the myths, are regularly edible, an incontrovertible requirement for any animal sacrifice that was made by the early Teutonic peoples.)

Most of the ancient gods of Teutondom were invoked by the people. It was held that each of the gods had certain distinct powers that were beneficial to the people, powers which, in one way or another, could make their coarse lives more enjoyable. The people regularly called upon the deities to work those powers in their behalf. Wagner was not unaware of these cultural practices, and he obviously felt that some replication of such invocation in his poem would augment the mythical ambience that he knew was dramatically necessary. It is for the stage setting of the second act of *Götterdämmerung* that he gives stage directions that include altar stones for Donner, Fricka, and Wotan, such dramatic properties silently but continuously suggesting the mythical assistance that the people requested of their gods. Then, shortly after that act begins he causes Hagen to call out to the vassals to prepare for the rituals of animal sacrifices to four of the gods, to allow the blood of these animals to flow upon the altar stones in order that the deities will bestow their divine blessing on the forthcoming marriage of Brünnhilde and Gunther. Gutrune offers an individual prayer to the goddess Freia, petitioning that she bestow her blessings on Siegfried, her husband to be. (The mythical Freia was somewhat of a goddess of love, a deity that was called upon by lovers and by married people, particularly women, who wished their marriage to improve through love. The Freia of myth was also fond of music and therefore 'love music' was thought to be one of her contributions to the universe.) In yet another invocation of the gods, the Gibichung vassals call upon the vengeful Donner to silence what they believe is the disgrace that Siegfried has brought upon them by his breaking of the trust between himself and Gunther, and the breaking of the vows of fidelity that he had made with Brünnhilde. It is then Gunther and Brünnhilde, individually, who call upon Wotan, the ultimate arbiter and final judge of all disputes, to avenge the betrayal that they believe Siegfried has wrought upon them, to restore the honor that the Volsung hero has stripped from them.

There is no serious doubt, and there really can be no question, regarding Wagner's skillful incorporation into his *Ring* drama of numerous and varied qualities, attributes, characteristics, and related activities that were associated with the deities of the ancient Germanic world. Yet, of all factors that he utilized to broaden the mythical ambience of the work and which he used to create a dramatic atmosphere that was conducive to his tale, there was one matter that was of greater overall importance in the development of that work's argument than any other. This mythical concern greatly influenced the ultimate dramatic content that Wagner brought to his drama, and that same concern became a factor of significance in the dramatic, climactic finale of the entire work.

The mythical matter that was related to the gods and which was so fundamental to the final dramatic formation of the *Ring* was really two-fold in nature, each segment essentially represented by cultural belief. The first of these two beliefs that early Teutonic society held pertained to the judgmental powers of the deities. The ancient Germanic peoples did not view their gods as exemplary of perfection, that is, these gods, despite the extensive magic powers that they had, and despite the religious control that they exercised, were not indefectible. These early peoples of the ancient Teutonic culture believed that their gods were fallible, that is, their deeds, their actions, and even their thoughts, did not always reflect rationality, logic, correctness of process, or at times, practical reasoning. Infallibility was not a part of the godhead of the deities of Teutondom! The ancient gods of the Teutonic world were capable of incorrect considerations. These gods were also able to misjudge, or they could judge badly, and they were capable of making incorrect decisions. Although there are reasonably few incidents that demonstrate these types of thought or action that make their ways into the myths, such evidence, nevertheless, is present in these tales, and indeed even to be found in what are considered to be the earliest of the stories, giving rise to the theory that these beliefs developed early in the history of the Germanic peoples. The matter of date of origin of these beliefs is not of any concern at present. What assumes significance is that Wagner saw thematic as well as dramatic qualities in this cultural concept and as he adapted it into the argument of his *Ring*, he was to make it a major and primary tenet.

It would be Wotan's dubitable pact with Fafner and Fasolt that was to reflect the fallibility of the gods, and it would be the factor that sets into motion the monumental action of Wagner's *Ring*. It is a bad judgment that Wotan makes when he enters a pledge that he will give Freia to the giants as their reward for their work on Valhalla, a faulty judgment which he later compounds by his attempt to renege on that pledge. These actions, which in and of themselves demonstrate a kind of divine fallibility, are then augmented with the god's flawed judgmental resolution to the dilemma, that is, to pay the giants with the gold that Wotan will steal from the Nibelung Alberich. How uniquely suitable Wagner thus found the mythical belief of the infallibility of the gods, for it would be that very concept that would serve as the solid understructure for all else that he was to bring into his drama.

It is these acts of incorrect reasoning, made by the King of the Gods, that swell in importance and lead, ultimately, to the outcome that Wagner would give to his *Ring*. That conclusion, however, that powerful theatrical final scene that culminates in one of dramatic art's most impressive and absorbing creations, was possible only because of the existence of the second of the fundamental Teutonic societal concepts that Wagner had found in the myths.

Heathen Germanic concepts held that the gods of Teutondom were not gifted with infinite life. The life of the divine beings of the universe was one of limited duration, that is it had a beginning and it would have an end. It is understandable that the early Germanic peoples believed that their gods had come into existence prior to their individual mortal births, and that the gods would live on for some time after their mortal deaths. A divine existence of that span would allow any mortal a certain concept of infinity because by means of such thought the gods were always present and available during the entire life of every mortal. Despite the religious convenience and the societal accommodation that such thought brought to the lives of the early teutonic peoples, their gods, the divine beings of Teutondom *were fated to die!*

The inevitable end of the gods is a major factor in the myths of early Teutondom. That end is called *ragnarök*, literally "dusk of the gods," and the matter receives expansive attention as a *volva*, a "wise woman," prophesied it in what is perhaps the finest and certainly the most famous of the poems that are found in *The Poetic Edda*. In these stanzas the *volva*, after whom Wagner developed his figure Erda, is queried by Wotan, and in a most vivid manner she tells of the last days of the world. There will be a final battle, she relates, a battle in which the gods will ride out from Valhalla, followed by the large army that the Heerfather has amassed. There, on Vigrid, the great plain that stretches as far as the eye can see, the gods will meet their many enemies, among whom are the Fire-Giants who will cross the Rainbow Bridge, burning it behind them as they enter the Land of the Gods. The *volva* recounts how all the gods will die, and she gives details of the violent deaths that Wotan, Donner, Froh, and even Loge will suffer. After the deaths of the divine beings, the Fire-Giants will set the world afire and soon all is ablaze in an intense fire, and all that is in the world burns. Then, the body of Midgardsorm, the monster World Serpent and child of Loge that has been slain by Donner, falls back into the seas and causes the waters to overflow their shores, to result in a flood of monumental proportions that now invades and overwhelms the entire universe. The "twilight of the gods" is at hand. As some of the verses of the Eddic poem then read:

> The sun turns black,
> The earth sinks into the sea.
> The hot stars down from heaven are whirled.
> The World Ash Tree shakes,
> Its ancient limbs shiver on high.
> Fierce grows the stream,
> and the life-feeding flame,
> till fire leaps high about heaven itself.

Wagner's gods thus meet their fated deaths. If the end that Wagner brings to his gods is not precisely that which is recounted and detailed by the *volva* of the *Edda,*, the climactic finale of the *Ring* does come about in a manner that essentially replicates the major matters of the Teutonic *ragnarök*. Wagner had found fire and flood in the myths of the early people of his native soil, a fire and a flood that destroy the evil, the greed, and the corruption that had permeated the ancient world. Wagner presents that fire and that flood that he had encountered in the myths, and he brings an end to the universe of his drama. Then, after a cataclysmic end of the world, he suggests the birth of a new and undefiled world, a world administered by virtuous and uncorrupted gods, almost in the same manner that the *volva* of Teutondom foresees.

(It should be noted that the finale of the *Ring* as it is known today was not the original ending that Wagner had prepared for his drama. His first ending was a scene in which Brünnhilde recognizes Wotan's dilemma, and despite her banishment from the world of the gods, seeks the forgiveness of the gods for their acts and brings them their salvation. The fire that she then brings to Siegfried's pyre is limited, and it does not reach into the heavens, into Valhalla where the gods await their end. In that original ending, the gods of Teutondom are saved, to continue their divine existence.)

Wagner's dramatic concern for the gods of Teutondom and their world is evident in the treatment that he gave them in his drama. His thematic care and his dramatic caution were uppermost as he incorporated into his *Ring* not only the essence of Teutondom's major deities, but also much of the lesser detail that was pertinent to these divine figures. There was little about the gods that he excluded, either of major substance or matter of a less important level, and the totality of his dramatic portrait mirrors remarkably the divine ones of the early Teutonic mythical world. Wagner's gods, like their prototypes, displayed attributes that were essentially mortal in nature, but on a scale that rises above, extends beyond, and exceeds in every way life as mankind has known it. Wagner's gods, like those of the ancient world love and hate, they are greedy, they are kind, and they are sensitive to their world. Above all else, however, Wagner's gods are fallible and finite, much in the manner as were the Teutonic gods of another day, and that fallibility resembles that of mortal beings, yet they are more perfect than man, and unlike man they are possessed of a magic that mortals can only dream of possessing, but cannot have. It is with that mythical magic that the gods produce the marvels of the world, and make real the wishes, the desires, the hopes for which man can only aspire. Indeed, Wagner's gods are much like his Germanic models, and, additionally, they also retain a Germanic quality that sets them apart from other divine hierarchies. If Wagner's gods reflect much of what can be called the human condition, it is that very quality that makes them personal, so very personal, so much in the pattern of the divine beings of an ancient Teutonic culture.

See also: *The Family of Gods*, Volume II

GOLD (General)

It has been said, and rightly so, that if one is familiar with the chronological journey of the gold as it makes its way through the complex thematic developments of Wagner's *Ring*, one knows the story of the monumental drama. The gold of Wagner's *Ring* is physically seen in the opening scene of the first of the four music-dramas, and from that moment until the final few climactic moments of this lengthy poem, the gold is essentially the silent, if not always present, unnamed, unlisted, and in its own way unheralded, protagonist of the drama. It is the hoard of gold in Wagner's drama, and the powers that this treasure holds, that fundamentally accounts for each and every major action of the work, and it is therefore the dramatic foundation on which and around which Wagner developed the numerous theatrical intricacies that emerge as the story is played out. Wagner seemed to signal his own awareness of the importance and significance of the gold, and the ring that was forged from it, that he brought into his poem when he referred to the entirety of his tetralogy as *Der Ring des Nibelungen* (*The Ring of the Nibelung*).

There is to be found in the mythical and legendary beliefs of the early Germanic peoples ample stimulation and inspiration for Wagner's use of a hoard of gold in his poem. Curiously, there are three historic traditions that are associated with treasures of gold, and each of these traditions figures prominently in the thought and activity that flourished throughout the ancient period of heathen Teutondom. Each of these traditions exists in and of itself, and each has its own variations that distinguish it from the others, yet it is rather a blend of these several qualities that Wagner enacted as he developed the role of the gold hoard in what has become known as his Siegfried drama.

The first of the trio of traditions that marked the views of the early Teutonic peoples held that there was, in the beginning, a great treasure of gold that was to be found in the Rhine River. This early belief, which is considered to be of Southern or German origin, was of significant import in the development of numerous songs, lays, and poems that tell of the riches that are to be found in this most important of Germany's rivers. So numerous are such works, and so fundamental is the belief to the German people that yet in the modern day there still abounds a belief that the sands of the shores of the Rhine will often give up some of its gold treasure to the seeker who is both diligent and patience in his search.

A second Southern or German tradition holds that there was a great treasure of gold that was buried within a mountain. This hoard, which is referred to as the treasure of the Nibelungs, one of Germany's most noted legendary royal families, lay deep in the bowels of the earth. From time to time, according to the beliefs, the treasure moved (earthquake), and it frequently came to the surface of the earth to sun itself. It was then that the gold could be easily seen because of the glint that its flakes made in the sunlight.

A third belief regarding gold treasure originated in the Scandinavian regions of Teutondom and this belief is referred to as the Northern or Nordic tradition. This concept held that there was a great gold treasure that lay in a waterfall. This hoard was guarded by a dwarf who had turned himself into a pike. This treasure, which included a gold ring, was stolen from the dwarf by the gods Wotan and Hoenir, who were aided in their actions by Loge. This treasure came into the possession of Hreidmar, who refused to share the gold with his sons, one of whom was Fafner (Fafnir). Fafner then slew his father, took the treasure for himself and fled to a forest where he changed himself into a dragon and became the hoard's guardian. Fafner is later slain by Siegfried, who then takes the treasure as his.

(Some aspects of this Nordic tradition held that there were snakes or serpents, occasionally dogs, that lay guard over a hoard or treasure of gold. From the earliest of times, serpents were the creatures most associated with gold treasures, and that antiquity is shown in the Old Norse words that called gold *orms bedr* ("worm's bed") and *Fafnis boeli* ("dragon's couch"). There is even one tale in which a toad is depicted as the treasure's guardian. It is this tradition and that single story that served Wagner as source for his dramatic action in which Alberich turns himself first into a serpent, and then into a toad as a means of demonstrating the powers of the Tarnhelm for Wotan and Loge.)

The southern traditions regarding the treasure of gold are included as part of *Nibelungenlied*, the poem that has become known as the epic of the German people. In this fascinating tale, a dwarf Alberich guards a vast treasure that lies deep within a mountain and belongs to King Nibelung. The treasure then comes into the possession of Siegfried who is later slain by Hagen. At Siegfried's death, the treasure belongs to his widow, Grimhild, but it is coveted by Hagen, who later sinks it in the waters of the Rhine in order that no one will ever have it again.

Wagner's thematic use of a treasure of gold is, essentially, a blend of the Southern and Northern traditions that dealt with such wealth. The gold, as first encountered, is seen in the opening scene of the *Ring* tetralogy, resting in its home on the bottom of the Rhine. In time, it is Alberich, a name and figure that is associated with the treasure in *Nibelungenlied*, steals the gold and claims it and its powers as his. From that point on, the gold takes a pathway, with attendant activities, that is quite similar to the activities that are recounted in *The Poetic Edda*, as well as in *Volsungasaga* and *Thidrekssaga*. Then, as Wagner ends his drama, the gold ring, representative of the treasure, comes into the hands of the daughters of the Rhine, who return it to its rightful home which, according to German tradition, is the waters of the Rhine.

GOLD (Payment)

Wagner's depiction of the method and manner of payment of gold to the giants Fasolt and Fafner for their labors during the construction of Valhalla has its source in an incident in a poem of *The Poetic Edda*. This scene in the *Ring* occurs in the fourth and final scene of *Das Rheingold* and its counterpart, unrelated to the event of the music-drama, is a part of "Reginsmol" ("The Ballad of Regin").

A major portion of the scene in Wagner's libretto contains a dramatization of the final negotiations between Wotan and the giant brothers for the magnificent castle Valhalla. In brief, and as prologue to the matter of gold as payment to the giants, the latter have been persuaded to accept the hoard of the Nibelung dwarf Alberich as payment, instead of Freia, the Goddess of Youth and Love. It was Freia who was pledged as payment to the giants in the original pact. At the frantic urging of his cohort gods, Wotan, aided by the cunning Loge, has wrested the treasure from the black dwarf.

When the moment arrives in which Wotan is to exchange the gold for Freia, who has been held by the giants, Fasolt hesitates. The giant is aware of the magic power of Freia's Golden Apples of Eternal Youth, yet it is more because of his attraction to the beautiful goddess that he hesitates to conclude the new arrangement. In this moment of hesitation, Fasolt suggests that he can best forget the goddess, and thus ease his saddened heart, if she is quickly hidden from his sight. The giant then asks that the gold be piled high in front of Freia in order that he can no longer see her. Wotan agrees with the request, and Loge and Froh then begin to stack the treasure in front of the frightened goddess.

The treasure is soon in place and Freia is hidden from view. Fafner draws near to the gold and examines it carefully. He complains that he can still see the sheen of Freia's golden hair. The giant demands that the Tarnhelm be used to block out the view. Reluctantly, Wotan allows the Tarnhelm to be placed atop the pile. Fasolt then approaches the huge mound. His actions and his words suggest that he does not wish to be separated from the goddess. The giant peers carefully at the treasure, drawing himself closer in order that he may examine it better. As his eyes examine the pile of gold, he suddenly starts back. Fasolt cries out that he can see Freia's eyes through a small crack. The giant steps forward, remarking that he cannot part with this beautiful creature so long as the radiance of one of her eyes is visible to him. Fafner looks about for more gold, but the treasure has been exhausted. Then, the giant sees the ring on Wotan's finger, the magic ring that Black Alberich had fashioned from the gold of the Rhine and which now bears the dwarf's curse of death. The giant demands that Wotan fill the crack with the ring, but Wotan refuses. The other gods urge Wotan to give up the ring. The god still refuses. Then, Erda, the Earth Mother, rises from a rocky cliff and her words of wisdom advise Wotan to rid himself of the cursed ring. Finally, the Allfather yields to the urging. The ring is placed in the tiny crack, Freia's eyes can no longer be seen, the new pact is fulfilled. Freia is now free to return to the gods.

As the two giants gather in the gold, they begin to argue about shares of their new wealth. The argument becomes quite heated. Finally, Fafner can no longer endure what he believes is Fasolt's selfishness. With all of his giant strength, he raises his staff and brings it down upon his brother. Fasolt dies immediately, after which Fafner takes up the gold and flees. We learn later that Fafner has fled to Neidhöhle, where he has changed himself into a dragon in order to guard his new-found wealth.

The parallel incident in *The Poetic Edda* is recounted in the first five stanzas of "Reginsmol" and the accompanying prose. This tale has enjoyed extensive popularity throughout Germanic regions where it is regularly known as "Otter's Ransom." This segment of the Eddic poem relates that Wotan (Odin), Hoenir, and Loge (Loki) have arrived at a waterfall in which a dwarf named Andvari lives in the form of a pike. Otr, a brother of Regin, after whom the poem receives its name, often went to the waters where he would change himself into an otter, catch a fish, and then sit upon the shore as he enjoyed his catch. Otr always closed his eyes when he ate because he did not wish to see his food disappear as he consumed it. Loge picked up a stone and threw it at Otr. The rock hit Otr and killed him. The trio thought themselves quite lucky so they skinned the dead otter.

The two gods and Loge (Loge is not a god in the mythical thought of early Teutondom) then continued their journey. That evening the trio spends the night in the dwelling of Hreidmar who, unbeknown to the travelers, is Otr's father. When the latter learns what fate has befallen his son at the hands of his guests, he seizes them and informs them that he will kill them if he is not paid a ransom. The price is to be gold, enough gold to fill the otter's skin and to cover it completely on the outside. Loge is sent to gather the treasure. He travels to the waterfall where he learns that Andvari guards a huge treasure of gold. Loge captures the fish and threatens to do him harm if he does not give him the treasure. When Loge sees that the dwarf is withholding a gold ring, he demands that he be given the ring immediately. Andvari hands over the ring, but not before he places a curse upon it.

Loge returns to the gods, delivering to them Andvari's treasure. The gods fill Otr's skin with gold, set him upon his feet, and then pile the gold on the outside so that the otter cannot be seen. When the gods have completed their work, Hreidmar steps forward to inspect what the gods have done. As he studies the mound, he sees a single whisker of his son through a crack in the stacked gold. Hreidmar demands that the whisker be hidden from his view. At Hreidmar's demand, Wotan brings forth the ring that had been cursed, fills the chink in the gold, and hides the whisker from further view.

We learn later that Hreidmar refuses to share his new wealth with his sons, one of whom is Fafner (Fafnir). The latter becomes angry, kills his father as he sleeps, gathers up the gold and flees with it to Gnitaheid, where he changes himself into a dragon in order to lie guard over his new-found wealth.

The scene in Wagner's *Ring* and that which is found in the *Edda* are unrelated, yet it is obvious to even the most casual reader that the manner of payment to the giants, as realized in the music-drama has as its dramatic source the method depicted in the Eddic tale. In essence, it is really only a matter of some of the names, the setting, and the incident of Otr himself that distinguish between a popular Teutonic mythic tale and a scene in Wagner's *Der Ring des Nibelungen*. Yet, the quality that gives the Eddic poem its mythicalness is also the same quality that Wagner was able to bring into his drama. It is not so much a matter of Wagner creating a tale out of the Teutonic myths, but rather Wagner creating myth itself, with his personal version of a theme. "The Ballad of Regin," which served Wagner so well for his scene in which the giants receive their payment of gold, also served him for additional segments of his giant work. Indeed, if there is any one Eddic poem that Wagner used for aspects of his drama more than any other, it is this poem in which the story of Otr's ransom is recounted.

GOLD (Rhine)

The gold in Wagner's *Ring* has the Rhine River as its home. The first sight of this treasure that plays so significant a role in this Siegfried drama is to be had during the initial scene of Wagner's monumental work. Alberich, the dwarf who entered the river bed from his home down in Nibelheim, is subsequently teased and taunted by the three daughters of the Rhine. As his lustful approaches are then rebuffed, the rays of the sun slowly penetrate the flowing waters and the poetic metaphor "awakens" the slumbering treasure. This is the gold of the Rhine, the gold that gives this segment of Wagner's *Ring* its name, *Das Rheingold*. This is the hoard that the Rhine King, father of the three nixies who swim about in the river, cautions them about, admonishing them to guard the treasure well, and carefully. Yet, before this scene terminates, the rejected Nibelung has taken the gold from its bed, has vowed to make a ring of the gold, and because he now has rejected love that ring will give him mastery of the universe. The dwarf flees with the hoard to his home in the bowels of the earth. From that moment in the opening scene of the *Ring* until the end of the drama, the gold passes through the hands of several owners, on each of whom an evil curse of death is brought to bear. Then, in the final climactic moments of the drama, the gold is returned to the

Rhinemaidens who happily welcome the treasure back to its home in the Rhine.

There can be no doubt that it was Wagner's intent to have the Rhine River to be considered as the home of the gold treasure. From the beginning of the drama, through until the end, by means of action as well as dialogue, the home of the gold is the flowing waters of the great Rhine. Curiously, such a thematic development is a matter of the composer's personal theatrical thought. There is no evidence in any of the source materials that recount that these waters were to be construed as the original or the permanent dwelling of this hoard!

Although it is fact that Wagner's dramatic treatment of this aspect of the hoard is of his own doing, there is some reason, if not logic, presented in the mythical and legendary literature that might allow such a realization without great deviation from the essence of that literature. There are references in numerous German stories and tales to the wealth of gold that is to be found in the vicinity of the Rhine. There was also the German tradition that flakes of gold could be found in the sand that lines the shores of the river. Then, too, there is an association of a gold treasure and the Rhine River that is contained in *Nibelungenlied*, the epic poem of the German people. In that work, Siegfried succeeds in taking possession of the gold treasure that belonged to King Nibelung and his sons, Schilbung and Nibelung, and which was guarded by the dwarf Alberich deep in the earth of a large mountain. In time, Siegfried is killed and the treasure rightfully belonged to his wife, Grimhild (Kriemhild). However, the evil Hagen, Siegfried's murderer, desirous to keep the hoard from the hands of Siegfried's widow, sinks it in the waters of the Rhine, where it will remain forever, where no one will be able to recover it. Although Hagen's actions do not signify that the river is the home of the gold, they certainly establish, or at least help to confirm, the German or southern tradition of an association of gold and the Rhine. That tradition, in its own feeble manner, apparently made its way northward during the migrations of the early centuries and into *The Poetic Edda* where its surfaces, if only infrequently. One of these Eddic poems recounts that treasure can be found "in the hills of the Rhine," while in another poem reference is made to the "gold of the Rhine."

Wagner's dramatic plan to make the Rhine the original and permanent home of the gold is one that is also somewhat in harmony with other concepts that are found in the Eddic literature. There are at least two poems in this storehouse of Teutonic mythical matters that reveal treasure in water as a prominent factor of the respective thematic material. There are those verses that tell of Aegir, God of the Sea, and the great banquet that he had prepared for the gods. The feast was held in Aegir's hall, which of course is the sea. There were no burning fires to illuminate the hall, as was the usual manner for lighting the halls of the other gods. Rather, Aegir's hall was lighted by the reflections that came from gold that had been placed strategically about the hall, placed in such a manner that the rays of the sun came down through the waters, struck the gold, and became the bright, warm light that so pleased Aegir. This use of gold, which has a striking resemblance to Wagner's setting in *Das Rheingold*, gave rise to such metaphorical terms for gold as "flame of the floods," and "water's flame." (Wagner apparently took note of such poetic usage regarding gold in water because he makes reference in his drama to the gold that is in the Rhine as a radiant star, a noble star of the waters that vies with the sun for brilliance and radiance.)

There is a second instance in *The Poetic Edda* of treasure that is found in water, a scene that is more kindred to the gold in Wagner's drama than is that of Aegir's feast. In these Eddic verses, which seem to represent the northern or Nordic version of the German tradition of gold in the Rhine, Andvari, a dwarf possesses a great treasure of gold that is housed in a *waterfall*. The dwarf guards his hoard in the form of a pike that swims about in the waters, a fate that was woven for him by a Norn. Wotan (Odin), Hoenir, and Loge (Loki) have been threatened with their lives by Hreidmar, whose son they killed, unless they pay for their action with a treasure of gold. Loge journeys to Andvari' waterfall and gains possession of the gold, which includes a gold ring, from Andvari by trickery, and the gods are able to ransom themselves. Wagner may well have been influenced by this Eddic poem which is titled "The Ballad of Regin" and which depicts the home of a treasure of gold in water, because it is this relatively short work that served him, more than any other single mythical tale, as source material for actions and activities that he placed in his *Ring*.

It is quite possible that Wagner was moved by poetic association of treasure in water, as depicted in both the southern *Nibelungenlied* and the northern *Edda*, to make the Rhine the original home of the gold. It is well known that he was most desirous to saturate his work with as much of the German nature and character as possible, and what, if not the Rhine as background, could serve him better in attaining that dramatic goal! Regardless of the specific stimulation for that action, however, certainly his dramatic actions of returning the gold to the waters of the Rhine as a conclusion to his work is without doubt a direct influence of a single stanza that is to be found in the more recent editions of *The Poetic Edda*, and which was definitely used by the compiler(s) of *Volsungasaga*, a second primary source that Wagner consulted. The Eddic poem is one that is concerned with the relationships of Attila (Atli), Gunther (Gunnar), and Hagen (Hogni), and the gold treasure after the death of Siegfried (Sigurd). In the Nordic tales, Attila had married Siegfried's widow Gutrune (Guthrun), and he believed that Siegfried's wealth therefore should now belong to him. Attila makes Gunther and Hagen, Gutrune's brothers, his prisoners and declares that he will not free them until they have bought their freedom with Siegfried's hoard, which they have now taken as theirs. These sons of Gibich (Gjuki) refuse to give in to Attila's demands. The Hun then orders Hagen killed. Gunther, now alone still refuses to surrender the gold. In his refusal, he cries out that only he now knows the "secret" of the gold, and to himself he says, in effect, that the Rhine River now holds this gold that has caused so much strife and concern, that this Nibelung gold, that once belonged to the gods, would now shine and glitter in the depths of the river, and its golden gleam would never brighten the hands of a Hun! (Gunther's reference to the 'Nibelung gold' is, of course, a reference to Siegfried who, in the *Nibelungenlied*, becomes known as a Nibelung after he gains possession of King Nibelung's treasure.)

There is no doubt that both the northern tradition regarding the final resting place of the Nibelung treasure, as found in the *Edda*, as well as the southern version, as presented in the epic *Nibelungenlied*, is in the waters of the Rhine. The details in each of these literary scenes differ, as do those that Wagner weaves into his story. Yet, the result is quite the same, and Wagner's hoard, like its model, will rest forever on the bed of the river.

It is most probable, given the concurrence of the traditions regarding the final resting place of the great treasure that are presented in Teutonic myth and German legend, that Wagner's theatrical mind conjured the scenic sense of making the Rhine both the original home of the gold as well as its final resting place. He was aware of the matter as depicted in the epic poem of his native culture, and he was also aware that his primary source above all other, the *Edda*, also named the Rhine as the ultimate resting place. He was also familiar with the numerous verses in the *Edda* that make reference to the treasure either as *near* or *in* water. It was dramatically practical to make those waters one and the same. Obviously, the Rhine, then, was the logical choice!

GOLD (Theft)

Alberich's act of stealing the gold from its home in the Rhine River, as the precious metal lay basking in the rays of the sun that filtered through the waters, has no exact counterpart in the myths and legends of Teutondom. There is, to be sure, an Alberich in *Nibelungenlied*, a dwarf who is a guardian of treasure that lies buried deep within a mountain, and this is that same treasure that Hagen, much later in the poem, sinks into the Rhine in order that no one should have its wealth.

Although the Rhine as the home of the gold hoard and the theft of that treasure by Alberich are dramatic creations that Wagner developed himself, there can be no doubt that he was stimulated to that end by a poem that is part of the collection know as *The Poetic Edda*. In these Eddic verses Wotan (Odin), the god Hoenir, and Loge (Loki) were traveling, and the trio came to a waterfall. They saw an otter beside the fall, eating a salmon. Loge threw a rock at the otter. The rock hit the otter and killed it. The gods and Loge then stripped the skin from the otter and resumed their journey. That night they sought lodging at Hreidmar's house. When the trio showed the otter's skin to Hreidmar and his sons, the latter immediately seized the three. Hreidmar was angry with Wotan, Hoenir, and Loge because the otter, whose name was Otr, was their son and brother who often changed himself into an otter and visited the waterfall to catch and eat salmon. Hreidmar said that the three must pay for their evil act, and he then demanded that they fill Otr's skin with gold and also cover it completely on the outside with red gold, so that he could not see it at all. Wotan then sent Loge to secure the gold. Loge went back to the waterfall, where he captured Andvari, a dwarf who had been condemned by a Norn to swim about in the fall in the from of a pike. When Loge asks Andvari what he would offer as reward if he were able to return to his regular from and once again live in the land of men, the dwarf-pike brought forth a large treasure of gold that Loge immediately seized. Andvari, however, had withheld a gold ring. When Loge saw the ring he seized that also. Andvari, who had now swum into a hole to escape with his life, then put a curse upon the ring.

It is doubtful that the incident about Andvari and the theft of his treasure from within a waterfall, and his curse upon a ring, in and of itself alone, could have stirred Wagner into the creation of Alberich's theft of the gold from the Rhine, and the Nibelung dwarf's curse upon a ring when the treasure is stolen from him. Yet, there are obviously certain similarities between the tale that is revealed in the Eddic verses and the story as Wagner developed it in his *Ring*. When more of the Eddic poem is revealed, the hesitation regarding Wagner's source and inspiration weakens.

After Loge takes Andvari's gold and the ring, he returns to Hreidmar's home and gives the treasure to Wotan and Hoenir. The gods then filled the otter's skin with gold and stood it on its feet. Wotan and Hoenir used the remainder of the treasure to heap about Otr's skin, to hide him from view. When all of the gold had been piled about Hreidmar's son, the father carefully examined the gold and announced that he could still see one of his son's whiskers. Wotan took the gold ring that had belonged to Andvari and plugged the chink so that the whisker could no longer be seen. Loge then tells the gods of the curse that the dwarf had put on the ring.

The resemblance between the Eddic tale and the related incident in Wagner's *Ring* is now unmistakable. As Wagner tells of Alberich, the giants, the building of Valhalla, and the payment of gold to the giants for their work on the castle, there is little except names that Wagner changed as he developed his story. It is essentially Wotan and Loge who steal the gold from Alberich, as did the Eddic Loge, stirred into the theft by the god. Alberich had taken the gold from its home in the Rhine, and it was from a waterfall that Loge had taken the mythical treasure. And, like Andvari, Wagner's Alberich places a curse upon the ring when the treasure leaves his possession.

The theft of the gold, as recounted in the *Edda*, reveals a serious flaw in the character of the Supreme God, Wotan. The theft in Wagner's drama of the ring from Alberich exposes that same flaw, a matter that lies at the foundation of the total character of the god that strolls about in the *Ring*. If, then, there are certain differences in the details of the theft of the treasure of gold, in both cases, that is in the myths and in the *Ring*, there is a theft and Wotan is involved in each incident. It is the theft itself, not the details, that exposes the true nature of the Allfather god, an act that allows the god to be suspect in other acts of a questionable nature, acts of less than honorable concept. It is this aspect of the god's character that is uppermost in both works as it emblazoned for all to see the black character that truly resides deep within the figure of the great god of Teutondom. In both cases, it is a theft that reveals that blackness for all to see.

GOLD (Treasure)

The role in the *Ring* of gold as treasure can be, and is, readily acceptable as integral to the drama's dramatic and thematic development. Such acceptance is automatic and unquestioned because the gold that Wagner depicts in his poem exudes those very qualities that man has associated with this most sought-after of nature's prizes throughout all of the history of mankind. The gold of the *Ring* is the gateway to wealth, opulence, and power of all manner and degree; it is an inducement to act, physically, mentally, and emotionally. Wagner's gold is even the symbol of base and often fatal corruption.

These several qualities that are associated with the gold are of such age and of such an extension throughout the cultures of the world that they can be considered today as natural to man's concept of this metal. Wagner understood this facet of mankind's thought and made no attempt to inject some kind of ploy to cause audience acceptance of these qualities. Instead, he offers a musico-dramatic portrait of gold as it has ever been envisioned in man's eye and conceived by his mind, and from that departure molded universal concepts into compatibility with his dramatic and philosophic intents. Wagner's thematic use of gold projects, then, an image that is at one with mankind's general perspective of the metal of the ages, as well as an idyllic vision of it as held by poet, pharoah, and peasant. Whatever singular or unique qualities that Wagner attached to the gold of his drama are, of course, the result of the composer's uncanny genius of poetic insight. Wagner early on in his work ennobled his gold with characteristics that are not regularly associated with the metal, yet such additions raise little if any philosophic controversy or doubt because these added qualities that stem from the composer are such that humankind, in the illusions of its fanciful mind, can accept them, without question, as part and parcel of the most regal, most treasured object of the ages.

There are two qualities that Wagner added to the nature of the gold of his poem that are most unique as well as significant. Each of these dramatic attributes is marrow to the drama simply because each becomes the basis, the foundation so to speak, for other involvements to appear in the drama, and then to be developed. It is obviously natural, then, that these qualities should be noted early in the work, in *Das Rheingold*, the first of the four music-dramas. Wagner's gold makes its initial appearance in the opening scene of the drama, and shortly after it begins to glow in the sunlight that filters through the waters the daughters of the Rhine reveal that universal power, mastery of the world, can be had by whoever fashions a ring from this gold, provided that he has renounced love! The second of these added attributes becomes known in the final scene of this drama, when the ring that Alberich has made from the gold is taken from him and the

Nibelung dwarf then places a death curse on each of those who shall come to possess this magic ring. These qualities that now are part of the gold of the *Ring* may seem to be fanciful, or at least imaginative, yet, in light of the mystical stronghold that gold has maintained so rigidly and so continuously on societies of civilization, they are neither alien nor improbable within the most introspective of human thought.

Wagner's use of gold as treasure, as determined in the course of history, is enhanced by a similar view that is found in the source literature from which he drew so copiously. Gold is ever-present in the Eddic poetry, although its significance in those verses is of a more subtle hue and of less all-around dominance than the gold in the *Ring*. The overall attraction of gold, as evidenced in the Eddic literature, is no less magnetic, however, than that of the contemporary day, and no less realistic than the picture that is musically drawn by Wagner. There seems to be no doubt that the composer was quite aware of the proverbial-like verses that are found in the second poem of *The Poetic Edda*, verses whose ideas still in the modern day are as readily pronounced as in the day of their unknown author. It is the substance of these verses that essentially enshroud the *Ring* like an ominous and foreboding cloud of an impending storm. The significance of these verses merits quotation:

A man knows nothing if he knows not
That gold oft apes begets.
Wealth is as swift as a winking eye,
Of friends, the falsest it is.

Verses that make reference to generic gold appear early in *The Poetic Edda*. One such account is found in the opening stanzas of the first Eddic poem, "Voluspo," which is at once the most famous of the Eddic works and also the most significant of the collection. The verses speak of World-Beginning, of the daily councils of the gods, of the decisions that the gods make and their resultant actions. Then, interspersed among the lines is a verse that announces that the gods of Teutondom had no lack whatsoever of gold! Such words not only denote gold as treasure, as wealth, but they also infer that there was no dearth of wealth among the divine ones. (Wagner obviously did not incorporate the essence of these words into his *Ring* drama. Had he done so, the dilemma that the gods experience in the matter of payment to the giants for their work on Valhalla, so necessary to the thematic argument of his drama, would not have been possible.)

Gold, as valued treasure, continues to appear regularly throughout the Eddic poems. If these Nordic verses make simple reference to the German traditions regarding the wealth of gold treasure that lay in the waters of the Rhine and to the gold that can be found in sands of that river, these same verses also contain their own Nordic concepts of gold as wealth and treasure. A partial list of some of the more explicit examples, with names that will be familiar to followers of the *Ring*, will certainly suffice to give evidence that the myths of Teutondom reflect a concept of gold as treasure that is essentially a mirror of cultural and societal ideas on the matter.

1. Wotan rewards the seeress with necklaces and rings of gold as reward for the wisdom and knowledge that she has given him.

2. Wotan and Saga drink from cups of gold. (Little is known of Saga. Some mythologists believe that Saga was a wife of the Supreme God, while others claim that she was his daughter.)

3. Heimdall, the Guardian of the Rainbow Bridge, had teeth that were made of gold.

4. The sons of the dwarf Ivaldi ("The Mighty") had made a wig of gold for Donner's wife, Sif, after Loge maliciously had cut off her real hair.

5. Skirnir, a servant, gave Gerd eleven golden apples on behalf of his master Froh, who wishes to win her.

6. Wotan regularly distributes gold to his followers.

7. Froh's boar has bristles that are made of gold and which light up the night as he rides the animal through the heavens.

8. The web of fate that the Norns weave has threads of gold.

9. Siegfried's sword is decorated with pure gold.

10. As a means of enticement, Attila (Atli) promises Gutrune (Guthrun) much gold treasure if she will become his wife.

11. Gunther (Gunnar) offers much of Fafner's gold to Oddrun if she will marry him.

12. When Attila (Atli) invites Gunther (Gunnar) and Hagen (Hogni) to visit him, he promises them many gifts, among which will be helmets that are adorned with gold, gold decorations that will be laid into the steering devices of their ships, and "treasures full huge."

13.   Gunther (Gunnar) tells Attila (Atli) that he has seven
        great halls that are completely filled with gold, and that
        the war helms of all of his soldiers are made of gold.

The foregoing prose interpretations of Eddic verses are but only a few developed from among the poems that are part of the Germanic mythical past and which demonstrate the early Teutonic concepts of and the attitude toward gold. It is interesting to note how the concepts of modern societies are very much in harmony with those concepts of a thousand or more years past. It is obvious, then, that Wagner strays little, if any, from the time-trod paths of these concepts as he goes about the business of developing the argument of his *Ring*. The gold of his drama is as much treasure as it would be in the present day. If Wagner was attempting at all times to bring an aura of mythicalness into his drama, as indeed he was, then in the matter of gold, he could relax creatively because the gold of then and the gold of now carries with itself a mythicalness of all time.

GOLDEN APPLES See: *Freia's Golden Apples* (Vol. I)

GÖTTERDÄMMERUNG See: *Doom of the Gods*

GÖTTERDÄMMERUNG (Name)

This German compound, translated as "Twilight of the Gods," is the title that Wagner gave the fourth part of his tetralogy of the *Ring*. The Old Norse term that designated the fated end of the universe was *ragnarök*, a compound word that consisted of the terms *ragna* and *rök*. The word *ragna* is the genitive plural of the word 'power,' a word that was synonymous with 'god.' The word *rök* can be translated as 'fate' or 'doom.' Thus, *ragnarök* meant literally "fate (doom) of the powers (gods)."

The term *ragnarök* was a partner in linguistic confusion. The pronunciation of the suffix *rök* was frequently made as rökkr, a word that meant 'dusk' or 'darkness.' Thus *ragnarökkr* was translated as "dusk (darkness) of the gods." This confusion permitted Wagner to draw from *ragnarök* for much of the theme and ambience of his *Ring* drama, and from *ragnarökkr* he gained a title of one of the drama's four parts.

See also: *Ragnarök*, Supplement C, (Vol. I)

GRANE

The mythological history of the stallion Grane is somewhat sketchy, but those facts about this celebrated horse that are to be found in the myths depict an exceptional animal that was a most faithful companion, and a kind of guardian, to his master, the hero Siegfried. This horse, called *Grani* in Old Norse, and according to the lays that are contained in *The Poetic Edda*, Grani was a stud that Siegfried had chosen from the herd that belonged to Hjalprek, the father of his stepfather, King Alf.

The *Volsungasaga* offers a beginning of the Siegfried-Grane relationship that is somewhat different from the Eddic version. In the saga the youthful Siegfried wishes to possess a horse. He visits his stepfather King Alf who in turn tells him to choose from the royal steeds that roam the forests. Siegfried goes into the woods where he comes upon a stranger who has a long beard. Siegfried asks if the old man can counsel him as to which horse to chose. Together, the two drive several of the steeds into a river. All of the horses quickly swim for shore, all that is except one. It is this horse that Siegfried decided was to be his choice.

The saga relates that Siegfried's stallion, which had the name of *Grani*, was a young animal. He was fair to look upon, and his growth had been excellent. Grane was a young horse, gray in color, and had never been ridden. The old man who had aided Siegfried in his choice said that Grane would be the best of horses because he was a descendent of Sleipnir!

It is most probable that the old man who befriended Siegfried is Wotan. The great god was old during the time of Siegfried's youth, and he had a long beard. Yet, the matter that seems to substantiate most concretely the supposition that the old man is Wotan is his statement that Siegfried's horse is Sleipnir's kin. Sleipnir was the name of the eight-legged horse that belonged to the Supreme God of Teutondom. Sleipnir was considered to be the finest horse in the world, partly because he could run through the heavens and over the seas faster than any other animal. Sleipnir had been born of the union between Svadilfari and the supernatural Loge who had changed himself into a mare to entice the stallion away from his giant owner and master. The giant had made a pact with the gods to build a great fortress. The agreement stated, however, that the giant was to finish his work within a given period of time. The giant's horse carried the huge, heavy stones that were used in the construction of the fortress. When the gods realized that the giant would finish within the stated period of time, and they would then have to give the giant the agreed upon payment which included Freia the goddess, the gods sought Loge to aid them. Loge's plan worked, and the giant was unable to complete his work, and the gods did not have to give him the goddess. However, Loge, as a mare, had lured the stallion far into a forest, and the subsequent union between Svadilfari and Loge produced Sleipnir, who was then given to Wotan.

The *Saga of Dietrich* (*Thidrekssaga*), also known as *The Wilkina Saga*, does not indicate an origin of Grane, but the work does reveal an original ownership different from that depicted in the *Edda* and in *Volsungasaga*. In this work that focuses on the life of the hero Dietrich of Bern, Grane originally belonged to Brünnhilde (Brynhild). (*The Poetic Edda* states that Brünnhilde's horse was an animal named *Vingskornir* ("Victory Bringer"). It was Siegfried's foster father, Mimir, who had advised the youth to go to Brünnhilde's palace, to ask her for the steed. The youth did as he was advised and Brünnhilde did in fact give Siegfried the stallion. Followers of the *Ring* will realize immediately that Wagner leaned more to *Thidrekssaga* and its version regarding original ownership of Grane rather than to those of the other of his literary sources, even though he was to make certain severe dramatic adaptations of those details.

Neither *The Poetic Edda* nor the *Volsungasaga* focuses on Grane in many of the stories and tales, although both of the works include him in the incident that features Siegfried and the dragon Fafner (Fafnir). After Siegfried had slain Fafner, he loaded the horse with much of the treasure that the dragon had guarded. As part of that treasure, the hero placed two chests filled with gold and gems, the helm of fear, and the sword *Hrotti* ("Thruster") on the horse's back. Despite the heavy load, Grane would not move until Siegfried had mounted.

It is not until Siegfried's death that Grane is again a principal factor in any of the details. (The *Volsungasaga* does state that Siegfried rode Grane through the flames as he made his way to Brünnhilde's castle.) The Eddic verses state that shortly after Siegfried died Grane so desired to feel his master's weight on his back once again that he ran at great speed, with thundering feet, ran until his entire body was bathed in sweat. When at last he stopped, he lowered his head, bowed it to the earth as if in homage to a true hero.

The *Volsungasaga* also makes due note of Grane and his reaction to Siegfried's death. The saga records that when the stallion knew full well that Siegfried had died, he fell drooping to the earth. The *Thidrekssaga* comments on Grane and Siegfried's death, in a manner that is perhaps a bit more stoic. This saga also tells how proudly Grane pranced as he bore the body of his slain master back from where he had been killed to his palace.

Grane is one of the more celebrated horses with a justifiable status in Teutonic mythical and legendary literature. Although this animal does not garner elaborate or extensive verse or saga attention to his activities, he is always somewhere nearby at those times when Siegfried is a part of the scene. There are distinct details as to how the animal became Siegfried's property, but there is not denial or refutation that he was the property of the hero Siegfried. Even Grane, in his own way, demonstrated that he belonged to Siegfried when he would refuse to move if any person other than the hero mounted him, or if anyone but Siegfried called to him. Indeed, Grane was a celebrated animal! However, perhaps Grane's position or status within the mythical scheme of things can best be depicted by an indication of one of the/ honors that was given him, an honor that in mythical terms was considered to be one of the highest. The runes of Teutondom, those special bits of magic that were the privilege of only a given few within the divine universe, could be written (recorded) on Grane's breast. To offer a parallel, or at least a comparison of the status that such a factor presents, those famed and celebrated Germanic runes could also be written in such other places as the tip of Wotan's spear, and on the bark of the World Ash Tree, two of Teutondom's most revered and venerated objects.

There is but one matter that is pertinent to Grane and his depiction in the mythical past of the Germanic peoples that is subject to some question. Curiously, it is a matter that is in doubt also when the subject is Sleipnir, the stallion that was the possession of Wotan, the Supreme God, and the animal that some tales depict as the sire of Siegfried's steed. The question at hand ponders Grane's color. A verse is one of the myths of the "Lays of the Gods" proclaims that Grane is a *gray* horse. In a verse that is contained in "Lays of the Heroes" it is Gutrune (Guthrun) who declares that Grane's color is *black*. In the matter of Sleipnir, the question of color was one of gray or white. Needless to say, Grane's color is significant only if that color is a determinant of some kind in a significant cultural or societal manner, and even then, perhaps it has importance only for a mythologist.

See also: *Horses*

GRANE (Name)

The meaning of the name of Brünnhilde's horse, which the daughter of Wotan presents to Siegfried as a wedding gift, is questionable, as is also its origin. There is a possibility that the name *Grane* is associated with an old German word *Grane*, which meant one of the hairs of a beard (*Grann*). The meaning of the name in that context is unknown. There is a slight possibility that the name is somehow developed from *Gran* ("grain"), but if that development actually occurred at some time in the distant past, the meaning of the word *Grane* has been lost.

GRAUEN

Grauen, correctly declined in the *Ring* from *Grau* (*Die Walküre*, Act III, Scene 1), is the name of the horse that is ridden by the Valkyrie Ortlinde.

See: *Horses*

GRAUEN (Name)

Grauen, which Wagner correctly declines from *Grau* in his text (*Die Walküre*, Act III, Scene 2), means *gray*.

GRIMGERDE See: *Valkyries*

GRIMGERDE (Name)

The ON prefix *grim* (OE and OHG – *grimm*) has several possible meanings. One such meaning is "fierce" or "savage," a meaning akin to modern English *grim*, in the sense of "harsh." A second meaning is that of *mask* (*masked*) or possibly *visor*. A third meaning, and probably the one that is most adequate and appropriate for the situation of the *Ring* and its story, is *helmet* (*helmeted*). These meanings were related in that each of the respective objects screened or concealed the eyes which, in ancient thought, were the means by which a harmful spirit could enter the body.

The suffix *gerde* is also a complicated word, in a semantic sense. It has an association with *gerdhi* or *gerthi*, which is akin to English "girth" or "to gird around." The word also denotes a "spear carrier," and in this case, "spear maiden" much as *hilde* can be accepted as "warrior maiden." At the same time, the term is an archaic form related to the OHG *warten* ("to watch" in the sense of "guardianship"). The modern English "warder" and "ward" are related words.

With this number of possible connotations, it is necessary to determine a meaning that seems to be one that Wagner may have had in mind when he created this Valkyrie's name. There are two primary meanings that filter through this semantic maze. One is "Warder of Fury" and the second is "Helmeted Spear Maiden." Either could be attached to this *Ring* figure.

GRIMHILD

Grimhild makes no appearance in the *Ring*, rather, she is mentioned only, and then almost in passing, as Hagen the Nibelung and Gunther the Gibichung acknowledge that she is their mother. (Gunther's father is Gibich, while that of Hange is Alberich, the Nibelung dwarf.) However, the name *Grimhild* is very prominent in the Teutonic mythical and legendary literature, and her importance cannot be overlooked.

In the *Nibelungenlied*, which is the southern or German version of the Nibelung story, Grimhild (Kriemhilt) is sister to the kings of Burgundy, Gunther, Gernot, and Giselher. In this epic of the German people, Gunther agrees to the marriage of his sister with Siegfried (Sifrit) after the Nibelung(!) has helped him win the hand of Brünnhilde (Brünhilt). In a disagreement between Grimhild and Brünnhilde, the former accuses the latter of being the mistress of the hero Siegfried, and makes public the ring and the girdle that Siegfried took from Brünnhilde on her wedding night as he won her for Gunther. Hagen does not accept Siegfried's denial of the incident and because of what he has done, he later kills him while on a hunting party. Grimhild swears vengeance on Hagen who has taken Siegfried's treasure and sunk it in deep in the Rhine.

Thirteen years later, Grimhild marries Etzel (Attila, the Hun). Etzel invites Grimhild's brothers to visit her. At Grimhild's insistence, Etzel's brother slays many of the Burgundians, after which Hagen seeks revenge by beheading a son of Grimhild. Grimhild then orders that the hall in which the Burgundians are housed to be set afire. There are only two survivors to this conflagration, Gunther and Hagen, both of whom are then made captive and bound over to Grimhild by the hero Dietrich von Bern. Grimhild imprisons the pair and then demands that Hagen reveal to her the site where he has buried Siegfried's treasure. Hagen says that he cannot reveal the location of the hoard so long as his master, Gunther, is alive. Grimhild then orders her brother beheaded, after which she shows Hagen his head. Hagen again refuses to tell Grimhild where the treasure can be found, at which Grimhild seizes Hagen's sword, the sword that is called Balmung and which once belonged to Siegfried, and with it she beheads Hagen. Grimhild at last has had revenge on her husband's killer. Because of what Grimhild has done, Hildebrand, a great noble in the court of Dietrich von Bern, slays her.

Much the same story is found in *Thidrekssaga*, the Norwegian work that focuses on the German hero Dietrich von Bern. It is in this saga that Wagner saw a detail that he had not found elsewhere, and which he brought over in his *Ring* drama, the explanation by Hagen (Hogni) that while their party was hunting in the forest, Siegfried had been killed by a wild boar. It is also in this saga that Grimhild (Grimilldr) is depicted as a most ruthless and insensitive person. At her urging, her husband Attila casts her brother Gunther (Gunnarr) into a pit of vipers. Later, to ascertain that her brothers Gernoz and Gisler are dead she puts lighted torches into their mouths. Dietrich (Thidrekr) slashes Grimhild in two when he learns of her actions.

It is in the Eddic tradition that Gutrune takes the place of Grimhild as Siegfried's wife. In the poems of *The Poetic Edda* Grimhild is the wife of Gibich (Gjuki) and the mother of Gunther (Gunnar), Gutrune (Gudrun), and Hagen (Hogni). Grimhild is looked upon as the Queen of the Goths, as her husband is the Lord of the Goths. (In the *Edda* the word *Goth* is used mostly to designate all of the southern Germanic peoples.) A similar arrangement is depicted in *Volsungasaga*, which in many ways is a prose paraphrase of the *Edda*.

Obviously, the prominence of Grimhild is not restricted to German works. Yet, despite the fact that Grimhild is a figure in several individual works, both in Germany and in the Nordic north, outside the epic-type works, there are few references to her. Then, for the most part, Grimhild is usually depicted as a greedy, lustful figure, bent on having her husband's wealth and the death of his slayer at whatever cost. This pejorative view is very much the concept that has surrounded Grimhild despite the fact that *Die Klage*, an addendum that was joined with the *Nibelungenlied*, justifies all her actions because she was loyal to her husband, Siegfried.

It is curious to note Wagner's turn to Eddic tradition rather than to the German version of the Siegfried tale as he developed the Grimhild-Gutrune aspect of his *Ring* drama. The relationships of these two characters with the hero Siegfried, and also some of their actions, are obviously those inspired by the story as it unfolds in the poetry of the Nordic *Edda*. Wagner's writings as well as the substance of many of his thousands of letters tell and retell of his wish to create a "national work of art." The composer even made an appearance after the premiere of his *Ring* in Bayreuth in 1876 to inform the audience of how far he had advanced toward that goal with his drama, and to urge the nation to continue work in what he had begun. Yet, one might wonder why Wagner, with his obvious national zeal, had not chosen the southern or German version to serve as his source material. Of course, it is true that the Grimhild-Gutrune-Siegfried relationship that he placed in his poem was not the only Nordic aspect of the Siegfried legend that was to find its way into his tetralogy. There were others. Yet, Wagner always maintained that he was creating that national work of art, and there is no doubt that his concern in that regard was something more than casual talk. Yet, it is obvious to anyone who is familiar with both the northern and the southern versions of this story that much of what he was to call his *Ring* is really substance that originated in the early Northern Teutonic thought.

Unfortunately, Wagner never spoke in detail to many of these matters and it remains only that it must be assumed that it was Wagner's astute dramatic mind that served him as he went about the business of selecting dramatic details that would best serve the overall purpose that he had set for himself.

GRIMHILD (Name)

The name *Grimhild* (*Kriemhilt, Krimhild, Kremhild, Grimilldr*) is a compound form that is similar in construction to most of the other names in Wagner's drama. As was demonstrated with the name of the Valkyrie *Grimgerde*, the ON prefix *grim* (OE and OHG – *grimm*) has several possible meanings. One meaning seems to be "fierce" or "savage," in the sense of modern English *grim* or "harsh." There is a possible second meaning that suggests *mask* (*masked*) or possibly *visor*. A third meaning is *helmet* (*helmeted*). These meanings were related in that each of the respective objects screened or concealed the eyes which, in ancient thought, were the means by which a harmful spirit could enter the body. When this prefix is joined to the term *hild* (See *Notes*), the name can render a translation of "Helmeted Battle Maid."

However, in this case, it is quite possible that another meaning is not only more appropriate, but also more correct. In the ancient literature Grimhild is not regularly considered to be a "warrior maid" or a "battle maid," but rather a fierce and spiteful person, often divisive. In such light, there are those linguists who maintain that the prefix of this name is not derived from *grim*, but rather from ON *gruma*. This latter word denoted a haunting, terrifying, or even sinister temperament that usually lay hidden behind a facade of apparent tranquillity. This invisible force was to be feared, even avoided, because at those times when it surfaced in an individual, almost always unexpectedly, the results were of a disastrous or tragic nature. (An excellent example of these semantics at work within the character of Grimhild is that of her actions in the second part of *Nibelungenlied*. In those pages she thrusts a burning torch into the mouths of her brothers to learn if they are dead, and later, she cuts off the head of her husband's slayer, Hagen.) Indeed, this prominent figure of the celebrated German epic is quite different from a 'helmeted battle maid.' She is very much a "Specter" in the basic sense of the word.

A second linguistic matter also makes its contribution to the suggested meaning. In the northern regions of Teutondom, Grimhild was regularly known as *Grimhuldr*. The suffix *huldr* did not carry the concept of a Valkyrie or "warrior maid" as did the word *hild*. Rather, the word conveyed more the idea of *maid* as a "youthful female." Since nowhere in the mythical or legendary literature is Grimhild presented as a "warrior" type, and because she is at all times very much the regal female, the term *maid*, or perhaps *maiden*, can be used to apply to her, but with the latter meaning.

A second consideration of the name *Grimhild*, then, infers that perhaps a more appropriate name for the mother of the Gibichungs Gunther and Gutrune, and Hagen is "Specter Maiden."

GUEST RIGHTS (Gastrecht)

The *Gastrecht*, or "Guest Rights," was, at one time, a familiar term in Germany, and in general the word, if not the custom that it depicts, is recognized throughout the Teutonic cultures and countries of Europe. Its use in the *Ring*, therefore, poses no serious concern in terms of comprehension or understanding. The word means the right of hospitality, that is, the right of a stranger to receive hospitality, particularly if one is a visitor in a strange or foreign land. This unique custom arose in the Medieval period of European history, a time when travel was slow and precarious, and later became embedded in most Germanic cultures. There are no geographic boundaries or border lines in Wagner's drama, yet the setting of the first act of *Die Walküre* involves one who is travelling in a new and strange region, and *Guest Rights* seems to be very much in order. Wagner includes the custom in this act, made operative there by Sieglinde, when the stranger Siegmund arrives at their dwelling, and then confirmed later by Hunding.

The first act of this music-drama opens with Siegmund struggling to find refuge and rest within Hunding's dwelling. Literally within moments after Hunding's wife, Sieglinde, discovers the stranger, she addresses him as "guest," a term that she will use several times throughout the first and second scenes and which reflects the initiation of *Gastrecht*.

One of the first acts that Sieglinde does is to offer the stranger-guest a cup of mead. Although some followers of the *Ring* may assume that this offer is one of kindness and generosity toward a beleaguered and weary stranger, it may very well reflect a mythical matter that Wagner uncovered in his extended studies of the Teutonic myths and which he felt had a rightful place in the story that his drama would tell. A Germanic custom dictated that promptly upon arrival a guest should be given a cup or glass of ale, and this drink should be given to the guest by the host's wife. The guest, however, must be wary of his hostess because it is possible that she has put a drug in the drink that she has offered, a drug that will *bewitch* the drinker. There were two ways by which the drinker could avoid this bewitching, either of which could work satisfactorily. One manner for detecting a drugged drink was to know the "Ale-runes," one of those bits of magic knowledge that was so important within the early Teutonic cultures. When the "Ale-runes" were 'worked' satisfactorily, the drinker became immune to the drug that was capable of bewitching him and he was able to consume the drink without any dire results. (The Teutonic myths include the *Ale-runes* as part of the wisdom and knowledge that Brünnhilde gives to Siegfried after the hero has penetrated the fire-girded mountain and awakened her.) A second means was to offer the hostess the opportunity to take a sip of the drink before that of the guest. In this way, if the drink contained the bewitching drug, the hostess would suffer the effects and the guest would then be free to reject the drink. Naturally, if the hostess refused to drink, the guest was immediately free to refuse. Wagner chose the latter method when he causes his Siegmund to request that Sieglinde drink first.

As Sieglinde continues to address the stranger as "guest," her husband, Hunding, arrives. He carefully eyes the stranger and then informs him that his house is holy to him and that he expects the stranger to respect that dictum. It is apparent that Hunding, as well as Sieglinde, is obeying the requirement of "Guest Rights" as he welcomes Siegmund, if suspiciously, into his home. Hunding then orders Sieglinde to prepare food for him and the guest. As Siegmund begins to explain how he came to be in Hunding's house, Hunding uses the word "guest" when he asks for the stranger's name.

It soon develops that Siegmund is a person on whom Hunding wishes to seek revenge. In the course of their brief conversation, Hunding learns that it was Siegmund who was responsible for the death of some of his relatives, and now that he is here in Hunding's house, he will avenge the death of those kin.

It is then that *Gastrecht* or "Guest-Rights" is made fully and completely operative. If, until now, the custom of *Gastrecht* has been in operation only partially, that is, when Sieglinde and Hunding have used the word "guest" several times as each addressed Siegmund, indicating, of course, that Siegmund is a guest in their dwelling, and offered him drink, it is now that the custom is found in its totally extended form. Hunding knows that he faces the killer of his relatives, and he is much angered, and desires revenge, yet he cannot harm Siegmund in any way at the moment because the latter is a "guest" in his home. The angered Hunding then tells Siegmund that he is a guest in his house, for the night, but, the next day Siegmund should arm himself because that is the time when Siegmund will have to pay for his past actions. There is, of course, in the words and the voice of Hunding the inference that he will not attack Siegmund while the Volsung remains a guest.

Hunding's words to Siegmund make complete the custom of *Gastrecht*. Although the person who slew his kin stands before him, in his own house, Hunding will make no move other than that of accepting Siegmund as his 'guest.' Such obedience and respect for custom is to be acknowledged, especially since Hunding is apparently a roughened warrior accustomed to the wildness of his age. Yet, the matter of *Gastrecht* had a rather long and certainly lasting effect of the cultures of times past, and it is to Wagner's credit that he uses the matter correctly and that the actions in these scenes seems most natural. It is a matter that may have skipped the attention of some followers of the *Ring.*

See also: *Brünnhilde's Wisdom*

GUNTHER

The figure of the *Ring's* Gunther has ample precedency in early Teutonic literature and history. In the Eddic tradition of northern (Nordic) Teutondom this individual is known as Gunnar (Gunnarr), and he is the son of Gjuki (Gibich) and Kriemhilt (Grimhild). He has two brothers, Hogni (Hagen) and Guthormr (Gotthorm), and a sister Guthrun (Gutrune). Gunther and Hagen swear oaths of blood-brotherhood with Sigurdr (Siegfried) who has married their sister. Siegfried changes from with Gunther and crosses through a wall of fire that surrounds Brynhildr (Brünnhilde) to win her for him. Gunther later believes that Siegfried has broken his oath to him by seducing Brünnhilde and concludes that he must die. Hagen will not carry out Gunther's wish because he will not break the oath that they have sworn, and so he and Gunther decide that their brother Gotthorm shall carry out the murder. Gotthorm slays Siegfried while the latter is in his bed, asleep. After Siegfried's death, Gunther and Hagen take possession of Siegfried's lands and the gold treasure that he had won when he slew the dragon Fafnir (Fafner).

Gutrune is distraught and much distressed over her husband's death. She accuses Gunther of having been responsible for Siegfried's death and swears vengeance on her brother's cruel deed. Gunther also becomes disturbed by Siegfried's death and by the words that his sister has spoken.

In time, Gutrune marries Atli (Attila). Atli invites Gunther and Hagen to Hunland. Gunther is warned that they must not take the trip. They travel to Atli's land, however, where they are soon made captives of the Hun's warriors. Atli wishes to know the whereabouts of Siegfried's gold treasure. Gunther refuses to reveal the secret as to where the gold is hidden.

Atli's men kill Hagen and rip his heart form his body, and when Gunther sees Hagen's heart, he is certain that the secret hiding place of the treasure is safe forever. Atli then orders that Gunther be thrown into a pit of vipers where he plays the harp with his toes until he is bitten and killed by a poisonous snake.

The *Thidrekssaga*, a work that was produced in Norway but based on German songs and tales, depicts Gunnarr (Gunther) as the son of Aldrian and Oda. Gunther is King of Niflungaland, sometimes called Gjukiland. Gunther has two brothers, Gernoz and Gisler, and one sister, Grimilldr (Grimhild). Grimhild's husband is Sigurdr (Siegfried). Gunther is a soldier-warrior who joins Thidrek (Dietrich) in his journey to Bertangaland where they wage combat.

Gunther marries Brynilldr (Brünnhilde). On their wedding night, Brünnhilde binds Gunther with her girdle and hangs him on a nail. Gunther promptly asks Siegfried to exchange clothing and take his place in the bridal chamber. Siegfried does his brother-in-law's bidding at which time he subdues and deflowers Brünnhilde, after which the two exchange rings.

In time, Grimhild sees Siegfried's ring on Brünnhilde's finger. She accuses her of unchaste acts. Brünnhilde believes that she has been dishonored by Siegfried and demands his death. Gunther is in agreement, and Hagen slays Siegfried while they all are on a hunting party in the forest. Gunther is very pleased and rejoices in the death of Siegfried.

Siegfried's widow Grimhild than weds Attila who, at her urging, invites her brothers to his land. Gunther's mother has a premonition of harm for her son, but he accepts Attila's invitation. Gunther is eventually taken prisoner by Attila's men and it is then that his sister Grimhild has her revenge by ordering that he be cast to his death in a pit of snakes.

The *Nibelungenlied* has yet another version of the tale in which Gunther is a primary figure. This epic poem, which is the only work of total German inspiration and origin that served Wagner as a source material for his *Ring* drama, is regularly credited as the poetic keystone for the numerous other related tales that circulated throughout the ancient Teutonic world. In this work Gunther is the son of Dankrat (Dancrat) and Ute (Uote). He rules as King of Burgundy with his capital at Worms. Gunther's brothers are

Gernot and Giselher, and his sister is Grimhild (Kriemhilt). Siegfried (Sifrit) the Nibelung, who has gained a vast treasure, wishes to marry Grimhild and so pledges his service to Gunther and his court. Siegfried then accompanies Gunther to Isenland, where the king hopes to win the famed Brünnhilde (Brünhilt) as his wife. Brünnhilde has said that she will marry the man who can defeat her at three tests of physical prowess. Siegfried dons his cloak of invisibility and performs the feats while Gunther goes through the motions. On the wedding night Brünnhilde tells Gunther that she will not submit to him until he reveals why a vassal like Siegfried has been allowed to marry his royal sister. Gunther remains silent and Brünnuilde then wraps her new husband in her girdle and hangs him on a nail that is in the wall. When he promises that he will not touch her, she takes him down. Later, Gunther again asks Siegfried for his help. On the next night, Grimhild's husband again becomes invisible by means of his magic cloak, and he then subdues Brünnhilde. As he departs the bridal chamber he takes with him a ring and a girdle that belongs to Brünnhilde. He gives these items to his wife. Later, during a quarrel between Brünnhilde and Grimhild, the latter accuses Gunther's wife of being unchaste with Siegfried and produces the ring and the girdle to support her claim.

Gunther is aware of all that has happened, but he remains silent regarding the matter. Hagen, Gunther's first vassal, convinces his master that Siegfried's death is the only way that Brünnhilde's honor can be restored. Gunther finally agrees with his vassal and Hagen then murders Grimhild's husband while they are on a hunting expedition in a forest, when he bends over to take a drink from a creek.

Gunther then devises a plan to seize Siegfried's treasure of gold. Hagen later takes the treasure and sinks it in the Rhine so that Grimhild can not take it as her own. All the while Grimhild is most distraught over these matters, and she is especially disturbed over the death of her husband. In time, however, her brothers are able to arrange a reconciliation between her and Gunther.

After many years have passed, Gunther gives permission for his sister to marry Etzel (Attila). Etzel then invites Gunther and his entourage to visit him in Hiunenlant (Land of the Huns). Hagen, who has urged Gunther not to accept Etzel's invitation, is extremely cautious and assumes charge of Gunther's forces as they make the journey. In the land of the Huns, Gunther and Hagen and the warriors go to Etzel's hall where they are soon attacked by 20,000 Huns. The fight is long and arduous and in the end Hagen and Gunther are the only survivors. They refuse to surrender, however, and it remains for Dietrich to capture them and turn them over to Grimhild.

Grimhild is now determined to learn the whereabouts of her late husband's treasure. She approaches Hagen who refuses to give her any information so long as his master Gunther lives. Grimhild then orders her brother beheaded and then she shows the head to Hagen. Hagen, now the only person living who knows where the treasure is hidden, still refuses to divulge the secret. Grimhild then grabs Balmung, the sword that once had belonged to Siegfried and which Hagen had taken as his after he had killed the hero, and beheads Hagen with it. Grimhild is then cut down by Hildebrand, a teacher and armor bearer to Dietrich.

The matter of Gunther, his role in any specific action or deed, his relationship and association with others, and his importance or significance in the matter of German legends, depends, in numerous ways, upon the version that interprets that role. Each of the several lengthy versions, plus those works that include some or most of this story, have variations as numerous as there are versions. It must be borne in mind, however, that the tale of the Nibelungs, that is, what has become known as the Siegfried legend, originated in the region of the Rhine as a Frankish tale. The *Gunther* of that original story takes his name and some of his character from the historic *Gundicarious*, the Latinized name that the Romans had given the first king of the Burgundians who invaded central Europe about 406 and who, by 411, had amassed a vast expanse of territory between the Rhine and the Alps. In 436, this king suffered a humiliatory defeat at the hands of the Huns under Attila.

It is obvious to a follower of Wagner's *Ring* that the Gunther of that argument is more the Nordic figure than that individual who has a role in the German cultural and literary past. Yet, if Wagner relied heavily on the Nordic version of the Siegfried tale for numerous major as well as minor details of his drama, he resorted to the *Nibelungenlied* for what can best be termed the German traits of honor, nobility, and pride. It was these aspects of the German culture that he stated that he had found in the epic poem, and which he desired to bring into his national work of art. The success or lack thereof that was Wagner's in this regard has often been discussed, and sometimes debated, since the premier of the *Ring* in 1876, and especially active have these discussions become when the focus centers upon Wagner's development of the character of his Gunther. Yet, it cannot be denied that the composer brought into his drama a total ambience that reflected much of the German thought, and if his Gunther's contribution to that thought is rather scant when viewed in light of the *Ring's* entire German consideration, the Gunther of his drama was, none the less, a figure of literary as well as historical renown.

GUNTHER (Name)

The name *Gunther* has no exact translation into English, although the root word is related to *war* and *battle*, and in one of its several variations was also used to denote a *bold* or *fierce warrior*. Perhaps a satisfactory interpretation of the name is "Battle Warrior."

The root of this name was ON *gunnr*. In ME the word became *gonne* and *gunne*, and *gun* in modern English. In the Nordic regions the term *gunnr* developed into the word *Gunnar*, and it is by that name that this figure is known in *The Poetic Edda*, *The Volsung Saga*, and *The Wilkina Saga*.

The root *gunnr* developed differently in other languages. The ON word *gunnr* was Latinized and applied by the Romans as the name of a king of the Burgundians, *Gundicarious*, who had become quite rich and powerful in the region of the Rhine but who suffered a resounding defeat in the middle of the fifth century at the hands of Attila the Hun.

The ON word *gunnr*, which the Romans had turned into *Gundicarious*, became *gunth* in the language of the Goths, a term that was once used to designated any of the continental Teutonic peoples. It is from the latter that the name *Gunther*, (and the variant *Gunter*) was developed. It is by this name that this figure is known in the southern or German version of the Siegfried tale as found in *Song of the Nibelungs* where he is a Burgundian king who becomes the husband of Brünnhilde.

GUTRUNE

The character that Wagner placed in the fourth drama of his *Ring* poem and to whom he gave the German name *Gutrune* is a major figure in the northern, (Nordic) lays, myths, sagas, and songs that recount the celebrated tale of Siegfried. Curiously, however, this same Gutrune is not a figure that is to be found in any of the southern (German) equivalents. This Gutrune has no role whatsoever in the popular Siegfried legend that originated and developed in the Frankish region of Germany, spread throughout the land, and went on to become *Nibelungenlied*, the national epic of the German people. In the simplest of terms, the Gutrune (Gudrun, Guthrun) of legend, the Gutrune of myth and folklore, and the Gutrune of Wagner's drama, is a product of northern thought, rather than an emanation that arose from German concepts.

Endless studies have been made regarding the chronology as well as the manner in which the Siegfried tale made its migratory journey from its native region of the Rhine in Germany into Nordic Teutondom, principally into Norway (and later into other Teutonic lands, and as far west as Iceland). Yet, without specific regard for that enigmatic history, it can be said that as the tale slowly made its way northward, most of the major characters of Germany's favorite story were retained, (with Scandinavian names), and many of its major occurrences were also preserved. The story never really lost the original substance and the aggregate that had given it its popularity in the south, an essence that evidently also pleased the northern people.

There was, however, one major change that did come about. It was to be a change that would provoke much intellectual consternation within the group of scholars devoted to the southern Germanic scene. Somehow, somewhere between the southern Rhine and the northern Baltic Sea and southern Norway, Grimhild (Kriemhild), Siegfried's wife and the sister of Gunther and Hagen, and a major player in the Nibelung tale, is replaced by the Nordic figure *Gutrune*!

In the *Niberlungenlied*, Siegfried, the son of King Siegmund and Queen Sieglinde of Netherland, marries Grimhild (Kriemhild), the daughter of Ute and Dancrat, and sister of the kings of Burgundy, Gunther (who later marries Brünnhilde), Gernot, and Giselher. Eventually, Siegfried is slain by Hagen, who is a kinsman to the Burgundian royalty. The Nordic version of the Siegfried legend, as recounted in the verses of *The Poetic Edda*, tells of Gutrune (Guthrun), daughter of Gibich (Gjuki), who becomes the wife of the hero. Gutrune is the sister of Gunther (Gunnar), and Hagen (Hogni). The three are half sister and half brothers to Gotthorm, and all are the children of Grimhild (Grimhilt). Wagner's arrangement is very similar to the Nordic scene, although he dispenses with Gotthorm, and makes Hagen the half brother through their mother Grimhild. In this northern version it is Gotthorm, who has been purposely fed a meal of boiled wolf, sliced snake, and mead, who slays Siegfried as the hero sleeps in his bed, but who, in turn, is killed by Siegfried before the latter dies. In the *Nibelungenlied* the children are referred to as *Burgundians*, and later *Nibelungs*, while in the Eddic tale they are *Goths*. Wagner becomes unique in this regard, and probably avoids numerous questions, when he causes Gunther and Gutrune to be known as *Gibichungs*, Siegfried is a *Volsung*, and Hagen is a *Nibelung*!

Although of a relatively minor nature, there are certain variations between the northern and southern versions in which Gutrune is a prominent figure. Suffice to say that after the death of Siegfried, as depicted in the German tale, the hero's widow, Grimhild, spends some twenty-six years mourning her husband's death and planning her vengeance upon his killer, Hagen. Those plans include her marriage to Attila, the Hun (Etzel in the German version) because she feels that she will be able to use his mighty military forces in her plans. Grimhild at last realizes her revenge when she strikes off Hagen's head with Balmung, the sword that had belonged to her husband. One of Hagen's warrior colleagues then steps into the fray and slays Grimhild with his sword. The *Nibelungenlied* ends with Grimhild's death. Because Grimhild was the last of the Nibelungs, the original title of the epic poem was *The Fall of the Nibelungs.*

The Eddic verses depict an arrangement that is slightly different from that of *Song of the Nibelungs.* After Siegfried is slain by Gutrune's cowardly half brother Gotthorm, she spends much time in mourning her hero husband. Her heart is bursting with grief, yet she does not cry or shed tears. Gutrune's lament for her slain husband then becomes the principal focus of no less than two lengthy Eddic mythical poems. Each lament tells of Gutrune's deep sadness, of her pain, of her distress, as the women around her try to console her. One woman, apparently in an attempt to soothe Gutrune's sorrow, tells how she lost seven sons, her husband, her father, her mother, and four brothers, all within a period of six months! After that emotional ordeal, the woman says that she was then made a slave to a monarch's wife, who beat her continuously!

(The Eddic Brünnhilde, who also had loved Siegfried, is greatly sorrowed at the hero's death. Apparently to join him in that death, this Brünnhilde orders eight of her servants killed along with five servant women. Then she commits suicide by killing herself with her sword. There is another Eddic poem which tells that Brünnhilde dies on a pyre that stood beside the one on which the body of Siegfried lay, and still another poem relates that Brünnhilde was burned on the same pyre on which Siegfried was cremated.)

Gutrune, still sadly mourning the loss of her beloved Siegfried, wanders about in a forest for five days, after which she travels to Denmark where she stays with Thora, the daughter of Hokon, for seven and one half years.

After Siegfried's death, the northern poems tell how Attila the Hun (*Atli* in the north) had wanted Gutrune very much as his bride. Gutrune did not wish to wed him. Finally, after some time, and at Gunther and Hagen's bidding, she weds Attila, who, as Gutrune had envisioned, tortures and kills her brothers Gunther and Hagen. (Attila was desirous of having Siegfried's treasure which Gunther and Hagen had taken over after the hero's death.) To have revenge on Attila, Gutrune kills their two sons and prepares their hearts for Attila's meal. In time, Hagen's son slays Attila in revenge for his father's death, after which, according to one Eddic poem, Gutrune kills herself. It would appear that the poem in which Gutrune commits suicide is a spurious one because most myths recount how Gutrune, after Atli's death, goes on to take a third husband, Jonak by whom she has a child.

By any standard, the depiction of Gutrune's existence, as presented in the Eddic poems, is uneven and indeed, at times, contradictory. While there are certain duplicities of thought and actions between the northern Gutrune and the southern Kriemhild, it is not possible to view a seamless, chronologically correct portrait of this northern figure. It is possible, however, with patience and careful study, to piece together a kind of image of Gutrune, although many of the literary details that are needed are at odds, or even missing. Essentially, however, the picture that results is that of the figure that Wagner brought into his drama. By and large, Wagner's Gutrune is the northern being, somewhat a secondary figure in that she is associated with two figures of truly major stature, Siegfried and Brünnhilde. For some unapparent reason, the northern Gutrune assumes only a less than primary role, even though she is the wife of Teutondom's greatest hero. In the southern *Nibelungenlied*, Siegfried's wife is not only a significant character, she is what may be termed a primary and fundamental figure in the Siegfried story, a major figure who will remain as such in any analysis. In the north, Siegfried's wife does not have the forceful and aggressive nature that is so apparent in her southern counterpart. Gutrune may have been a faithful being as she lamented her husband's death, but unlike the Grimhild of Germany, she does not convert that lament into a scorn for her husband's killer, or into a rage of hatred, or into an unconditional vow of violent vengeance. Gutrune's role is less than primary when viewed beside that of Grimhild, even secondary when viewed beside the major figures of the Nordic tale. Gutrune is not a 'Grimhild' in her nature or in her heroic being. Rather, the northern Gutrune is more a fragile, emotional, being, a kind of romantic spirit that obviously appealed to Richard Wagner.

So it is in Eddic literature, and so it is in Wagner's *The Ring of the Nibelung*. Gutrune is the necessary stimulus to Gunther, to Hagen, to Siegfried, to Brünnhilde, but, at the same time, she must not assume an importance that overshadows those very individuals. It is the existence of each of these other individuals that must unravel, their natures must unfold, and their roles must be played out to the very end. The same cannot be said for Gutrune. It is true that after Siegfried's death the Eddic Gutrune continues on, but it becomes her lament that is important rather than any of her actions. In a sense, Wagner's Gutrune has only her lament, which is not nearly so grandiose as that of the Eddic verses. Wagner's Gutrune, much as her northern model, simply fulfills the necessary spaces that the argument demands, and then she dissolves into dramatic nothingness. In Wagner's poem, Siegfried dies, and after a most brief expression of sorrow, Gutrune seems to fade away, and in such a manner that few if any of an audience are even aware that she is no more.

GUTRUNE (Name)

The compound name *Gutrune* is the Germanized form of the ON *Gudrun* and the later form *Guthrune*.

The suffix of this name, *run*, is the ON for "rune," or in more practical language, "knowledge" or "wisdom."

The prefix of this name, *gut*, allows for a double meaning of the name. There are those who maintain that this prefix is the ON word for "god," and therefore a translation of "Divine Knowledge" is appropriate. However, there are those who suggest that this prefix is the adjective "good," and therefore, the name is really "Good Knowledge." Given the fact that the Gutrune of literature as well as of Wagner's drama is a mortal with nothing of a divine nature in her figure, her life, or her character, it would seem most appropriate that the latter translation be attached to this name.

HAGEN

It is perhaps curious as well as interesting to any follower of the *Ring* to note that other than the Volsung Siegfried and the Burgundian Grimhild, the *Hagen* of the Teutonic world is perhaps the most prominent and the most significant character of all those who emerged from the extensive Germanic thought and literature. Such is true in the numerous tales, sagas, and Eddic poetry of the Nordic north (Norway, Sweden, Denmark, Iceland) as well as in the stories, poems, and epic literature of the southern Germanic peoples (continental Europe). Yet, it seems apparent that any reference to this figure outside the rather vast array of German heroic works depends in substance on those tales that were to become the thirteenth-century German epic poem *Nibelungenlied*.

The figure known as Hagen can be, and is, distinct from one Teutonic region to the next. The role of this legendary being, his relationship to others, his function within his specific societal group are all dependent upon the version of the Siegfried legend that is foremost in any given area. Among other aspects of this fascinating figure, Hagen can be an evil schemer or he can be a figure who at times shows tinges of an honorable and proud stature. He can be a stalwart and brave warrior or he can demonstrate unforgiving disdain and haughty contempt for fellow man. He is at once a brother to rulers, or the son of a demonic father and therefore a half brother to proud warriors, or he is a fearless vassal to the royal family of ancient Burgundy. Yet, throughout the literary existence of this fascinating figure, in all of the numerous versions of the Siegfried tale that are to be found throughout all of the vast region of the Teutonic countries and peoples, there is one factor that is constant, unswerving, and ever-present: Hagen is involved, in one way or another, in the plot that will culminate in the death of the hero Siegfried!

It is in *Nibelungenlied* that Hagen is the vassal to his Burgundian king, Gunther. (Reference is usually made to the Burgundian "kings," Gunther and his brothers Gernot and Giselher. It is Gunther, however, who is the foremost ruler of this land.) This Hagen is an awesome figure, handsome in his ferocious ways, keen to strike an enemy, suspicious of others, always prepared to enter combat, and fiercely loyal to his lord and king.

It is in the plot to murder Siegfried (Sifrit) that Hagen assumes an indispensable role in this very German work. Brünnhilde (Brünhilt) and her husband Gunther have been humiliated by Grimhild (Kriemhilt), Siegfried's wife. The latter had proved openly that it was Siegfried who had taken Brünnhilde's virginity after her marriage to Gunther, and not her husband. It is Hagen who says that the only way in which honor can be restored to the royal couple is through the death of Siegfried. Brünnhilde and Gunther are in agreement and Hagen then plans the action that will bring about the death of Grimhild's famed husband.

Hagen goes to Grimhild. He tells her that it is his desire to protect Siegfried whenever he is in battle, and therefore he must know where on his body he is vulnerable. Grimhild reveals that Siegfried's vulnerable spot is between his shoulder blades. Siegfried had been rendered invulnerable when the blood of a dragon that he had killed covered his entire body, all that is except a spot between his shoulder blades where a linden leaf had fallen.

Hagen plans a hunting party. When the party pauses to rest, Hagen says that he has not brought wine for the meal, and therefore all must drink from a stream. When Siegfried bends to take a drink, Hagen hurls a spear at his spot of vulnerability. The sword sinks into Siegfried's back, and after a death lament, the hero dies.

Grimhild mourns her husband's death. She knows that it was Hagen who killed Siegfried, and it was not robbers as had been claimed. When Siegfried's coffin is put on display Grimhild vows revenge on Hagen. When Hagen passes before the coffin, Siegfried's wound begins to bleed, which, in the eyes of all, is further proof of the vassal's guilt.

Grimhild mourns for three and one half years. She forgives all except Hagen. Siegfried's vast treasure of gold that he had won from the sons of

King Nibelung is brought to Burgundy. When Grimhild begins to distribute the wealth, Hagen is angered. He seizes the entire treasure and sinks it in the waters of the Rhine, believing that one day he could make it his.

Grimhild mourns for thirteen years, at the end of which she marries Etzel (Attila). Hagen opposes the marriage, but Grimhild looks forward to it because Etzel has told her that as his wife she will be able to avenge Siegfried's murder. Grimhild then mourns her husband's death for thirteen additional years, after which King Gunther and his vassals are invited to visit Hunland. Hagen does not wish to venture into the land of the Huns, but when Gunther insists that the journey be made, he assumes personal command of all of Gunther's warriors. En route, on the shores of the Danube, the entourage meets two nixies, Hadeburg and Siegelind, who prophesy that of the entire retinue only the king's chaplain will return alive from this journey. To test the words of the nixies, when they are in a boat on the water, Hagen throws the chaplain overboard. When he sees the man reach home shores safely, he knows that the water spirits had predicted well. Thus, when all the forces land on Etzel's shores, Hagen destroys the boat and tells all the men of the fate that awaits them.

Shortly after all arrive at Etzel's court, Grimhild confronts Hagen. She asks Gunther's vassal why he had not brought Siegfried's treasure on the journey because it rightfully belongs to her. Hagen tells her that he had sunk the hoard in the Rhine. Hagen then admits that it was he who killed Siegfried and he flaunts Siegfried's sword, Balmung, which he had taken as his own. Hagen's countenance and total bearing instill great fear in Grimhild's warriors, and they retreat instead of challenging Siegfried's killer.

As many of the Burgundians had feared, the Huns attack them, this time while they are asleep. Hagen and Volker defend the Burgundians against this attack which had been prompted by Grimhild. Later, at a feast in Etzel's great hall, Hagen learns that Etzel's men have killed some respected Burgundians, and as repayment, he beheads Ortlieb, a son of Grimhild and Etzel, and the boy's tutor, and then cuts off the hand of Etzel's messenger.

A battle ensues. The hero Dietrich leads Grimhild and Etzel out of the hall. The Burgundians fight valiantly, but all are slain by the Huns except Gunther and Hagen. Then the hero Dietrich fights with Hagen, wounds him, and then is victorious over him. Dietrich hands Hagen over to Grimhild who orders him to be put in a dungeon. Dietrich and Gunther now fight and, finally, Dietrich subdues Gunther, who is also delivered to Grimhild. Dietrich then requests freedom for the pair because they have fought so bravely. Grimhild separates the two and announces that they will have their freedom if the treasure is handed over to her. Hagen refuses because he has taken a vow that he will never reveal the secret of the treasure so long as his master Gunther lives. Grimhild is angered both by what Hagen has said and his arrogance. She orders that her brother Gunther be beheaded, after which she dangles his head before Hagen. Hagen again refuses to divulge the hiding place of the treasure and declares that now the treasure will be kept safely from her forever. Grimhild can resist no more. She grabs Balmung from Hagen and with it smites off Hagen's head. The noble Hildebrand then cuts Grimhild down.

(The *Klage*, a relative short addendum to the poem of *Nibelungenlied*, finds fault with Hagen whom it holds responsible for the entire matter. It casts no blame on Grimhild because she merely seeks vengeance on the killer of her husband to whom she is ever loyal.)

The Nordic version of the Siegfried legend is found in *The Poetic Edda*, in "Lays of the Heroes." In these verses Hagen (Hogni) is the son of Gibich (Gjuki) and the brother of Gunther (Gunnar) and Gutrune (Gudrun). The two brothers swear an oath of blood brotherhood with Siegfried (Sigurd), the husband of their sister. Because of Siegfried's supposed betrayal of Gunther, his murder is planned and plotted. Hagen, however, refuses to take part in the action because of the oaths of brotherhood that the two had sworn, and it is the half brother Gotthorm who slays the hero.

In other of the Eddic verses Gutrune marries Atli (Attila), who invites Gunther and Hagen to visit them in Hunland. Hagen interprets a warning that tells them not to make the trip, but Gunther makes the trip, and Hagen travels at his side. Once in Atli's hall, they are attacked by the Huns as Atli demands to be given the great treasure of the Nibelungs. Gunther is very quickly overpowered, but Hagen fights ceaselessly, and kills a number of the Huns before he too is overpowered. Atli demands that Gunther reveal to him the secret hiding place of the Nibelung hoard, but Gunther demands that he be shown the heart of Hagen before he will reveal the secret. The heart of a man is shown to Gunther, but he knows it cannot be Hagen's because it palpitates and trembles too much to be that of a man who is collected at all times, fearless, even of death. Then, the Huns cut Hagen's heart from his body and show it to Gunther. In his own way Gunther now rejoices, because on seeing Hagen's heart he knows that he is now the only person who knows the hiding place of the Nibelung treasure and that it will be safe forever, deep in the waters of the Rhine.

(The 'Nibelung treasure' that is noted in the German *Nibelungenlied* and in the verses of the Nordic *Edda* is not the treasure that Siegfried won when he fought and killed the dragon Fafner (Fafnir). In the original southern stories that served as basis for the Nordic versions, the name *Nibelung* was used by no less than three distinct clans or families. The first of this trio was King Nibelung who ruled in Nibelung Land. Siegfried waged war with two sons of King Nibelung. Siegfried was victorious and took possession of all the Nibelung land, the people, and a gold treasure that the king had kept buried deep in a mountain. Siegfried also took the Nibelung name. Siegfried then married Grimhild, sister to the Burgundian king Gunther. In time, Gunther's forces and those of Siegfried join ranks and the entire group now takes the name Nibelung. Gunther is now known as a Nibelung, as are all the Burgundians. When Siegfried is slain, his widow becomes the rightful heir to the treasure, but before she can claim possession, Hagen seizes it and sinks it in the Rhine. Throughout this succession of events, the treasure also bears the name *Nibelung*, and as such it will remain throughout the entire poem. In the *Edda*, Gunther, the King of the Burgundians, possesses a huge treasure. Apparently this is the same hoard that came over to the Burgundians at Siegfried's death because in these verses, as in the southern poem, it is called a Nibelung treasure and it had been sunk in the Rhine.)

Although Wagner will turn primarily to *Nibelungenlied*, and in a secondary manner to *The Poetic Edda*, to extract the essence of the Hagen that will be a part of his *Ring*, this figure who plays such a pivotal role is a known figure in the literature of other countries. In *Thidrekssaga*, the saga about the German hero Dietrich which came into being in Norway, Hagen exists with the Nordic name of Hogni. This figure was the son of Oda who was married to Aldrian. Hagen was conceived one night when Oda was raped by a demon as she slept in her garden. Hagen is thus a half brother to Gunnar, Grimhild and Gisler, the children of the pair. There are verses that originated in the Faeroe Islands that tell that Hagen is killed when he slays an enemy who, before he dies, kills Hagen by breathing poisonous breath on him. There are also some Danish poetic verses that tell of Hagen (Hagenn) who marries Brünnhilde (Bryneld) who had been won for him by Siegfried (Sivard). In time, Brünnhilde sees some jewelry on the finger of Siegfried's wife, Grimhild (Kriemhilt), and she urges Hagen to slay him. Hagen decapitates Siegfried with his own sword, Adelryng. Hagen then brings the severed head to Brünnhilde, slays her by slashing her into pieces, and then he commits suicide by falling on the sword.

It is obvious to the follower of Wagner's *Ring* that the character that the composer called Hagen is at once a blend of the natures of the several figures that were so named and which were found in the literatures of the ancient Teutonic past. Like each of those several literary figures named Hagen, the character that made his way about in the *Ring* is very much involved in the murder of Siegfried. Yet, in his own way, Wagner seemed to desire to blend into his character more of the essence of the figure that he had found in his native *Nibelungenlied* than that of the other works.

Wagner's Hagen, like the prototype in *Nibelungenlied*, is indeed a striking figure. At first glance, he reflects a proud, a noble being that extends an unswerving loyalty to his lord, Gunther. Yet, there lies just beneath that gilded surface a nature much to be feared, a being of suspicious ways and equally ferocious manner. Wagner's Hagen, like his source in the German epic, is always prepared to scheme, to plan, to plot, to cause the evil incarnate of his being to come down so unsuspectingly on others. Wagner's Hagen, like the German figure, envisions the Nibelung treasure as his, as his alone, and to that end he will guide all action, manipulate all persons, resort to any means.

Gunther and the others, in the German epic and also in Wagner's *Ring*, believe that Siegfried had been intimate with Brünnhilde as he went about the business of causing the maid to become Gunther's wife. Hagen plays with the emotions of the weak Gunther and he talks to the pained Brünnhilde, bringing the matter entirely to his side, causing the pair to believe that the only way in which each may regain his individual and personal honor is through the death of Siegfried. It is the Hagen of both the epic and the *Ring* who incites the desperate pair to action, the one who skillfully causes them to be in agreement with the plan that he has conceived, a plot that he secretly believes will ultimately give the great treasure to him. It is Hagen who tricks out the secret of Siegfried's vulnerability, it is Hagen who plans a hunting party, it is Hagen who slays the hero by running his weapon into his back. And, later, when Hagen approaches the hero's body, the hand of the dead Siegfried hand slowly rises, as if in a final rejection. (In the epic Siegfried's death-wound begins to bleed when Hagen approaches the corpse.) It is at this point that Wagner's genuine resort to the epic of his native Germany terminates. The composer has no further need of additional matters of character and action, and the epic tale now shifts entirely to the life of Siegfried's widow, Grimhild, and her search for revenge against her husband's killer.

Although Wagner found much in *Nibelungenlied* that he could bring over into his Hagen, there were matters in the non-German works that obviously pleased his dramatic palate. From the *Edda* he took the relationship of Gutrune as sister to Gunther, rather than that of Grimhild, whom he then converted into the mother of the pair. Likewise, he deemed the matter of an oath of blood brotherhood, which is found in the *Edda*, to be of significant dramatic purpose. However, in the Nordic version of the tale, Hagen participates in the act, whereas in the *Ring* it is only Gunther who swears fidelity to Siegfried.

In the matter of Hagen, Wagner could also turn to *Thidrekssaga* for inspiration. In his drama, Wagner makes Hagen a half brother to Gunther and Gutrune through their mother, Grimhild. To enhance the rather degraded and base character of Hagen, the composer causes the conception of Hagen to have been effected when the Nibelung dwarf Alberich uses the gold of his treasure to lure Grimhild, the wife of Gibich, into an affair. This specific arrangement was the product of Wagner's dramatic thought, although there can be no doubt that he was influenced by the details that he found in the saga. It is in that work that Oda, the wife of Aldrian, lay asleep in her garden when she was ravished by an incensed demon. The resultant child of that pairing is Hagen, who is then a half brother to Gunther (Gunnar, Gisler, Gernoz, and Grimhild (Grimilldr)).

Finally, it seems that Wagner was not satisfied with the manner in which Hagen dies in the several literary works. In the *Nibelungenlied* Hagen is beheaded by Grimhild. In the Eddic literature Hagen's heart is ripped from his body and used as means to make Gunther tell where the treasure is hidden. In some poetry Hagen is killed by poisonous breath, and in other verses he kills himself by falling on his sword. None of these methods of death seems to be appropriate for the Hagen of the *Ring*, at least in the mind of the dramatist. Wagner seemed to feel that Hagen's death should become an action that was related to the drama, an action that would enhance the details of his argument. Thus it was that death by drowning was to be the cause of Hagen's death, but it was not a drowning at any place, in just any water. Rather, he would cause Hagen's death to be in the Rhine, the waters that are so significant throughout his drama and the waters that had served as the original home of the gold and to which it would be returned by Brünnhilde in her final moments. And, as yet another way in which to show the true character of his Hagen, Wagner causes his death to occur because the greedy Hagen, ever bent on reclaiming the treasure as his, attempts to take it from the Rhinemaidens' hands, from the hands of those nixies who long have drawn unsuspecting victims to a watery death, and about whom Fricka had commented much earlier in the drama.

Hagen remains today as one of the truly well drawn characters in the argument of the *Ring*. Despite his somewhat brief appearance, in only the final drama of Wagner's tetralogy, Hagen's sardonic, mocking, and derisive character becomes an artfully developed nature, a being who rides the waves of his culture, always much concerned regarding his own welfare with little heed to who and what are to suffer because of his actions. The Hagen of the German epic is very much his own man. Wagner recognized this aspect in the character of Hagen, and he sought mightily to bring that facet of amoral nature into the Hagen of his drama. It seems that Wagner was quite successful in his attempt.

HAGEN (Name)

This figure appears in several works of early Germanic mythical and saga literature, usually with either *Hagen* (*Haghen, Hagene, Hagenn*) or *Hogni* as his name. The precise meaning of the name is uncertain although linguistic history suggests individual interpretations that can readily be associated with the character of either genre.

It is most probable that the original ON word *Hakon*, with *Hacon* and *Hacun* as variations, developed into *Hagen* and also *Hagene*. Some linguists propose that the word *Hagen* is related to the early word *hagge* (OE – *haga*; ME – *hagge, hegge*) which was the feminine form of a noun that denoted an ugly or evil-looking person, one who was thought capable of wicked or contemptible acts, possibly an untamed, wild person, or a witch. This word survived in English as *hag* and the variation *haggard*, and in German as *hager* ("coarse," "uncultivated," or even "clumsy"). It is this depiction, that is as "The Vile One" or "The Coarse One," that seems best to relate to Wagner's son of Alberich. Others relate the ON *Hacon* to *hagr* which meant "useful," "deft," or "handy," a depiction that is not readily applicable to Wagner's Hagen.

There are those scholars who propose the name Hagen as an equivalent of OHG *hagustalt* or "man without a wife," possibly "vassal." There is also the possible relationship with OHG *hagupart* or "mask." Then, too, there are those who relate the name to a Swabian word *Hackel*, which translates as "boar," the animal that, according to Hagen of the *Ring* as well as he of *Thidrekssaga*, killed Siegfried.

The Icelandic name *Hogni* seems to be a derivation of ON *hogg*, which meant "blow" or "stroke." The references of this word to physical matters can readily be associated with this figure's participation in the incident of Siegfried's death, both in the literature as well as in the *Ring*. This name, however, was never used in continental Europe.

The name *Hagen*, however, should not be confused with *Haagan*, which was a Danish and Norwegian name that meant "high kin," and which, according to some scholars, is a descendant of *Hogano*, which translates roughly as "forest man" or "dweller in a grove."

HAMMER See: *Donner's Hammer* (Vol. I)

HEGELING See: *Sintolt, the Hegeling*

HELLA

The name *Hella*, a word frequently used in the Teutonic myths to refer to the mythical figure *Hel*, is found no less than three times in the *Ring*. Siegmund, in *Die Walküre*, says that he will not go to Valhalla because Sieglinde cannot travel there with him, in which case he prefers Hella. In *Siegfried*, Alberich warns Wanderer (Wotan) that once he has the ring again in his possession, he will use its powers to call up Hella's army, and together they will then conquer Valhalla, the Home of the Gods in the *Ring*. In the final music-drama, the drugged Siegfried, disguised as Gunther, penetrates the fire that surrounds the mountain top and confronts the terrified Brünnhilde who asks if he is one of Hella's army of the night. Wagner's use of the term *Hella* in each of the three scenes is correct mythical usage, and these scenes become yet more examples of the composer's correct and proper use of mythical terms and dramatic use of their functions.

In the myths of Teutondom, Hel, frequently referred to as Hella, is one of three monster offspring of Loki (Loge) and the giantess Angrboda. The others are Fenrir, the wolf, and Jormungandr. When Wotan learned of the potential dangers to the deities that these monsters could become, he ordered that each be prevented, in one way or another, from mingling among the gods or entering the Land of the Gods. Fearing the huge and powerful jaws of Fenrir, the gods bound him with the marvelous chain Gleipnir. Jormungandr was tossed into the waters of the oceans where he grew so big that ultimately his body encircled the world and he became known as Midgardsorm, or World Serpent.

Hel, whom some mythologists consider to be a goddess, was ordered to the netherworld. This was a land of total and permanent darkness that lay beneath one of the three roots of Yggdrasil, the World Ash Tree. It was here that Hel (Hella) would reside in her own hall which was "far from the sun," from which drops of venom fell, and around which serpents twined. It was from here that Hel would rule her kingdom. This world of darkness was regularly called *Hel*, after the figure that ruled there, although at least one Eddic poem calls this land Nastrond. At times, it was also called *Niflhel* ("Hell of Darkness"), and *Niflheim* ("Home of Darkness"). The inhabitants of Hel were the dead, that is, those mortals who had died but who had not met an heroic death in battle and therefore had not been selected by Wotan to be privileged to an afterlife in Valhalla. It was in Hel that the dead wandered about in the darkness, and the wicked and the evil underwent painful and agonizing torture. Hel (Hella) was thus both the figure who ruled over the Land of the Dead and that land itself.

Hel (Hella) had an army whose soldiers were these dead, and because these dead carried out their afterlife in the subterranean regions of the earth, that army was called *Army of Darkness* and *Army of the Night*. (Wagner causes his Brünnhilde to use those very words, "army of the night," when she is confronted by Siegfried who, in the guise of Gunther, arrives to take her as Gunther's wife.) Mythical beliefs held that at *ragnarök*, the fated day of destruction and defeat for the gods and the world that they had created, Hel (Hella) would gather her army and on a ship that would be captained by Loki (Loge), sail out from the north to the field of battle where that army would attack its enemies, the gods. (In The Final Battle, Fenrir the wolf would devour Wotan, and Donner would slay the World Serpent and then fall dead from the poisonous slaver that the serpent had breathed upon him.)

Hella, her function, and her netherworld play a significant role in the mythical beliefs of the early Teutonic peoples. This guardian of the dead and enemy of the gods, in her own way, is really as important to the total

Germanic religious thought as is, for example, Wotan himself. Wagner knew of Hella and her Hel, yet if she did not have an appropriate role in his *Ring* drama, certainly she could not be excluded from the total makeup of his mythical argument. The composer refers to her, and not once, but three times. He does not expand on her character, however, and neither does he give her any function within his story. Yet, in the few words that are included in his drama, in those words that single out this very important mythical figure, Wagner demonstrates the extension, and possibly also the profundity, of his knowledge of his culture's mythical past, and he further demonstrates his unique talent for bringing into his drama the significant aspects of his native culture, if even those details seem at times to be of a secondary tier of mythical matters.

HELLA (Name)

Hella, frequently called Hel, is the guardian of the dead in Hel. It would seem that there is no specific meaning to the name, or to its abbreviated form. Yet, conversely, the name Hel has firmly implanted itself in Christian religious thought in which this Hell resembles in numerous ways the Hel that was so foremost in the minds of the early Germanic peoples. Suffice to say that the Teutonic Hel cannot be defined, only interpreted.

HELMWIGE See: *Valkyries*

HELMWIGE (Name)

The modern German word *Helm* (ON – *hjalmr*; OE – *helan*; ME – *helmen*; Goth – *hilms*) used here by Wagner as the prefix for this Valkyrie's name, is best translated into English as "helmet." The archaic term "helm" is used occasionally, most often in poetry. The word is preserved in the popular masculine name *Helmut* ("Helmet Courage"). (At one time, the English verb that derived from the ON original term meant "to hide" in the sense of "to cover with a helmet.")

The suffix of this name, *wige*, is a variation of the modern German *Weg*, a word that is akin to English "way" in the sense of "road" or "thoroughfare." (The galaxy known in English as "The Milky Way" was called *Wotan's Weg* by the early Germanic peoples.)

The two parts of the name Helmwige, when joined, produce a word that can best be translated as *Helmet Way*. If such a meaning stimulates some semantic ambiguity, perhaps further interpretation is in order. The concept inspired by the original words seems to depict a roadway that is paved, or at least lain, with the helmets of battle soldiers. In that light, the name Helmet Way seems to be an appropriate name for Wagner's Valkyrie.

HEROES

The early Teutonic concept of *hero*, the ideas concerning the *hero*, and the mythical factors associated with the *hero* are fundamental to a full understanding of certain matters that Wagner included in his *Ring* drama. Throughout those sections of the drama in which Siegfried has a role, the Volsung is spoken of, and frequently referred to, and even addressed as *Held* ("hero"). Although it is probable that the word 'hero' has little semantic force in modern cultures whose first language is English, the word, as used in documents that date from the Middle Ages through the Romantic period of the early nineteenth century, was as fundamental to the societies in which it was used as were such other words as *King*, *Queen*, *Lord*, and even *God*. Wagner, always desirous that his poem reflect the ambience of a distant era of the past, swayed naturally toward use of the word *Held*, but always in a manner that was correct and appropriate for both the scene and the activity involved.

The word *Held* developed in German from ON – *halr*, which became AS – *haele*, OHG – *Halid*, and MHG – *Helet*. In its original semantic uses the term denoted a man of outstanding courage who accomplished feats that were just beyond the capacity of ordinary humans. Thus it was that matters of regular life, matters of every day, were the concern of rulers, such as kings, and men (noblemen), while "heroic" matters always were dealings between the divine ones, that is, the gods, and men. The matters that evolved when the hero was part of the situation always dealt with battle and combat of some kind, and combat that resulted in victory for the hero.

The early Teutonic societies held that all families of heroes originated with Wotan (Odin). Thus it is that Siegfried, at least in the northern or Nordic cultures, is shown to be a direct descendant of the Supreme God. As the genealogical chart that prefaces *Volsungasaga* reveals, Siegfried is the son of Siegmund, who is the son of Volsung, who is the son of Rerir, who is the son of Sigi, who is the son of Wotan! The relationship in this case is also linguistic: *Sigi* > *Sigimunt* > *Sigifrit*.

The ancient Teutonic peoples, that is, those who existed throughout the extensive Germanic regions prior to the advent of Christianity, readily accepted the concept of man made in a god's image. This belief was especially strong when the mortal involved was a 'hero.' The belief held that the hero was a human in human form, but that he had been created in the image of Wotan, and that hero, like all others, went about in the universe either as a Wotanic man or as a humanized Wotan. The Grimm brothers, Jakob and Wilhelm, the formidable team of nineteenth-century German scholars that essentially gave credence to the concepts and beliefs regarding German heroes, did much in their voluminous writings to make known such an idea and to assure its understanding.

The heroes of that ancient Teutonic era were recognizably human in form. They were not like some heroes and some gods of other cultures in that they had several limbs or numerous heads or several eyes. These Germanic heroes, however, could suffer handicaps or disabilities, like their gods. One hero who is not a part of the Volsung clan, Hagano, had but one eye, like Wotan. Another hero, Walthari, had but one hand, like the god Tyr.

Gunthari was lame, as was Loge, and Mayare was blind, as was the god Hod, son of Wotan and Fricka.

Teutonic heroes were usually formidable in their stature. They were like all other mortals in general shape and size, but that shape and size was just sufficiently beyond those physical characteristics of regular and normal humans. This size was indicative of their anomalous, often supernatural qualities, and to accompany this factor of size, there was always a special sheen and glimmer, or glint, that was present in their eyes. (Curiously, the heroes of Teutondom usually had names that were compound words, with both the prefix and the suffix having specific meanings. This matter of compound names for heroes was just the opposite of the names of the Teutonic gods whose names may have been bi- or multi-syllabic, but were regularly simple words.)

There was one additional factor of major importance that was regularly associated with the Teutonic hero. In the main, the Teutonic hero had not had a normal birth, that is, he was frequently cut from the womb of his mother, who then died. At such time as the hero had experienced a normal birth, the mother usually died shortly after giving birth. Either form of birth regularly left the hero motherless, which often became a matter of concern in the hero's later life.

There can be no question regarding Wagner's keen awareness of the several criteria that were necessary in the makeup of the Germanic hero. The Siegfried that the composer made a part of his *Ring*, and to a lesser extent his Siegmund, are dramatic examples of the hero that developed out of the heathen Teutonic mind. By means of dialogue and dramatic actions, Wagner made certain that these mythical criteria were part and parcel of his Volsung clan, and the application of these criteria would be another of the techniques that he would use in order to bring to his work the aura and ambience of a mythical past.

Wagner's dramatization of mythically correct heroic qualities in his pair of Volsungs, and especially in his Siegfried, was mythically possible because the composer satisfied one of the primary criteria necessary to the early Teutonic concept of 'hero.' Both Siegmund and Siegfried are direct descendants of the Supreme God. While it is true that the Nordic version of the Siegfried legend also causes Siegmund and his son Siegfried to be descendants of the god Wotan, Wagner makes a slight rearrangement of that relationship, one that will contribute to the dramatic continuity of his poem and, at the same time, make more substantive and pertinent the relationship of god and hero. Wagner's Siegmund and Siegfried are the son and grandson of the god, respectively, rather than the great grandson and the great, great grandson that they are in mythical thought and as shown in *Volsungasaga*. Wagner's closely woven relationship is then viewed more in detail within the framework of the drama itself, with the revelation that the relationship of god and men came about because of Wotan's union with mortal woman, which, of course, places Siegmund's divinity and his mortality in an equal setting. Wagner's arrangement of this foundation for the existence of a hero is most obviously the application of the mythical concept, but it is also an application that is made most ideal by the simple technique of having all the parties involved in the argument and present in the drama, either in person or by designation.

Wagner does not allow the mythical basis for the existence of a hero to be the only factor to be associated with his two heroes, Siegfried and Siegmund. The dramatist was careful to display in his heroic duo the catalogue of characteristics that was mythically associated with the early Teutonic hero. First and foremost among these mythical qualities was the hero's fearlessness. Siegfried, as well as his father Siegmund, are both courageous, essentially fearless men. It is Siegmund who is unafraid as he defends Sieglinde and rejects all that the supernatural Brünnhilde tells him about an afterlife in Valhalla. It is Siegfried who seeks out, confronts, and slays a dragon, a deed rather uncharacteristic of mere mortal courage. It is this same Siegfried who fearlessly penetrates the flames of a fire-girted mountain, not once but twice. Wagner even attempts to make his Siegfried the unique hero by endowing him with a nature that knew absolutely nothing of the meaning of fear, or of fear itself, a matter that the composer then threads into the development and unfolding of the *Ring* plot.

As Wagner guided his father and son through their respective heroic paces, he was ever mindful of the nature of the activities in which they were involved. Like the activities of Teutonic heroes of another time, Wagner's pair, and especially his Siegfried, carried out actions that were not representative of activities that occurred and evolved between one mortal man and another. Rather, the activities of the pair were such that in one way or another they had an association with the gods of Teutondom, and if not with the gods themselves, then with supernaturals of the divine universe. It is, after all, Wotan who thrusts the sword into the trunk of a tree, to give his son a weapon in the hour of his greatest need. It is, then, only Siegmund, of the many who tried, who is able to withdraw that sword. It is Brünnhilde, the Valkyrie who seeks to aid the brother-sister pair in their plight. It is Siegfried who is raised by a Nibelung dwarf. It is also this Volsung youth who woos Brünnhilde after she has been kissed into mortality. It is also Siegfried who masters a Valkyrie's horse, Grane, the mortal who uses the Tarnhelm to assume another's form, the hero who uses that same Tarnhelm to transport himself immediately from one place to another. It is also this same hero who cavorts with the nixie daughters of the Rhine. This mortal-divine relationship, so frequently displayed in the drama, had really reached its dramatic apogee when Siegfried met face to face with the Supreme God of Teutondom, and then fearlessly pushed the Allfather of the Teutonic people aside as he let himself be guided to a mountain that was surrounded by fire by a forest bird whose language he understood!

Wagner made dramatically clear one remaining major aspect that figures in the makeup of the early Germanic 'hero.' That factor, if such it can be called, is the matter of Siegfried's birth. By means of the dialogue in the first act of *Siegfried*, Mime finally reveals that Siegfried's mother died while giving birth to the hero. This matter becomes of some importance to the motherless hero who often expresses his dislike for the dwarf who would like to have Siegfried accept him as both father and mother, the youth who wonders what his mother was like, and who repeatedly asks that he be told about her. Wagner makes much of this mythical criterion that pertains to a hero's birth and which figures so prominently in the list of 'hero' qualities that dominated heathen Teutonic culture, and it is to his creative credit that he was able to weave the matter into his argument, not merely as just another mythical fragment, but as a matter of serious dramatic concern.

Wagner's duo of heroes, the father and son of Teutonic myth and legend, behave and conduct themselves like the Germanic heroes that they represent. Wagner obviously takes full advantage of the several concepts that early Teutonic peoples associated with heroes, and his Siegmund and his Siegfried become remarkable dramatic clones of the Teutonic heroes that made their way through the minds and the thoughts of those who made Wotan their Supreme God. It is of no consequence that Wagner did not endow his descendants of Wotan with superior physical stature, perhaps because he also had made integral to his argument the giants Fafner and Fasolt, and neither does his drama suffer any thematic weakness because he did not cause his heroes to suffer any disability, however slight, perhaps because the culture of his own day seemed to look askance at less than a total human condition. Of course, he had no worry regarding the names that he attached to them. The compound names that he used were part of the Teutonic past, and he found it necessary only to use the German form in preference to the Nordic terms.

There was, however, one final criterion that concerned the hero and which came into play in the Teutonic past, one which Wagner quite discreetly made very dramatically real. It would seem that Wagner had no wish to be faulted regarding the total makeup of his most legendary figures, and, therefore, he made thematically evident, as well as dramatically significant, that last, and probably weakest, of the heroic qualities. Ancient Teutonic concepts held that heroes *always* possessed only the most intelligent horses! Such a concept, minor though it may seem, was paramount in the total depiction of the hero because at times it became the animal whose actions actually determined the outcome of a given situation. The heroic stories and tales are replete with such situations. Yet, Wagner's Siegmund had no horse! Neither did the more significant hero of the *Ring*, Siegfried! Although it may be argued that there was no thematic need that the Volsung hero of the *Ring* possess such an animal, Wagner, ever the Teutonic mythologist, deemed it necessary that at least his Siegfried should have a horse, and what better animal than the very horse that had been his in myth and legend, Grane. So it is that Grane, the swift, strong, loyal, and wise animal that was second in the mythical universe only to Sleipnir, the horse of the Allfather, comes into the hero's hands, the gift to him from his bride. But again, as he had done so often before, Wagner takes advantage of all aspects of his source material, and in the case of Grane, he uses the animal not simply as Siegfried's horse, but in a twofold manner, exploiting the heroic qualities in both cases. The horse Grane, in the *Ring*, belongs to Brünnhilde. The animal has served her well, and is her great pride as he so often carried her and her cargo between Earth and the celestial fortress Valhalla. As a supernatural, Brünnhilde could only have ridden what was a supernatural horse. When, however, the daughter of Wotan is made mortal, when her divine qualities no longer serve her, her need of a divine animal is no longer paramount, even though Grane remains loyal to her and stays by her side. What better gift to her Siegfried, as he sets out to seek new heroic adventures, than a horse befitting the hero. Grane thus becomes Brünnhilde's wedding gift to Siegfried, somewhat in exchange for the ring that he has given her. This arrangement in which Grane first belongs to Brünnhilde and then to Siegfried is of Wagner's own doing. Yet, in his arrangement of this situation, with the supporting dialogue that pertains to the horse, he has really used the mythical Grane to serve a double purpose, and in so doing, to convey a mythical value that is greatly intensified, almost to the point that Grane might well figure among the *dramatis personae* of his drama.

There can be no question, once Wagner's Siegfried and Siegmund are compared to the heroic concepts that were part of the heathen Teutonic thought, that it would be readily shown that the composer followed the concepts of the Teutonic past in great detail. If he varied some aspects, if he made others less or perhaps more significant than those of Eddic times, if he made adaptations of the heroic quality within his argument, he was, nevertheless, essentially true to the Germanic mythical past, dramatically faithful to the Teutonic culture of another day. Wagner's "heroes" are indeed the "heroes" of the mythical and legendary past. It is only their activities that are distinct from those of an earlier Siegfried and Siegmund, and then, even those are quite frequently themselves part of the heroic tradition.

See also: *Siegfried, the Hero*

HOLDA See: *Freia* (Vol. II)

HOLDA (Name)

The name *Holda*, which Wagner associates with the goddess Freia, is represented in modern German by the adjective *hold* (fem. *holde*) which translates into English as "gracious," "friendly," "charming," "lovely," and "pleasing." Variations of this name are *Hulda*, *Halle*, and *Hulle*, and in some stories she is known as *Frau Holl*.

This popular figure from Germanic folklore is known in the Nordic regions as *Hulle*. In northern Teutondom, Hulle was associated with cattle, which she guarded while they grazed in the fields. The Nordic word *haldan* and the Old Icelandic *halda* meant "to graze" in the sense of leading cattle to pasture.

In the southern region of the Teutonic world, which included Germany, Holda had at least two distinct roles. In some locations, she was a wife who presided over the cultivation of flax, which she later used as she wove. In other regions she rode about in a wagon and caused the snow to fall. In all of continental Europe, Holda dressed in a blue garment and she wore a white veil. She was a fair, white lady, young and lovely to look at. Holda had a merciful spirit, a joyful nature, and she was given to song and music. It was believed that Holda could be seen at noon on pleasant days as she bathed in lakes and waterfalls, and one could reach her home by penetrating those waters.

Wagner's use of this name and figure from German folklore to be enmeshed with the gods of Teutonic mythology has been questioned frequently. There is no thematic reason for this action, and the only significance that the association of Holda and Freia has in the drama is one of providing the composer with an unusual but nevertheless pleasant assimilation of sounds.

See also: *Freia* (Vol. II)

HORN CALLS

The second act of the third drama of the *Ring* includes a brief scene in which Siegfried attempts to learn what a bird is saying. In order to communicate with the bird he carves a reed pipe (horn) from the stem of a nearby plant. When that action produces no results, Siegfried then turns to the silver horn that he wears at his waist. As the Volsung issues his horn calls, he admits that once he used this method to communicate with friends, to call friends to meet with him. Sorrowfully, Siegfried then adds that no friend answered his call, only a bear and a wolf. Without concern at this moment for Siegfried's success or lack of success in gathering friends together, by means of his horn call this son of Siegmund has voiced a prominent and much practiced activity that was very much a part of the ancient Teutonic societies' behavioral patterns.

Siegfried's horn calls represent a method of communication, primitive though it may be by modern standards, that was quite natural to the early Teutonic culture. History indicates that all early societies utilized some similar method to convey a message of some kind, or to indicate location. Wagner was not to be dramatically deprived of this cultural activity, the horn call. If indeed they were 'calls,' they were also physical acts with which he could work in musical terms.

There are no less than four situations in the *Ring* in which the generically named "horn call" becomes prominent. The first call was that of Siegfried and his attempt to communicate with Forest Bird. The second of Wagner's horn calls is to be heard in the second scene of the "Prelude" to *Götterdämmerung*. The Volsung has left his new bride, Brünnhilde, to seek new adventures. Brünnhilde, listens intently as Siegfried, now far below in the valley, sounds his horn to let all who may be in hearing distance know who he is and where he can be located. This call is followed in the second act of that drama by a call that is made by Hagen. This call, made on a steer horn, is one that signals urgency, and calls the Gibichung vassals together.

Hagen's call is returned by two similar calls which are made by the vassals as a signal to Hagen that they have received his message and are on their way to meet him. The fourth and final call of the *Ring* occurs in the last act of the fourth music-drama. There is a hunting party in the forest. Siegfried has become separated from Hagen and the other of the group. A horn call is heard in the distance as Hagen's group calls out in sound as to their location. Siegfried hears the call, and then answers with his own call. These two horn calls quickly allow the two groups to meet in a clearing of the woods. (There is yet another horn call that is part of the *Ring*, but it is not a call that is used or made in the manner as those others that have been mentioned. The call in question occurs in the first act of *Die Walküre*, and is made on an alpenhorn. The call serves as the musical announcement, or perhaps it may be termed a motive, of the pending arrival of Hunding.)

The matter of horn calls in the *Ring* may not be a subject that normally evokes extensive discussion when compared to numerous other themes that are available in that work. Yet, the matter becomes one of some consequence when placed in the creative sphere that Richard Wagner inhabited. It would seem that there are at least two basic reasons that justified the composer's use of such techniques, one which allowed dramatic results while the second became a matter of musicality. Firstly, it must be assumed that Wagner inserted the several horn calls into his drama as another of his many attempts to replicate a setting that projected an aspect of mythicalness. Such insertions, each thematically individual, are more than merely frequent in the drama, and it is basic knowledge that one of Wagner's most intense wishes was to create, in any way possible, a setting that truly reflected the primitive timelessness that myth offered. The literature that he had studied so assiduously over the years, especially *Nibelungenlied* and *Volsungasaga*, had included horn calls essentially as a matter of regular routine in the conduct of affairs. The calls in those works are several in number, and each receives a remarkably sufficient depiction as well as description. Wagner was aware of these calls and he understood their fundamental utilitarian purposes within the society they served. There could be no doubt in his mind of the societal and cultural significance of such calls, that these calls were an integral part of the mythical and legendary process, and as such they had their dramatic place in his poem.

The second of Wagner's justifications for the use of horn calls became a ramification of his concept of the dramas that he was composing. He refused to call his works *opera*, rather they were *music-dramas*. As such, dialogue and music were to function as a single medium, and Wagner obviously saw the horn calls as musical matters that could also convey the meaning of the words with which each was associated. In Wagner's creative mind, therefore such calls could also have thematic status. Wagner thus viewed these horn calls as something more than mere musical notes. Even the least musical of the several horn calls that he included in the *Ring*, that made by Hagen on a steer horn, and a response made by Gibichung vassals on two similar instruments, was made musical by Wagner's unique tonal instructions. His orchestration for this situation specifically called for steer horns (cowhorns), which are hardly a musical instrument as instruments are regularly viewed. Yet, he also directed that these animal horns, be *tuned*, that the notes that they issued were to be C, D, and D flat!

Wagner made the matter of horn calls in the *Ring* more than mere incidental orchestral sounds, or busy stage work. It was because of his desire as well as ability to make words and music function as one medium, that his horn calls became a musical message. The musical aspects were present, to be heard at the proper time. Yet, those sounds also conveyed the semantic substance of the words that were part of the dialogue, or if not the full meaning of the words, then certainly the meaning that the dramatic situation offered. In either case, Wagner's horn calls may be understood as music as well as dramatic situation.

HORSES

The horse was, without question, the most important animal in the era of the early Teutonic tribes and clans. In addition to the many stories and tales that abounded in the culture in which the horse played a major role, this creature also received ample mention in the myths, legends, and sagas of these peoples. In *The Poetic Edda* alone there are no less than twenty-six horses called by name!

Most of the gods of the Germanic mythical world were the owners of horses. These animals were their principal means of transport. The gods rode their horses across the Rainbow Bridge each day in order to travel to the World Ash Tree, beneath which they met in council and made their decisions regarding the world. These horses are named in the verses of *The Poetic Edda.*

The Valkyries of the Teutonic supernatural world also had horses. It was by means of these animals that the warrior-maidens rode through the heavens and carried select fallen heroes from the field of battle where they had died to their new celestial dwelling, Valhalla. (It was believed that the sweat that fell to earth from the manes of the Valkyries' horses as they sped through the world with their heavy loads was the dew that came each day.) Wagner duplicates the physical aspect of heathen Germanic belief by causing each of the nine Valkyries of his *Ring* drama to possess and to ride a horse. The composer even gave names to three of these animals. There is *Grauen* and *Brauner*, and, of course the famed horse that belonged to Brünnhilde and which she presented to Siegfried as a wedding gift, *Grane.* (In the mythical literature, the horse Grane belongs to Siegfried and Brünnhilde's horse is named Vingskornir.)

The most celebrated horse of all Teutondom was that which belonged to the King of the Gods, Wotan. This horse was named *Sleipnir.* It had eight legs and could run through the air and over the seas faster than any other animal of the mythical world.

Sleipnir was the offspring of the stallion Svadilfari and the demigod Loki (Loge), who had changed himself into a mare. Svadilfari belonged to a giant who had made a pact with the gods to build a great building which he had to finish by a specific deadline if he was to be paid. The payment to the giant was to be the goddess Freia, the sun, and the moon. Svadilfari hauled the huge stones with which the giant performed his work. When it became apparent that the giant would meet the terms of his agreement, and that he would complete his work by the deadline, the gods became most concerned.

The deities did not wish to give the giant the agreed upon payment. They turned to Loki and accused him of involving them in this arrangement. Then, they threatened that if he did not come to their aid, he would suffer great harm. Loki feared the wrath of the angry gods. He turned himself into a mare, and then enticed Svadilfari away from the work site and into the forest. The result of that union was the horse Sleipnir, which became the property of Wotan.

Wagner's Wotan also rides a horse, the only god of the *Ring* to do so. Although this horse never becomes a part of the dramatic stage action, Wagner causes the matter to be known by means of dialogue that the Valkyries carry on as they meet at Valkyrie Rock. These battle maidens are quite excited, even fearful, as they tell of the frenzy and furor that Wotan is causing as he rides his horse at full speed, from the North. This action occurs at the opening of Act III of *Die Walküre*, as the angered god searches for Brünnhilde, to punish her for her disobedience of his command that she permit Hunding to win out and to live in his combat with Siegmund. Unlike Wotan's mythical horse, the gods' horse in Wagner's drama is unnamed.

There can be no doubt that Wagner was alert to the matter of the horse and its mythical role in the supernatural world of the early Teutonic peoples. In accordance with the major placements of these animals in the myths, he brought the horse into his drama and made it integral to his story. The appearance of the horse in the *Ring* is, in and of itself, a relatively insignificant factor. The matter has no bearing on the development of the tale. Yet, the inclusion of this animal, at the proper times and with the proper relationships, is another of the numerous mythical matters that sounds an important mythical tone in the total mythical ambience that is so evident throughout Wagner's lengthy work.

See also: *Grane*

———————————

HOYOTOHO (Hojotoho)

It is interesting as well as curious to note that the Valkyrie greeting of *Hoyotoho* that Wagner gives to his nine supernatural daughters is mythical in essence. This greeting, often called a *cry* as well as a *war cry*, is first used in the *Ring* drama by Brünnhilde as she makes her initial entrance, and then later by the other Valkyries as they pause at Valkyrie Rock on their journey to Valhalla with their fallen heroes.

The mythicalness of this greeting is found in several individual tales, although neither the word nor any equivalent finds its way into Eddic literature. In those tales in which the cry is used, it is shouted by the frenzied troops, possibly berserkers, of an army in its charge against an enemy. This cry is also shouted during the wild chase of The Furious Host (Das wütende Heer), that is, Wotan and his savage troops as they ride through the black of night. This same cry is heard in a slightly different form, *Hohotoho*, when it is shouted by a wild, raging hunter who rides a headless horse through the dark of a forest.

Wagner's use of the cry of The Furious Host is most significant. Heathen Teutonic beliefs made Wotan the leader of The Furious Host, and, therefore, the war cry itself is clearly associated with the Supreme God. It is indeed mythically possible, if not probable, that Wotan himself uttered this cry as he traveled about in the vast universe, as was his habit. Wagner accepts the cry in its German form, and then makes it synonymous with the Valkyries who in the *Ring* are associated with Wotan, not only because they are his Valkyries, but also because they are his daughters!

Wagner's use of this famous cry as a detail in the extensive panorama of his *Ring* drama is yet another of a myriad of examples that gives evidence of the careful attention that he gave to the mythical ambience of his poem. Wagner was most desirous of creating a seriously authentic mythical atmosphere that would envelop all that was to be his settings, his themes, and his figures and their actions. As can be understood through the war cry of his Valkyries, it was not only the major factors of the mythology that emerged from his creative pen.

See also: *Bear*

The Furious Host

HUNDING

It is most probable that of all the characters that Wagner placed in his *Ring* drama, that of Hunding became the most difficult to depict as well as to name. Such difficulty arose because the figure, as he is developed in the drama, has no prototype in Teutonic mythology or German legend, and the single figure that is called Hunding in Eddic literature is associated with Danish legends rather than with the German Siegfried tales.

The Poetic Edda contains three poems that are regularly known as the *Helgi* lays. These poems focus on Helgi the hero of Denmark and the nearby regions of the Baltic Sea. These works have their own sets of characters which function in their own environment and in their own ambience, untouched by the heroic stories that came out of Germany. These Helgi lays originated in Denmark, went northward into Norway, and then westward, where the works circulated throughout the islands. The inclusion of these poems as part of the Eddic depiction or interpretation of the Siegfried matter is a subject that has been of serious question literally since the discovery of the original Eddic manuscript, and yet today there is still much debate as to how these poems became associated with the Volsung tragedy.

Saxo Grammaticus, in his *Gesta Danorum*, a history of Denmark which he wrote in Latin sometime between 1200 and 1210, writes that Hunding was a celebrated Saxon king who ruled in Jutland. Certain verses in *The Poetic Edda* depict Hunding as a king of many lands, and then specifically state that he is the King of Hundland. Helgi enters the tale when he slays King Hunding, after which the latter's four sons seek to avenge their father's death. They, too, fall before the Danish hero.

It is at this point in the story that Helgi's association with the Volsung matter becomes apparent. Some verses of the Siegfried cycle of poems, as well as *Volsungasaga*, state that Helgi, along with Hamund, were sons of

Siegmund and his second wife Borghild. The grown Helgi had confronted King Hunding because he was a great enemy of Siegmund, and their two armed forces had fought many times. These two statements, succinct and unimposing as they are, represent the only words that tie Helgi and Hunding to the otherwise lengthy tale of Siegfried, and, of course, that relationship exists only in the Nordic version of the legend!

The Siegfried story now focuses on that aspect of the tale in which Siegmund now woos and weds Hjordis. King Lyngvi, a son of King Hunding, also desired to have Hjordis as wife. (This Lyngvi is not one of the four sons earlier slain by Helgi.) The angry Lyngvi now challenges Siegmund. As the two battle, an old man (Wotan) causes Siegmund's sword to break and Siegmund is mortally wounded by Lyngvi. As Siegmund lies dying, he tells his wife to save the pieces of the sword for their yet unborn son. Siegmund says that with the sword, the son will grow to become the greatest of heroes. The son of Siegmund and Hjordis is, of course, Siegfried, who is eventually given his father's sword with which he avenges his father's death by slaying Lyngvi. Again, these details, some of which will be familiar to followers of the *Ring*, belong to the northern version of the Siegfried matter, and have no counterparts in the southern or German story.

The character of Hunding, as found in the Eddic verses and the saga's prose is very much a secondary one. He has but a minor role in legendary matters, essentially that of serving as a kind of pivot around which other more significant matters are played out. Such, too, is the role of Hunding in Wagner's *Ring*. He is secondary to the Sieglinde-Siegmund segment of the story, yet he must be cast as somewhat of a dark figure, one who is suspicious of his wife's actions, yet not certain as to what he should do or how to accomplish the deed. The situation that Wagner brings to his drama, that is, the Hunding-Sieglinde-Siegmund trio, is of his own creation. In his search for that third party, the composer understood that he would be unable to make some prominent figure of the Volsung story into a Hunding, that he would be unable to bring into the role a figure whose poetic life was well projected in myth and legend. He needed a quiet figure, one who was a part of myth and legend, but yet one who lurked in the background and one whose actions represented the dark side of otherwise joyful situations.

Wagner's choice was opportune. The Hunding of Teutonic myth and legend met all the criteria that the composer had established. This Hunding was not a prominent figure of mythical tales, his role in the Siegfried cycle was most secondary, almost non-existent. This Hunding of myth was really a dark figure, perhaps even sinister in that he was a great enemy of the Volsung Siegmund. It is obvious that Wagner was unconcerned with Hunding's Danish origin and history, that he had been a king, and that his relationship with the Volsungs was tenuous at most. The Hunding of Danish myth would become the Hunding of the German *Ring*, holding sway in his own realm for but a relatively short period, under his own name, which perhaps gave Wagner another reason for his choice.

HUNDING (Name)

The name *Hunding* was a popular masculine name during the Middle Ages, after which time it fell into disfavor. (During the era of its popularity, related and acceptable nicknames were *Hundt* and *Hund*.)

The word that Wagner chose as the name of Sieglinde's husband offers at least two primary interpretations, one of which seems to be of more dramatic consequence than its companion. Both of these meanings utilize the regular understanding of the suffix *ing*, which, as explained in *Notes*, denotes "Child of" or "Offspring of."

The word of concern in this mortal's name is the prefix *Hund*, which can be approached from two distinct points of semantic view. The most popular route, as well as the most convenient, is to accept this word which is derived from ON *hundr* (OE – *hund*; Goth – *hunds*) and which meant "hunt" in OHG, and in modern German, "hound" or "dog." Combined with the suffix, the full name of Wagner's character then translates as "Son of a Dog." Such a translation, while at once semantically correct, is, nevertheless, derogatory in a societal sense and therefore, according to some followers of the *Ring*, is not appropriately applicable to the Hunding of Wagner's drama.

There is, however, a second view of *Hund* which seems to be more appropriate to the situation in the *Ring*. The word *Hund* now is *Hun*, a word that is not mired in the baseness of popular German speech, but rather reflects a concept that was developed early in Germanic history. This meaning, interpretation is perhaps a better word, relates *Hun* to the word *Hunne*, derived from late Latin *Hunni*, which is a generic term for a member of the Mongolian hordes who, under Attila, invaded and gained control of much of Europe in the fifth century. (Although there was the ON *Hunar* which gave OE *Hune* and *Hunas*, it is very possible that the modern German *Hunne* and its English equivalent English *Hun* are derived through medieval Latin from *Chuni*, which was the native name of those Asian people who were Chinese as *Hiong-Nu* and also as *Han*.) Those armies became known for their vicious, vandalistic activities that were carried out with formidable physical might. These warriors were looked upon as ill-tempered, ruthless fighters, as individuals much to be feared and avoided. The warrior of Attila's forces, the 'Hunne,' became synonymous with "raw power" and "brutal force." When the prefix Hun bears this concept, and it is combined with the suffix *ing*, with the transitional *d*, the name *Hunding* projects quite adequately the substance of such a concept. In this light, then, the Hunding of the *Ring* is, essentially, an unshackled, primitive strength, a power to be used for mastery and subjugation. It is in that metaphoric sense that Wagner's Hunding is very much the "Offspring of Power."

INCEST

The matter of *incest* is a regular topic of discussion among followers of the *Ring*. In the modern day, the term *incest* is usually understood to mean sexual intercourse between individuals who are closely related by blood, and between whom any marriage would be adjudged as illegal or forbidden by cultural or societal custom. The word in English is derived from the Latin neuter *incestum*, from *incestus*, a combination of *in* meaning "not," and *castus*, meaning "pure" or "chaste." The brother-sister twins in Wagner's drama, Siegmund and Sieglinde, are those against whom the charge of such unchasteness is routinely made.

Moralists of the modern day are quick to remind followers of Wagner's music-drama that the composer penned into his poem an incestuous relationship. There are among those followers those who condemn this relationship, which results in the birth of the hero Siegfried, and there are also those who attempt to defend Wagner's actions by means of the very mythology that gave the composer the basis and framework of his argument.

Those of the first group adhere strictly to the contemporary thought that revolves around the word *incest*. These individuals find that the act denoted by the term is a serious sin, a violation of the basic goodness of man, an act that breaches all codes of civil as well as religious conduct. Further, these followers also point out that an act of incest is illegal in most societies, that is, it is an act that can result in penal sentence, quite often one of some duration. Then, too, there is the sense of social embarrassment, a cultural rejection, even revulsion, that follows revelation of an act of incest.

It is not unusual for those who have studied the *Ring* as well as the sources from which the drama was derived to take a distinct tact. These forces will note that Wagner's *Ring* takes as its sources the ancient and heathen Teutonic thought that dominated that society in its time. It will be noted that in the earliest of those times the deities were regarded as bisexual. Loge, for example, turned himself into a mare in order to attract a stallion into a forest, a union that produced Sleipnir, the famed horse of the Supreme God Wotan, and in some tales the sire of the horse Grane. There also myths that relate that Freyr and Freyja, who became Wagner's Froh and Freia, were the children of Njorth and his sister, Nerthus. In the Eddic literature it is Loge who speaks of Njorth and his relationship with his sister, but a similar situation is supported in *Ynglingasaga*, a brief discussion of the gods by the Icelander Snorri Sturluson. At the Creation of the Universe, according to early Teutonic thought, Ymir, a male giant 'gave birth' to the first male and the first female. They emerged from the giant's left armpit. (Some scholars contend that Ymir's two offspring are Ask (Ash) and Embla (Elm), the first mortals of the universe, but other students of these myths maintain that the gods created Ask and Embla out of trees that they felled in the forest.) The giant Ymir also rubbed his feet together and produced a son who had six heads. In time, the Germanic gods became individual males and females, but the mythical thought continued to view the male and female deities as two segments of the same idea, counterparts, perhaps, of a single concept, and as such they were looked upon as brother-sister, and on occasion as husband-wife.

The relationship as brother and sister that Wagner gives to his Siegmund and Sieglinde was not one of his creation. It is true that he took the names for this duo from the German epic poem *Nibelungenlied*. However, it is to the Icelandic *Saga of the Volsungs* that he turned for most of the other matters that serve as dramatic foundation for the pair. It is in this saga that Siegmund and his sister are descendants of Volsung who, in turn, is a descendant of Wotan. It is in this saga that Siegmund's sister comes to him one night, and stays with him for three nights, and that a son was born of that union. That the saga names Siegmund's sister as Signy, and that the son is Sinfjotli rather than Siegfred, is of little importance in the matter at hand; the account does bring the brother-sister relationship to the fore, and without the stigma that would be attached to such a relationship were it a reality in later times.

Although Wagner accepted the mythical relationship of brother-sister, and allowed a son to be born of that union, it is perhaps true that he sensed a possible concern, however slight, that current audiences might express regarding such a depiction. There can be no doubt that the composer was aware of his society's modern thoughts regarding such a sexual union of brother and sister, yet, he was building his work with myth and legend, and in that light any such matter certainly was appropriate to his argument. Nevertheless, there seem to be at least three specific times in the drama, in addition to the totality of the dialogue that unites the pair, when Wagner attempts to soften the potential impact of the Siegmund-Sieglinde union, three bits of the dialogue that he may have included to give some substance to the thought that this relationship had at least a modern sheen of legality, even though that legality was mythical. In the final moments of the first act of *Die Walküre* Siegmund and Sieglinde declare their newly awakened mutual love, and, in their own way, profess their vows to each other. In the course of that dialogue, which alone satisfies the matter of legality in the eyes of some students of the *Ring*, Siegmund uses three words that speak to the matter of Sieglinde as his legal mate. First, he uses the word *Frau*, a term that is not a stranger to most persons who recognize the term as one that signifies a married woman, a 'Mrs.' Siegmund uses the term in that context, a married lady, and it is Sieglinde whom he calls his 'Frau.' Shortly after the utterance of that word, Siegmund uses another word that has somewhat the same meaning. The word is *Weib*, which in daily speech means 'woman,' but which is also a poetic term for *wife*. Twice, now, Siegmund has called Sieglinde his 'wife.' Then again, for a third time he refers to his sister as his wife, this time with yet another distinct word. Releasing the great joy that he has found his love and that he also has found the great sword that his father had promised him in the hour of his greatest need, Siegfried offers the sword to Sieglinde as his *Brautgabe*, literally a "gift to the bride." Mrs! Wife! Gift to the bride! Those specific and quite definite words which are all a part of a dialogue that either directly or metaphorically suggests 'vows,' 'fidelity,' and marriage!

Such action was, after all, that of marriage, in a day when legality and certificates and clergymen were unknown factors.

The relationship of Siegmund and Sieglinde occurs in a distant past, at a time that is primeval in the age of man. Given, then, the dialogue that Wagner gives to Siegmund, what more could have been done to accept his actions, as well as those of Sieglinde, as *marriage* in the full sense of the word? Wagner did all that was necessary, at least that which was necessary in accordance with his creative genius. Yet, there was always present the matter of the blood relationship, a brother-sister relationship which, despite the age in which that relationship occurs, is still to many of another day, a cultural taboo. It seems that there are those who would apply the standards of one age as the standards of a bygone time, or put in other terms, there are those who would accept the mythical standards of an ancient past at all time except when their current thought deems that such though should be rejected, a standard that can be accepted, so long as it pleases and sets the nominative person at ease.

Regardless of the shades of innocence or guilt that may be present in the scene from *Die Walküre*, the scene of the brother and sister and their declarations of love for each other, and the resultant sexual union, Wagner was satisfied with what he had composed, both in word and in sound. He was obviously a creative spirit that understood the human condition, and he was not about to violate the nature of a distant age simply because a society of another day did not agree with what he had brought into his drama. His Siegmund and Sieglinde remain brother and sister, husband and wife, parents of Siegfried, Volsungs, and children of the Allfather, Wotan!

INVULNERABILITY (Siegfried)

The matter of the invulnerability, of the hero Siegfried is more a subject of legend than it is of myth. In Nordic versions of the Siegfried story, which is spotlighted by *The Poetic Edda*, the major source of early Teutonic myths, and by *Volsungasaga*, which is essentially a prose paraphrase of the

Edda, Siegfried's invulnerability is not a factor in the hero's life. The invulnerability of the Siegfried that Wagner writes into his *Ring* drama is a theme that originated within the southern, that is, the German concept of the hero's adventures. In the opening segments of *Nibelungenlied*, the celebrated epic of the German people which dates from the early thirteenth century, Hagen tells how Siegfried slew a dragon (unnamed), and then bathed in the beast's blood. This blood caused Siegfried's skin to become so hard that no weapon could cut it. (In one version of the northern tale, the dragon's venom is spewed on Siegfried and in another it is the dragon's blood that spills down upon him. However, Siegfried had been advised to build a trench into which the blood could flow, and be carried away. In neither tale, however, is the aspect of invulnerability a factor.) Some time later in the German story, when Hagen plots the death of the champion, he swears to Siegfried's wife, Kriemhild, that he wishes to protect Siegfried and asks her how he can shelter the Nibelung from attack. (In this work Siegfried is a Nibelung because he conquered the two Nibelung brothers and took their great treasure for himself.) Kriemhild believes that Hagen is a friend and explains that as the dragon's blood flowed over Siegfried's body, a leaf from a linden tree floated down and lodged itself on his back, between his shoulder blades, effectively prohibiting the blood from reaching that skin under the leaf. It was that spot that was beneath the leaf that was the one place on the hero's body that was vulnerable to weapons. The remainder of Siegfried's body was invulnerable to any weapon. Hagen then asks Siegfried's wife to sew a piece of cloth on the hero's clothing so that he will know where he must guard him when they are in battle. Kriemhild complies with Hagen's request.

Kriemhild's words to Hagen, and later her compliance with his request that she signal Siegfried's only vulnerable spot, proved to be the factor that allowed for the untimely death of the champion. Siegfried, Hagen, Gunther, and their vassals go on a hunting party. The group stops in the forest, to rest and to refresh itself. Hagen has brought no wine, and therefore the hunters must go to a stream that is nearby, to drink. Gunther and Siegfried decide to race to the stream. Siegfried wins the race, but then as he bends to drink, his back is exposed, and it is at that instant that Hagen thrusts his spear into the one vulnerable spot on Siegfried's body. (The

Northern versions of Siegfried's death have the hero in bed, asleep, when he is fatally stabbed by a drugged brother of Gunther and Hagen. Although one of the Eddic poems debates whether Siegfried was slain out of doors or in his dwelling, the debate is neither lengthy nor convincing, and the northern myths continue to make reference to Siegfried's death as one that occurred while he was asleep.)

The manner in which Siegfried achieved his invulnerability in *Nibelungenlied* is essentially duplicated in *Thidrekssaga*. This latter work, which is also titled *The Wilkina Saga*, has some content that deals with Siegfried, although the major theme of the work is an account of the exploits and adventures of Theodoric the Great (454-526), ruler of the Ostrogoths from 475, and king of the Romans from 493. Theodoric is known in German as Dietrich von Bern, the latter part of his name derived from the name of one of his two capitals. Dietrich appears in *Nibelungenlied*, and it is he who conquers Siegfried's murderer Hagen and then delivers him to the hero's vengeful wife Kriemhild. In this saga, Siegfried kills Regin, the dragon, and then bathes in the animal's blood, which makes his skin become hard, like horn. Siegfried is able to place the blood over his entire body except in the one place his hands cannot reach, between his shoulders. Siegfried's body thus becomes invulnerable to weapons, all of his body, that is, except that small spot on his back.

The account of Siegfried's invulnerability remained quite popular in the tales of Siegfried that circulated in continental Teutondom. A manuscript that dates from 1472 is titled *Lied von hürnen Seyfrid* (*Song of the Horned-Skinned Siegfried*). Hans Sachs, a prolific writer on the sixteenth century and whose figure appears in Wagner's *Die Meistersinger von Nürnberg*, composed a seven-act tragedy that he titled *Der hürnen Seufrid* (*The Horn-Skinned Siegfried*). F de la Motte-Fouqué, perhaps the most widely read romantic of his day, titled the first of his many Siegfried sketches *Der gehörnte Siegfried in der Schmied* (*The Horned-Skinned Siegfried in the Smithy*). Seven years later, in 1810, this sketch became a part of the author's trilogy of plays that he titled *Der Held des Norden* (*The Hero of the North*).

The matter of Siegfried's bathing in the dragon's blood and the effect that this incident has upon the physical character of Siegfried had not escaped Wagner's dramatic eye. It is obvious that he sensed that the concept of invulnerability to injury or death from weapons was vital to his dramatic picture of his Siegfried. The concept was fundamental to any figure who was to be not merely a hero, but a national hero, and the major literary pieces of his culture had made heavy note of this aspect of Germany's legendary hero. Thus, the composer caused his Siegfried to become invulnerable to weapons and, like the legends of old, over most of his body. What is distinct in Wagner's version, however, is the manner that the composer chose to effect the invulnerability of his hero, rather than drawing on the popular idea that Siegfried bathed in the blood of a dragon that he had slain.

The scene in which Wagner divulged the matter of Siegfried's invulnerability is the last one of the second act of Götterdämmerung. Brünnhilde has been handed over to Gunther by the disguised Siegfried who took her by force from her mountain top. The former Valkyrie is offended, embarrassed, and greatly angered by all that has happened to her, including the supposed unfaithfulness of Siegfried through his new relationship with Gunther's sister, Gutrune. She pleads that someone come to her aid. The scheming Hagen taunts Brünnhilde, and he then tempts her to action by stating that she can trust him, and that he will avenge her shame, her loss of honor. Brünnhilde defends Siegfried when she tells Hagen that one look from the Volsung's eyes would frighten him no end. Hagen then asks Brünnhilde to reveal the magic spell that will weaken the brave hero. In her anger and because she seems to trust Hagen, much as Kriemhild trusted Hagen in *Nibelungenlied*, Brünnhilde then reveals the secret of Siegfried's vulnerability.

Siegfried's invulnerability came about through the divine magic of Brünnhilde, when she was a Valkyrie, before she was changed into a mortal woman. She tells the evil Hagen that she used her skills in magic to protect the hero from any wound, so long as you did not attack him from the back. She reveals that when she gave Siegfried her protection, she gave it to him for only the front of his body, not the back part. Her unique action in this regard was because she knew that Siegfried's bravery was such that he would never turn his back to a foe. Thus, Wagner's Siegfried has the invulnerability of old, but the protection that he also enjoys does not include any part of his back, unlike that small part of the legendary hero's body that was not covered with dragon's blood. At last, now, Wagner's Hagen has learned where he must send his spear to kill Siegfried, an action that he will take in the last act of the tetralogy of the *Ring*.

Wagner obviously complied with the demand from myth that Siegfried be essentially invulnerable to weapons. Wagner's method of achieving that state differs from the mythical actions, but it would seem that Brünnhilde's explanation makes the Volsung into a braver and more valiant individual than his counterpart in myth, simply by the fact that he is so brave that he would never turn his back and flee from a foe. Yet, it is also true that Wagner made no effort to emphasize this aspect of the hero's figure. It appears that he was satisfied with the nature and character of his Volsung as he had depicted him, and as he made his way through the other mythical matters that contributed more substance in the argument of the drama.

See also: *Dragon*

IRMING See: *Wittig, the Irming*

-K-

KISS

The final scene of *Die Walküre* is often regarded as one of the most sincerely touching, one of the most compassionate scenes of the *Ring*, and indeed of all musical masterpieces. It is in this scene that Wotan, ever the Allfather, deems that he must punish his favorite daughter, Brünnhilde, because she disobeyed his command that she not give her supernatural protection to Siegmund in his struggle with Hunding. The scene develops to an intense climax as the daughter explains to her father that it was not a command that she disobeyed, but rather his will that she fulfilled. The god stands firm in the matter of Brünnhilde's punishment, even though his decision is one that strains at his personal love for this Valkyrie daughter. The god tells Brünnhilde's that he will put her into a deep sleep, and as he softens his initial harshness, he states that he will accede to her request that he surround her rock with fire in order that it will be only a mortal who does not know the meaning of fear who will brave the flames, then awaken her and take her as his wife. Wotan then slowly approaches his daughter and gently kisses her on the forehead. This action of the god, that is, the kiss, is one that places his daughter into a deep sleep and, at the same time, takes from her all supernatural qualities that she possessed as a Valkyrie. The god then calls to Loge, God of Fire, and orders that the mountain be girded by flames. Brünnhilde now sleeps as a mortal and will eventually be awakened from the sleep by the fearless Siegfried.

Much of this scene between Wotan and Brünnhilde that Wagner wrote into this part of his *Ring* was inspired by almost identical scenes in two of the poems of *The Poetic Edda*. However, the act of a kiss to cause the Valkyrie to fall into her sleep and to take away her godhood is a dramatic device that originated with Wagner, and is not to be found in this mythical literature. It would seem certain that the composer, versed as he was in the mythical and legendary matters of the Germanic past, was aware of the beliefs that the ancient people had regarding the use of one's lips to produce a kiss. Among other beliefs, the concepts of that early day held that a kiss, in and of itself, held great powers. At times, a kiss could place the recipient in a state of complete forgetfulness, or it could revive forgotten memories or remembrances. A kiss could cause one to enter a stuporous state, much like that produced by the sweet fragrance of the blossoms of the linden tree. A kiss could also intensify the emotional state, and thereby cause one to sense a personal satisfaction in all things, a state in which no evil would be perceived. It was not, however, a kiss that caused one to enter into a deep sleep.

Germanic beliefs held that Wotan, the Supreme God of the Teutonic world, had powers to perform any task that he desired. In many situations he merely had *to wish* a matter, and it was realized! It was therefore mythically possible that Wagner's god could have accomplished the desired action upon Brünnhilde with only a wish, or by the simple mythical desire that a kiss produce the same result. However, Teutonic mythical beliefs regarding the divine act of causing one to fall into a sleep were quite specific and included neither a 'wish' nor a 'kiss.' In the Eddic literature, it is Wotan who places his daughter into a sleep because of her disobedience of his command, and to achieve that sleep, he pricks her with a *sleep-thorn*. This dramatic property, which is possessed by Wotan who alone among the gods is able 'to work' its powers, is not further described as to kind or species of thorn, as are such other items of nature as the World Ash Tree, the linden tree, the fir tree, and others. The sleep-thorn is mentioned several times in the Eddic poetry, but Wotan limits its use to Brünnhilde. As a matter of cultural history, however, it was believed that some of the *volvas*, the seeresses or wise-women of early Teutonic days, were able to work the sleep-thorn, although in religious thought its magic was the privilege of only the Supreme God.

Wagner never discussed his reasons for the substitution of a kiss for the mythical sleep-thorn. Neither did he make any mention of the matter in his extensive writings. It seems reasonable to conclude, however, that the composer felt the kiss, more than a sleep-thorn, conveyed more of the emotional ambience that he wished to create with this father-daughter relationship. It is also possible, if not probable, that Wagner sensed that his scene was really one that could be more easily developed, understood, and appreciated as a mortal rather than as a divine or mythical matter, in which case the kiss between father and daughter would be more readily accepted than any magic that a sleep-thorn might have. Regardless of what were or were not Wagner's reasons for the details of this scene, the final moments of this music-drama remain one of the most memorable of the *Ring* drama.

(Curiously, Brünnhilde is also awakened from her sleep by a kiss. Now, however, the kiss is from Siegfried, a mortal, and the kiss is therefore a kiss which, in the heathen thought of the early Germanic peoples, carries no special magic.)

See also: *Fear*

KNOWLEDGE See: *Brünnhilde's Wisdom*

-L-

LANGUAGE See: *Bird Language*

Language (of the Ring)

LANGUAGE (of the *Ring*)

In 1853 Wagner invited a group of select friends to read his recently completed poem, *Der Ring des Nibelungen*. Each of these individuals was well acquainted with the arts of the day, and each had a special attraction to the world of music as well as an extensive knowledge of *opera*. The results of this activity, that is, the reactions of the readers, were not exactly what Wagner had expected or anticipated. Indeed, these reactions were something more than he ever could have deemed possible. The readers of Wagner's poem expressed puzzlement at what they had read. They said that they could not understand how Wagner's work could ever serve as a libretto for opera. They related that this drama of the Nibelungs and the Volsung Siegfried could never be sung, that none of the dialogue could be put to melody, and that whatever music that was composed to accompany the verses could never be orchestrated!

Wagner had erred in one crucial way. Each of his readers was indeed quite knowledgeable in the field of music and opera, but that knowledge was deeply embedded in the style of opera that was the popular form of the day, the Italian, and to a lesser degree, the French. The libretto that Wagner had placed in the hands of his readers, that is, the poem of the *Ring*, was not only outwardly dissimilar in content to the popular and successful operatic stories of the day, but the poetic style, the language in which he had developed his argument had none of the linguistic characteristics that the libretti of the popular operas of the day boasted, none of the poetic attributes with which his readers were familiar and by means of which they were prepared to make reasoned judgment. Wagner's readers had never before encountered the kind of libretto that the composer had prepared, and that newness, that strangeness, that deviation from the standard of the time obviously stirred within them a negative reaction!

Those who had judged Wagner's poem were emotionally and intellectually comfortable with and adjusted to the major characteristics of the standard libretto that served Italian Opera. These attributes were six in number:

1. The verse line was relatively long.

2. The end words usually rhymed, and that rhyme was usually masculine, although it is rather extensively known that Verdi constantly requested his librettist that he be given "feminine vowels."

3. The metaphor of the poetry was regularly of a romantic type.

4. Standard grammatical and syntactical language structures were expected.

5. The vocabulary of a libretto was contemporary to its day.

6. A libretto should contain frequent repetition of words, phrases, and lines.

Wagner's poem boasted none of the six major characteristics of the dialogue of an opera, or at least none of those linguistic characteristics that were prominent in the Italian opera of the day, and which were deemed necessary for any operatic work to enjoy a critical as well as a popular success.

Wagner immediately set about to defend his work. In mid-1853 he wrote a letter in which he supported his poetry by discussing the low level in which the poetry of the day found itself. The essence of his ideas affirmed that modern poetry had now developed its own artform, its own manner of artistic expression, and that form and that expression had become so accepted in his time that poetry was now unquestionably divorced from music. Poetry and music, he continued, now had little concern for each other, and each now went its own artistic way. This separation of poetry and music was, in his mind, especially noticeable when the poetry was intended to represent human speech, which, of course, was the primary linguistic demand in opera. Wagner also maintained that there was a naturalness in human speech, and that naturalness must also be present in opera, if the operatic work was to be effective. Wagner then concluded that if naturalness of speech is to be realized in opera, the poetry that represents that human speech must not be limited or bound by fixed and rigid rules of language. Wagner's defense of his *Ring* poem, at least his defense of the language in which he had created the poem, was an outright rejection of all language standards that had enveloped the opera of his day, because, as he staunchly maintained, he was not writing simply *opera*, rather he had written *drama*, and this *drama*, eventually would be joined with a *music* that he would compose specifically for that drama, and together this drama and this music would be *music-drama*.

Wagner was not unaware of the importance of language in any dramatic work. He had read and had studied carefully the *Edda* and associated Teutonic myths and legends, not only their content but also the language in which they had been recorded. He readily understood how each was far removed from the counterparts that were present in his day. He was convinced that myth and mythical thought were far removed from contemporary society and manners, and therefore a mythical dramatic work could not be presented in the language of that contemporary society. He also believed that it was impossible to present the antiquity of his *Ring* theme in any combination of ancient and modern language, that such a language would be, at best, contrived, and would dilute the universality that was to be found in myth into dramatic trivia that he believed 19th-century opera to be.

Wagner had given special note to what can be termed *divine language*. The terminology *divine language*, as used here, refers to that language specific to the gods and other supernaturals of heathen Teutondom, that language with which those figures communicated with each other as well as with those of other regions of the mythical universe, particularly the communication of the divine ones with the mortals of earth. Wagner was aware of the manner in which the Eddic literature had generated an overall language for the myths, and specifically a language for the supernaturals. He understood also that those linguistic characteristics had been really matters that the early Germanic culture had conceived. Yet, as he studied the distinctiveness of that language, and as he pondered how that language had set the gods apart, both from man as well as from other supernaturals of the mythical universe, he understood the difference of that speech, a difference that, in its own manner, created a striking, yet expressive metaphor. He was somewhat intrigued by this speech. As his mind developed the story of gods and dwarfs and giants, he was obviously cognizant that theirs was a world far removed from the reality of his day. Yet, he also understood that that world of old, at least the concepts that had conceived that world, had been the cultural parent of much that was to be found in his contemporary society. Wagner also understood equally well that the story of that ancient world had been told in a language equally removed from that of his times, but in a language that had been the *linguistic* parent of his modern German. He concluded, then, that he must tell his tale in a language that bespoke the language of the gods, a language that conveyed convincingly a sense of Teutonic antiquity, a language that imparted the nature of myth, but which, at the same time, was a language that was recognizable and acceptable to an audience of his day! It must also be a language that would mirror the naturalness of speech, and it must also be a language that lent itself readily to expression in music.

Wagner gave much thought to "language" as he made his way through the mythical literature that served him as source material. In time, he determined that the *poetic* structure of his drama would be *Stabreim*, a verse form that was popular in early (fourteenth-century) German and English cultures, but nevertheless, a from that had long faded from the poetic scene. Wagner's idea was to present his story in a verse form that had indeed once existed and which numerous scholars would recognize immediately, a language which, at the same time, would be understood by an audience, yet be distant enough to allow that audience to believe that just perhaps it was indeed *divine language*.

Wagner felt that the Stabreim verse form would satisfy all the language needs of his drama. This verse form had no fixed metrical pattern. This fact freed him from the long lines of the operatic fare of the day, and there would be no need to count the number of syllables in each line, to consider the stressed and unstressed syllables of each verse. Neither did Stabreim exact an elegance of words. Wagner was most pleased that its metaphor therefore was simple, concise, and unelaborated. Stabreim had no end rhyme, although it did boast an alliteration that Wagner later would praise most highly. Wagner was most pleased with the Stabreim poetic form, probably mostly so because, in addition to all else, with this poetic structure he was free to make whatever adjustments he deemed important or necessary to achieve what he considered to be the naturalness of human speech.

Wagner's decisions about the "language" of his poem included, in addition to the Stabreim verse form, certain matters regarding vocabulary. He would weave into his verses what may be termed three kinds of vocabularies. One of those vocabularies would be, of course, the regular and standard vocabulary of the day. However, at any such time as he felt that a specific character or event or situation or action could be mythically enhanced, or could be more indelibly imprinted in the mind of the audience, he would do all possible to include a second kind of language, that is, special words or terms that he felt would contribute to that end and which would also automatically convey the ambience of a remote and distant universe. The language that allowed this mythical enhancement focused on ancient German words. Wagner's concern here was with those ancient words that were still to be found in modern German, but whose basic meaning or meanings had somehow been altered by time or by design because of distinct cultural developments. Included in that language were words which had remained in the modern speech but which had essentially been replaced by more contemporary terminology.

The second kind of unique language that drew Wagner's attention was that speech whose words were principally of his own creation. These terms, and there were more than just a few, usually were words that he had developed by means of one of the salient features of the German tongue, the compound word. He accomplished these words by means of one of three avenues of creation. It was not unusual for Wagner to create a new word by joining into compound form two or more ancient words that had lost some of their original semantic potency. A second technique that Wagner regularly employed was to join an ancient word with a modern German term and offer the creation as a single word. On occasion he placed the ancient word first in his compound, and at other times he placed the ancient word last in his compound form. The results of these arrangements were usually quite startling in a semantic sense.

A third language to which Wagner resorted quite frequently to assure himself of just the correct terminology in any given situation was perhaps more a technique. Wagner often selected a standard German compound term from the modern tongue, and then employed that word in a dramatic situation that forced it to take on a meaning that was distinct from that associated with regular usage.

These several techniques, woven into the alliterative verse of Stabreim, formed a truly special and singular language, a kind of mythical speech that seemed to be most fitting and most appropriate for the supernatural beings that would populate his drama. At times, the language of the *Ring* seemed foreign, yet, interestingly enough, also strangely familiar. This unique language that Wagner had designed to tell his tale also was inordinately complex, providing to be puzzling even to modern day native speakers of German. In the end, however, the language of the *Ring* was not unlike the essence of the mythical world of the gods that it served, that world that was fundamental to the drama that its creator desired to be a true national work of art.

LENZ (*Spring*) See: Moon

LOGE See: *Loge* (Vol. II)

LOGE (Name)

Loge, like Erda, is a deity, but only in Wagner's *Ring* drama. The composer developed this figure as his God of Fire despite the fact that the overwhelming nature of his character is drawn from a mythical figure who is not only not a god, but also a figure that has no connection whatsoever with fire, a figure which he then endowed with the minuscule attribute of another Teutonic being, a very ancient figure who has been essentially forgotten. The two mythical beings who were fused into the singular Loge of the *Ring* were the Eddic *Loki* and a figure that predates him, a supernatural known as *Logi*.

The *Loki* of Teutonic myths stimulates the essence of the Loge that Wagner was to place in his drama. This mythical being is a clever and shrewd figure, one who is ever alert to his situations, and very quick to provide answers or actions that will be to his own benefit. The Loki of myth was not above lying, cheating, or even murder, if he felt that he personally could somehow gain from the occasion. Loki was a masculine name that was used by the Germanic people until about the fifteenth century, after which it fell into societal disfavor and disappeared completely from the German language. The development of the word *Loki* into *Loge* would have been a relatively simple linguistic process, the voicing of a consonant and the opening of a front vowel. This process takes place as a most natural occurrence within the Germanic sound system.

The second supernatural that forms a part of Wagner's Loge is the being known as *Logi*, who apparently was the second of three sons of the giant Fornitor. Little is known about these brothers except that the first of this trio was Hler, who represented *water*, the second son was Logi who represented *fire*, and the last was Kari who represented *air*. The name *Logi* appears only in *The Prose Edda* in which this supernatural is called "Wildfire."

The name *Logi* seems to be derived from an earlier name, *Lothur*, which meant "blaze" or "glow." It was Lothur who gave "heat ... and goodly hue" to the newly created mortals Ask ("Ash") and Embla ("Elm"). (Wotan gave these mortals "soul" while Hoenir gave them "sense.")

It was a simple linguistic task for Wagner to take the two names, Loki and Logi, and then to create from them the name for his figure, Loge. Although the name Loge in itself apparently has no semantic value, it does bear a relationship with the Lothur of old, and after all, Wagner's figure is the fire and flame of the *Ring*. Given the nature of the character Loge and the semantic of the original words, it would seem that the name of Wagner's God of Fire is "Blaze," or "Glow," or possibly "Heat."

-M-

MAY (Wonnemond) See: *Moon*

MEAD

Mead, a fermented drink whose primary ingredients are honey and water, is a dramatic factor in Wagner's *Ring*, and it is also a drink that figures prominently in mythical Teutondom and its literature. The appearance of this popular beverage of the mythical past occurs for the first time in Wagner's drama of the *Ring* in the first act of *Die Walküre*. It is Sieglinde who, in this act, offers mead as a drink of refreshment to the exhausted stranger Siegmund who has lost his way in the forest and who seeks refuge in her dwelling. This use of mead, that is, as a drink to soothe fatigue, reflects a similar use that is depicted in verses of *The Poetic Edda*. The poem tells how Gerd, the fair giantess of whom Froh had become enamored, welcomes the god's servant Skirnir, who had been sent to speak for the god, and then offers him a drink of mead after his long and tiring journey. Mead again becomes a factor in this same drama of the *Ring* as Brünnhilde later, in the second act, attempts to describe the pleasures of Valhalla to Siegmund, one of which is that the divine *Wunschmädchen* ("Wish-Maidens"), that is, the Valkyries, will attend him there, adding that she herself will bring him his drink. Brünnhilde does not identify the drink, but the reference obviously is to mead which, in Teutonic mythical thought, was the only drink worthy of Valhalla's heroic warriors, and it was a liquid that was furnished in endless supply by the she-goat Heidrun. (In a similar vein, the only food that was consumed by these heroes was the meat of a boar, Saehrimnir ("The Blackened"), an animal that was 'raised' each night in order to be slain and cooked again the next day.)

Wagner caused mead to appear once again in this drama, in the final act, as the Allfather Wotan laments the act of banishment that he feels compelled to place on Brünnhilde. The King of the Gods informs his favorite daughter that because of her defiance of his command to withhold her divine protection from the mortal Siegmund, she no longer can attend him in Valhalla, that she no longer can serve him his mead at mealtime. This brief dramatic relationship of Wotan and mead reveals in a most subtle manner Wagner's knowledge of the Teutonic past. An association of mead and the Supreme God of Teutondom infers that the drink is the 'supreme drink' of Teutondom, that it possesses some special quality, a magic perhaps, some special character that would rank it above all other drinks. Such would be an obvious relationship, and a logical conclusion in view of the historical fact that mead was known in the culture as *Wotan's Drink*. As a second regard, it should be noted that it is only mead that Brünnhilde no longer will be able to bring the god at mealtime. No other food is mentioned, and, mythologically, Wagner was correct to exclude any reference to food. He was well aware that in the ancient belief, the King of the Gods consumed no food other than mead, a liquid that was both food and drink for him. All solid food that was set before the god was fed to the two wolves that sat at Wotan's side. (The mythical belief that Wotan consumed no solid foods is in conflict with another accepted mythical concept, that which viewed the gods as able to preserve their youth through the consumption of the special apples that were in the guardianship of the goddess Idun.)

Mead also appears in the fourth drama of the *Ring* In anticipation of the wedding of Brünnhilde and Gunther, Hagen summons the Gibichung vassals. He then orders that they celebrate the occasion of this wedding with mead, which will be served to them by the lovely Gibichung maidens. If Hagen's words, while at once intended for the scene at hand, seem to be a depiction of the scene of the Valkyries serving the slain heroes and the gods in Valhalla, they are also a kind of metaphor that relates that mead is the drink to be offered to celebrants on special occasions. This latter use of mead is compatible with cultural belief that mead was indeed a drink intended for more than mere regular consumption, and its use in the *Ring* as a drink of celebration parallels a similar use as found in one of the poems of *The Poetic Edda*. In the poem, an elaborate feast was being offered by Aegir, the sea-god. Many of the deities and their wives, as well as their servants, had been invited. As part of the festivity, Aegir had prepared great quantities of mead, which was spiritedly consumed by all the guests, including Loge, who was uninvited and who, because he drank too much of the potent mead, became a disrupting factor during the celebration.

Mead was indeed the special drink of the ancient Teutonic culture and its mythical beliefs. The Vanir (Wanes) gods called it *The Foaming*. The race of giants knew mead as the *Bright Draught*, while the sons of Suttung, a giant, called it *The Feast Drink*. Those who inhabited Hel, the Land of the Dead, called it *mead*, mortals called it *ale*, and the gods called it *beer*. Scholars have long agreed that the Eddic poem in which these several names are presented contains sparse mythological authenticity, and that the verses that constitute this poem are more in the tradition of the skaldic verses that so pervaded Old Norse literature. If such is true, the several compound terms that are used as names for *mead* can be accepted only as kennings of some learned poet, and the English renderings of *beer* and *ale* as synonyms for *mead* are more approximate linguistic interpretations of otherwise untranslatable ancient words than they are expressions of cultural reality. Despite the skaldic flavor of the original poem, and the apparent inaccuracies of language that are natural to translations, the appearance in an Eddic poem of such a series of terms to denote the drink gives ample evidence not only of the widespread presence of mead in the heathen world, but also of a certain acclaim and renown that ancient Teutonic thought had attached to it.

There are yet other Eddic poems that speak of mead as the special drink of the gods. These numerous references to mead, in their totality, serve as an undeniable indication of the commonalty of the drink in the divine world, which of course, reflects the thought that originates in the mind of man. In one such poetic work the gods are disturbed about dreams of foreboding evil that come to Balder, the favorite son of Wotan and Fricka. The King of the Gods sets out on a journey to learn the meaning of these dreams. Wotan travels to Hel where he raises a Wise-Woman from her grave, and asks her to tell for whom all the preparations of a feast of welcome have been made. The Wise-Woman answers that the celebrations will be given and the mead has been especially brewed for the reception of Balder into the Land of the Dead. In another Eddic poem, Donner, disguised as a bride, has journeyed into the Land of the Giants, to attempt to retrieve his missing hammer. At the wedding supper the god consumed an ox, eight salmon, and he drank three tuns of mead. (A *tun* equaled 252 gallons.) A third poem of *The Poetic Edda* tells of Heimdall, the Guardian of Bifrost, the Rainbow Bridge, who sits in his dwelling and gladly drinks good mead. In yet another poem of the *Edda*, it is the *volva* or Wise-Woman who reveals that the eye that Wotan had given for a drink from the Spring of Wisdom lies in those waters, and that the god's pledge serves as the vessel from which Mimir, the guardian of the spring, drinks mead each morning. In what is the most aphoristic of the Eddic poems, and a work that is fundamental to the understanding of early Germanic religious thought, there are those verses that tell that Wotan hung, head down, from a branch of the World Ash Tree. The god hung there for nine nights. Then, he saw the runes, there beneath him, on the ground. Wotan quickly took them up, then fell to the ground. It was then that the Allfather god came to possess nine mighty songs, which in turn enabled him to win a drink of precious mead.

Of all the references to mead that are found in the Teutonic myths, there is none that is more meaningful or more significant within the totality of ancient Teutonic beliefs than that which speaks of the *Mead of Poetry*, often called the *Mead of Inspiration*. The complete and separate tale that focuses on this mead is one of the most important of all Teutonic myths, a poem that illustrates the elevated status of mead, endows it with the vital potency of wisdom, and further allows that with the wisdom that this mead bestows, all things are possible. Of course, it is Wotan who is the only divine being that is superior enough to be closely associated with this special mead. The myth is worth recounting because of its unique association of mead, Wotan, wisdom, and the human race, all of which, in their own way, have a place in Wagner's *Der Ring des Nibelungen*.

The first great war of the universe ended with a pact of peace between the two warring races of gods, the Aesir, the clan that was headed by Wotan, and the Vanir, a clan of sea-spirits that was once prominent in the Baltic Sea region. The truce was made valid when each god spat into a vessel. The gods so valued this spittle that they made a figure from it, the figure of a man. The gods named this man Kvasir, and they had endowed him with such wisdom that there was no question whose answer he did not know. Kvasir traveled about the world intent on teaching mankind the wisdom of all ages. On one of these journeys, Kvasir became the guest at a feast that was being offered by two brothers, the dwarfs Fjalar and Galar. These dwarfs overcame Kvasir while he was participating in the celebration. The dwarfs then killed the wise Kvasir, and then drained his blood into two crocks and a kettle. The crocks were called Son and Bodin, and the name of the kettle was Odrorir. The brothers then poured honey into the blood and the liquid became mead. This, now, was very special mead because it had been made of the blood of the wise Kvasir and, therefore, when it was drunk it gave its drinker intellectual inspiration as well as the treasured art of poetry and scholarship. The gods were upset at Kvasir's death, but the dwarfs gave some comfort to the gods when they told them that Kvasir had choked to death on his own learning because there was no one in the universe intelligent enough to compete with him.

The dwarfs then invited the giant Gilling and his wife to their dwelling. The brothers did not care for Gilling, and so they took him into their boat and rowed far out into the sea. They steered the boat into a rock, and the impact overturned the boat and Gilling was thrown into the water and drowned. When the dwarfs told the giant's wife about her husband's death, she wept loudly and long. Fjalar became very disturbed and upset at the cries and the wailing of Gilling's wife. Finally, to stop the noise, Fjalar told his brother to kill the woman by letting a millstone fall on her as she went through the doorway of the dwelling. When Gilling's son, Suttung, heard of the deaths of his father and his mother, he seized the two dwarfs, took them out to sea, and put them on a large, isolated rock that the tide had covered. The dwarfs were frightened, and they begged to be spared. In exchange for their lives, they offered Suttung the precious Mead of Poetry!

Suttung quickly agreed to the offer. He took the mead to his hall which was deep in the interior of a mountain. He hid the mead in a room that was called Hnitbjorg. This was the room that belonged to his daughter Gunnlod, whom he appointed as guardian of the coveted mead.

Wotan had long wandered throughout the universe in a constant search for knowledge. He had drunk once from the Spring of Wisdom, he had learned the charms of the world, he had learned the redes, he had learned the runes and how to work their magic, he had gained the special songs of learning. However, of all his acquisitions, that learning and knowledge that was the greatest of all was that of poetry, the knowledge of words, of how to use them, a knowledge with which all things were possible because through words true wisdom could be gained. Wotan had not gained that knowledge and wisdom, and he had long sought this supreme power that was possible through a drink of the Mead of Poetry. The Supreme God of the Teutonic world set out now on a journey to find and to possess the celebrated Mead of Poetry. As was his usual custom, Wotan donned a disguise and took on a special name for this trip. On this journey the god would call himself Bolverk ("Doer-of-Ill").

The god had traveled some distance when he came upon a huge field that was near Suttung's mountain. The field was ripe with growing grain. Wotan saw nine serfs who were busy mowing the grain and its hay. The god watched them for a while, and then told them that their scythes were dull, that he could sharpen them, and thus ease their work. Wotan then took a hone from his robe and began to sharpen one of the scythes. In due time, the god put a sharp edge on the scythe, an edge that was so sharp that each of the nine serfs wanted to buy the hone. Wotan sharpened each scythe and then agreed to sell the instrument, but he stipulated that the one who purchased it must pay for it with a great feast. When all nine of the serfs readily agreed to the terms, Wotan decided to resolve the matter by throwing the hone into the air and whoever could catch it would be the new owner. The god tossed the tool high into the air, and there was then a great scramble by each of the serfs who tried frantically to catch the hone. So physical were the attempts of the serfs to catch the hone that they cut each other's throats with the sharpened blades of their scythes.

Wotan then invoked *Gastrecht* (Guest-Rights) and spent the night in the home of Bragi, Suttung's brother. The god's host complained that nine of his serfs had been killed that day and that he did not know where he could find workers to replace them. Wotan offered to do all the work that the serfs were supposed to do, but that his payment was to be a drink of Suttung's mead. Bragi admitted that the mead was not his to give, but he was so desperate to have his field mowed that he agreed that he would do all possible to gain the drink. Bolverk (Wotan) performed the work that he had promised that he would do, but when he asked Bragi for his wages, Bragi answered that his brother had refused to part with even a drop of the mead. Bolverk then said that they must get the mead by any means whatsoever, even by trickery, if necessary.

Bolverk then brought out an auger which he said was named Rati (Traveler). Bolverk handed the auger to Bragi and told him to bore a hole through the mountain, into Gunnlod's room. Bragi wanted to satisfy his pledge, that is, to pay his debt, so he did as Bolverk had ordered. After Bragi had drilled the hole, Bolverk changed himself into a serpent, slid into the narrow passage, and slowly made his way into the mountain, all the way to Gunnlod's room. Once in Gunnlod's room, Bolverk changed himself from a serpent into his regular from and began to ply Suttung's daughter with some of his magic. Gunnlod succumbed to Bolverk's advances and the disguised god then seduced the maid. Bolverk slept with Gunnlod for three nights. (Wotan once boasted that there was never born the maiden that he could not know.) Gunnlod was so pleased with her visit from the god that she then offered him a drink of the mead that she guarded in the room. Bolverk eagerly accepted the offer. With his first drink, Bolverk emptied the kettle of its mead. With his second drink, the god emptied one of the crocks. Bolverk's third drink emptied the second crock. Bolverk then went outside, changed himself into an eagle, and began to fly toward Asgard, the Land of the Gods. When the Aesir deities saw Wotan in the heavens as he flew toward them, they hurriedly placed receptacles in the courtyard. Bolverk finally arrived and he spat the mead that he had drunk into those vessels. Wotan changed back into his regular form and then gave the magic mead that he had spat into the crocks to the gods and to those mortals who would be wise and learned poets. It was from that day that the gods and certain mortals had the magic power to become inspired and then to write elevated, sublime poetry. The Teutonic Mead of Poetry, however, was not intended for every mortal. During Bolverk's flight back to the Land of the Gods, some of the mead that he was carrying spilled from his mouth and fell to the ground. Some mortal men gathered up the drink and immediately attempted to put its magic to use. All that these men could produce, however, was mediocre verses because the mead that they had gathered was not the principal liquid, but a less potent liquid with less magic in it. This mead then became known as the *poetaster's share*, and all those who tasted of it from that day forward would be less than principal poets.

The belief that poetry and its words were associated with knowledge is one of the most significant concepts to emerge from early Teutonic thought. Special to this belief was the mythical idea that a drink of the Mead of Poetry granted the gift of poetry, and with that art came wisdom. The perception of this unique drink, its special powers, and the dramatic results that followed a drink of the mead was extensive in the Teutonic lands, and these images were so accepted in the Germanic cultural mind that the drink became known by several names which, if viewed collectively, reflect the chronology of the story of the mead from its creation until it came into the hands of man. The drink was called first *Kvasir's Blood*. Then, the mead became known as *Dwarf's Drink*. Then, it was called *The Drink of Odrorir, Wotan's Drink*, and followed then by *The Drink of the Gods*. Finally, when the concept that the gods had shared the drink with mankind became standard, this beverage became known to the universe as *Wotan's Gift*.

Wagner felt no dramatic compulsion to be concerned with Wotan's adventure in the acquisition of the Mead of Poetry, or with the magic mead itself. Neither matter was of consequence to the version of the tale of the gods as he would write it. Overall, the matter of mead in the *Ring* was to be one of little thematic prominence. However, in light of the frequency of the references to mead that he included in his poem, and the functions that he attached to this liquid, it is obvious that Wagner understood the significance of mead in early Teutonic thought, the matter of its association with the gods, and particularly its close relationship with the Supreme God, Wotan. It is in this consideration that the composer was meticulous in his intent to be as mythically correct as possible, as was his usual turn in similar concerns.

It is apparent that in Wagner's mind mead was one of the lesser matters in the development of his drama. Despite that thematic truth, he was aware, nevertheless, that mead was a most basic and fundamental matter in heathen thought, and therefore, despite its unimportance as a segment in the development of the argument of the *Ring*, his mead merited fundamental consideration. Wagner rightly viewed mead as a factor that was integral to the authenticity of the Germanic ambience that he wished to bring to his drama, and in its own ways that mead that he brings to his poem, the uses to which it is put, and the occasions on which it is used, artfully combine to make a unique thematic and dramatic contribution to the thoroughly mythical coloring that shades Wagner's drama.

MIDGARD

Of the nine worlds that the early Teutonic mind conceived as the universe, one was the world of mortals, the world that was known as *Midgard*. This world, whose name translates as "Middle Enclosure," was sheltered within the branches of Yggdrasil, the World Ash Tree, which also housed, in one form or another, the other eight worlds.

The gods had fashioned Midgard from the body of a great giant, Ymir, who was the first living creature of the universe. The gods then used the giant's brain to make the clouds that would be found in this world. The gods would house those clouds in the dome of the giant's skull which became the firmament. At the base of the skull there were four dwarfs, each positioned at one of the four corners, and in such a way that together they could hold the world of man firm and fast. As with all else that achieved an importance or significance in the heathen Teutonic world, each of these dwarfs had names. In the geographically conscious Germanic culture these dwarfs were called *Northri (North)*, *Suthri (South)*, *Austri (East)*, and *Vestri (West)*. This work that the dwarfs performed was quite important in the early Germanic scheme of things and it became known as the "Burden of the Dwarfs."

There is a second feature of heathen Teutonic beliefs that was also known as *Midgard*. This mythical concept was that of a formidable serpent, one of the three monster offspring that were the result of the union between Loki (Loge) and the giantess Angrboda. (The two other offspring were Fenrir, the wolf, and Hel, Guardian of the Dead.)

This second Midgard had the given name of *Jormungandr*. However, when the gods had Loki's offsprings in captivity, they came to realize the serious and dangerous threat that this serpent posed for the divine ones. They then concluded that Jormungandr should be removed as far as possible from the land of the gods. Their decision was to throw him into the sea. Wotan himself assumed this responsibility, which he carried out as the council of the gods had determined.

Jormungandr fared well in the waters of the seas. In the vast waters, the serpent grew in size until he was so large that his body soon circled the world and he could bite his tail. It was because of this great size, and the fact that the serpent's body circled the world of man, that this child of Loki soon became known as *Midgardsorm*, or "World Serpent."

Midgardsorm, the World Serpent, was to figure in the Final Battle of the universe. When the destruction of the gods and their world (*ragnarök*) commenced, and the gods of Teutondom marched out to meet their enemies, it was Donner who was to do battle with this monster serpent. The great god would slay this creature with his mighty hammer, but he would die also, killed by the venom that the World Serpent had breathed upon him.

Wagner included the world of mortals in his *Ring* drama but he did not give that land a name. Neither did he resort to any use of Midgardsorm, although it may be argued that the giant serpent influenced, if only indirectly, one of the major scenes of the drama. The scene in question comes in the final moments of the *Ring*, when the Rhine rises and overflows its banks, flooding the land. It is most likely that Wagner received inspiration for that scene from the mythical thought that when Donner killed the monster Midgardsorm, the creature fell back into the sea out of which he had come.

The serpent was so large that when his body hit the water, it caused the sea to rise, to flow beyond its shores, and to flood the world.

MIME

The Mime that Wagner brings into his *Ring* drama is not a single mythical or legendary figure as are, for example, Siegfried, or Brünnhilde, or Fafner, among others. Rather, the Nibelung dwarf that he would call Mime was really a composite figure in that the dramatic role that he plays in the drama is drawn essentially from the Nordic mythical thought, while the name as well as some details of the character of this figure are to be found in the folk and literary lore of northern continental Europe.

It is to *The Poetic Edda* that Wagner would turn to gain source material for his Mime, a move that he would make quite frequently during the composition of his *Ring* drama. There, in the verses of those tales, he would find *Regin* ("Counsel Giver"), the mythical being who became the foster father of the Volsung Siegfried (Sigurd), the figure who would serve as teacher to the youth. (Although the *Edda* is neither necessarily concerned nor singularly attentive to the matters that Regin 'taught' to Siegfried, the prose paraphrase of these stanzas, *Volsungasaga*, reveals that the self-appointed teacher Regin taught his charge all forms of the arts, as well as chess, how to speak in several languages, and the lore and magic of the runes!) This Eddic Regin is one of three sons of Hreidmar, the other two being Otter (Otr) and Fafner (Fafnir). The verses state that Regin is a dwarf who is wise, fierce, more ingenious than others, and quite skilled in magic. The *Volsungasaga* adds that he is also very talented in the working of iron, silver, and gold. One day Regin tells Siegfried the story of his family. He recounts that his brother Otter, who regularly took the form of an otter, hence the name, had been killed accidentally by the gods, who then had to ransom themselves by giving Hreidmar a large treasure of gold. The gods had learned of a vast treasure that lay in a waterfall and which was guarded by a dwarf named Andvari who had changed himself into a pike to swim about in the waters and to guard his hoard. They took this gold from Andvari, by force, but not before Andvari had placed a death-curse on it. Regin's brother Fafner wants the gold treasure for himself, and thus he kills his father and flees with the hoard to the forest, where he takes the form of a dragon, to lay guard over his wealth. Regin wants his share of the gold, as his inheritance, and he convinces the fearless Siegfried that he must journey to Fafner's den, to slay the dragon. The naive Siegfried and his master teacher travel into the forest, to the lair in which Fafner has hidden the treasure. In time, Siegfried and Fafner meet, the latter warning the youth that Regin will later betray him. The cowardly Regin runs into the forest as Siegfried slays the dragon with the sword that his foster father had forged for him. When Regin returns, he uses his sword to cut out his brother's heart, and then eats it as he drinks his blood. After a brief time, in which Siegfried learns to understand the language of the birds, the youth is convinced of Regin's intended betrayal, and he slays his treacherous teacher.

The follower of Wagner's *Ring* immediately recognizes the Eddic Regin and his role which become, essentially, Mime and much of his dramatic action in the drama. What is somewhat more enigmatic in the matter of this figure is the reason or reasons that the composer had for the change of name from *Regin* to *Mime*. As a point of departure, it should be pointed out that there is in *The Poetic Edda*, the same work from which Wagner had extracted the major actions for his Mime, a supernatural character who already bears the name of *Mime*, or at least that name in its basic form, *Mimir*. The Eddic Mimir is not in any way associated with the Siegfried theme, but is, rather, a water spirit whose mythical charge is that of Guardian of the Spring of Wisdom. It is from this spring, whose waters contain the wisdom of the universe, that Wotan once drank, and gave an eye as payment for that drink. That payment was known as *Mimisbrunni*. Mimir then uses the god's eye as a cup from which he drinks each morning. The Eddic Mimir is later given as hostage to another race of gods that beheads the Master of Wisdom and sends the head back to Wotan, whose magic caused it to continue to talk and render sage advice. Much the same tale of Mimir as that found in the *Edda* is recorded in the *Ynglingasaga*, a work of fifty-five short chapters that was based on the Norwegian poem "Ynglingatal" and which served as a preface to *Heimskringla*, a history of Norwegian kings by the Icelander Snorri Sturluson (1179-1241).

The existence of a mythical Mimir in the work that served as primary source material obviously did not deter Wagner from the use of that name for his thematically unrelated Nibelung dwarf. It is possible that Wagner was resorting to the names that he had found in *Thidrekssaga* (*Dietrich's Saga*), also known as *Wilkinasaga*, a work to which he frequently makes reference in his writings. This saga, which dates from the late thirteenth century but whose place of origin is disputed as either Iceland or Norway, contains much that pertains to Siegfried despite the fact that the work focuses on the German hero, Dietrich. The Mimir of this saga is a cunning and shrewd metalsmith who comes upon a young boy who is wandering about in a forest. Mimir takes the youth to raise as his foster son, to whom he gives the name of 'Siegfried.' In time, this Siegfried grows to early manhood and confronts the dragon that in this saga is called Regin! The young Siegfried kills the monster, and then smotes off the head of Mimir because of his intended treachery.

It is equally possible that Wagner decided, after his long and intensive study of Germanic and legendary matters, that Mime would be the name of his Nibelung dwarf simply because it was one of the most popular names in all of early Germany. There is a *Mimo* in a ninth-century German work, and in a fifteenth-century variation the name is given as *Mimmung*. Mime (Mimir) was the name of the teacher of the celebrated Wayland (Wieland), the smith, a figure about whom Wagner once proposed to write an opera. In the epic poem "Biterolf und Dietleib," composed about 1260, there is a *Mime* who is a master smith who lives and works near Toledo (Tolet), a city famed throughout history for its excellent work in metals. This Mime was known for the swords that he had forged. There is a *Mimering* (Miemerinng) who wanders through numerous ballads that originated in Denmark. Curiously, this Mime of the ballads is a dwarf knight! It is the *Gesta Danorum*, the history of Denmark that was written in Latin about 1210 by Saxo Grammaticus, that tells of a dwarf named *Mimingus* who was captured by Hod, a son of Wotan and Fricka, but who ransomed himself by giving the god a special sword and an arm ring that held the magic to increase its owner's wealth.

The popularity of the name Mime is also noted in other ways. *Mimelo*, a diminutive of Mime, was once used frequently, both as a masculine and a feminine name. The name *Mime* also became the linguistic base for the names of certain geographic sites. The present day *Minden*, for example, was once called *Mimidun*, and modern day *Munster* was once known as *Mimigerdiford*.

It is not at all presumptive to state that all the mythical factors that formed the framework of Wagner's *Ring* argument lay like a foundation of great strength at the root of the composer-dramatist's thoughts. All that he attempted to achieve dramatically, all that he had hoped to accomplish artistically, rested enveloped in that Teutonic mythical lore that he had accumulated during his years of study. He was well aware of the fact that the myths that he had studied, those tales that were to serve him so well in the formation of his argument, were products of northern Teutondom. He also understood that the figures with which he was to populate his drama as well as numerous situations and events that he would include, were, in the main, those that had found expression or variation of some kind in the Nordic regions. There was little in his work that was purely German. Yet, Wagner was constantly attempting to bring to these matters as much of the German tradition as possible. If many of his figures spring from that northern Teutonic palette, it can also be said there is usually a southern or German tint that colors their character or their actions, in one way or another. So too was it with Mime. Wagner knew all there was to know about the Nordic Mimir, or at least all that he needed to know, and he had encountered figures with the same name in other works, works that depicted this figure with a nature and character that he felt were more of the German sort. It would be from that non-Nordic thought that he would extract the dramatic foundation for his Nibelung dwarf who was to inhabit the bowels of inner earth and who would exhibit much of the lust and greed that is so much at the core of the drama. To this nimble figure he would give the role that the Nordic minds had developed to be closely associated with their Siegfried figure, and despite the mythical existence of a figure of distinct qualities who bore the name of Mimir (Mime), Wagner would crown his figure with that same name, a name that was very German and one that once enjoyed a unique popularity among the natives of his own German soil.

See also: *Dwarfs*

MIME (Name)

The use of the word *Mime* as the name of one of the two principal Nibelung dwarfs is essentially of Wagner's own design. If he had extracted the principal features of the character *Mimir*, who is found in the saga of Dietrich von Bern (*Thidrekssaga*) as the basis for his *Mime*, it was also that name that he sought to Germanize for use in his *Ring* drama. Wagner felt strengthened in his decision to use the name because he not only had found numerous variations in scattered literary works, but also because he was aware that the word had enjoyed a rather extensive linguistic history.

It is most probable that the name *Mime* can be associated with a Germanic prototype **mim*, which inferred "measure" in the sense of "think." Old English produced the word *mamrian* and Low German had the term *mimeren*. By the ninth century, German had the term *Mimo* (*Memmo*), and in the fifteenth century the word had become *Mimmung*. There are also the several variations that existed in separate regions of the Teutonic world, including the Eddic *Mimir*, the Danish *Miemerinng* and *Mimering*, and the Latin *Mimingus*. There is circumstantial evidence that the word, without the German suffixes *ing* and *ung*, served as a geographical name.

It is also possible, however, that the composer, in his choice of this word as a name, was influenced further by the German verb *mimen*, which carries a meaning of "to feign" or "to pretend." In conjugated form, the first person singular of the present indicative tense, *mime*, translates as "(I) feign" or "(I) pretend," actions which are specific to the *Ring* and its Mime, especially in the first and second acts of *Siegfried*. It is in those scenes that the Nibelung dwarf pretends kindliness and warmth and affection for the

Volsung while all the time he is making plans to slay him once the youth has killed the dragon and the treasure of gold that the beast guards can be had.

MOON

The moon, like the planets, like the sun and the other stars that had their places in the skies, was created by the gods of Teutondom when they tossed into the heavens the sparks and embers that had drifted their way from Muspellsheim. The latter was one of the nine worlds of the mythical Germanic universe. It lay 'to the south,' and was the home of the fire-giants who would one day cross the Rainbow Bridge, set it ablaze, and then confront the gods in the final battle of the universe. It would be this mythical moon that Wagner would bring to one of the climactic scenes of his *Ring*, that scene that would bring to a conclusion the dramatic first act of *Die Walküre*, an ending that establishes beyond any doubt the newly-found love of the Volsung twins, Siegmund and Sieglinde.

The moon of Teutonic myths is one of those special elements of nature that at once bemused the peoples of early Teutondom, and also attracted them in unusual ways. These people believed that a special steed named Hrimfaxi ("Frosty Mane") brought the moon into the sky each night. The moon was chased through the heavens by a wolf. This animal was named Hati, and it was an offspring of Fenrir, the mighty wolf. (Fenrir was a child of Loge and a giantess, and it would be this animal that would swallow Wotan at the fated destruction of the universe.)

The moon had its phases, and those phases had an unrelenting hold on the way that culture measured time. The early clans had reckoned that since the moon had changes, changes that they could see, they would count time by those changes. Hence it was that these early Germanics counted time not by days, but rather by nights. As a result of this societal practice, there was a lunar year of what would equal about thirteen months as measured by the modern calendar, a year that would have more import in many ways than the solar year of twelve months.

The moon had an influence on the kind of work that should be done in its light. If man was guided to perform the work that supplied the necessities of life in the light of the sun, it was in the light of the moon that important decisions should be made. It was at night, beneath a moon, that counsels and advice were to be given and received. It would be at night, in the moonlight, that councils should be held, and that the rules of conduct and behavior should be laid down. (It should be noted that Wagner does not specify the light of the moon, but he does bring in his Norns at the dark of night, and his Erda appears twice, both times in the dark of night.)

It was also in the full of the moon that marriages should take place. Those marriages that could be realized during the period of the full moon in the month of May received a special blessing that no other marriages could receive. That period that is now called May was a very special period of time in early Teutonic thought. Although it did not have a specific date, it was a holiday period, the time when summer (which is known today as spring) began, when the flowers began to open, when the birds returned from the winter sojourn in some distant land. It was the time, after the relentless cold and gloominess of winter, that brightened people's life. It was the time of songs and dances, the time of festivals, of feast, the time of sacrifices, and the time for youthful love.

It was this moon and this period of time that Wagner would bring to flood down upon the lives of his Siegmund and his Sieglinde. It would be the moon that announces the arrival of Spring, the moon that would spur love and suggest the fertility of life. It would be the moon of that distant age that would announce to the pair that the joy of life would open its fullest rays upon them, on this pair who only now had discovered each other. In the simplest and briefest of terms, it would be the moon of *Wonnemond*, literally "Blissful" or "Rapturous Moon," and a poetic name for the month of May.

Wagner begins this thoroughly mythical scene that involves the moon with stage directions. He writes that the entrance door to Hunding's abode suddenly springs wide to reveal a beautiful, calm evening's night. He continues his directions, writing that there is a full moon, a moon whose rays stream down upon the earth, making all things visible. It is now that Siegmund and Sieglinde, in the light of that moon and under the influence of its rays, declare themselves, one for the other, and admit a love that neither of them had ever known before, a love that represents the complete surrender of one to the other.

Siegmund begins the duet that is regularly known as "Winterstürme," the scene in the *Ring* that Wagner's wife, Cosima, claimed as her favorite and which she called "Spring Song." As the couple stands in the moonlight that floods the scene, Siegmund declares that the storms of winter have vanished before the might of 'Wonnemond,' that the essence of Spring surrounds them, and that the two now know a love that only they can have. As Siegmund is stirred by the rays of the moon, so too is Sieglinde, who also declares her love. She refers to Siegmund as the 'Lenz,' which is a term that refers to the season Spring, much as does 'Wonnemond,' but which infers more the vitality and vigor of that time of the year, the joy and rapture that is associated with the springtime, rather than simply one of the seasons of the year.

(There is an interesting, if ever so subtle, grammatical maneuver that Wagner arranges in these final words of *Die Walküre*. Siegmund is depicted as the *Lenz*, that is the Spring with all its vitality and sprightness. Sieglinde is referred to as *Liebe*, the German word for "love." In the German language, the word "Lenz" is masculine and the word "Liebe" is feminine. Thus it is that when the duet speaks of "Lenz" as a liberator, it is the masculine term that signals Siegmund, and it is the feminine "Liebe" or Sieglinde that has been liberated.)

The moon of *Die Walküre* is the moon of the Teutonic mythical past. It is a 'rapturous moon,' it is the moon of love, it is the moon of May, a time when all nature begins to stir, a time when mortal man begins to feel rejuvenated after a long winter. Wagner's moon is the poetic "Wonnemond," Siegmund is the "Lenz," and the delicate Sieglinde is indeed the "Liebe." This trio comes together in such a way that there is produced one of the most dramatic and climactic moments of the entire *Ring*, a vibrant scene that truly reflects the Teutonic mythical past.

See also: *Sun*

       Seasons

MORTALS

The semantic limits that regularly govern the use of the word *mortal,* that is, a "human being," cannot be rigidly set when certain 'mortal' figures of Wagner's *Ring* are a consideration. No one will question seriously, if at all, that Wagner's drama transcends material experience and existence, primarily by means of its mythical and legendary substance and, therefore, the mortals that figure in the drama's *dramatis personae* can and are designated as such only according to that substance.

The concept of 'mortal,' at least that which pervades within the ambience of the *Ring,* is exemplified by interpretation rather than by definition. Siegmund and Sieglinde must be accepted as mortals, only because their mother is designated as 'mortal woman,' and despite the overriding thematic fact that their father is Wotan, The Allfather, the Supreme God of all Teutondom. Their son, Siegfried, in whose veins runs the blood of the Allfather, must also be seen as a mortal, one who can take a dethroned supernatural as his bride. Hagen is also looked upon as a mortal although his father is a dwarf, a figure who was truly a supernatural being by early Germanic standards. It would seem, then, that as one approaches the final scenes of the *Ring* that Gunther and his sister Gutrune, the Gibichungs, are mortals in the manner of modern societal concepts. Yet, even they are tinged with the hue of the supernatural, bound as they are to their half brother, Hagen, the son of Alberich. It remains for Hunding, the Neiding, to stand alone as mortal man if the accepted definition of today's world is to be applied to the characters of Wagner's *Ring.*

Followers of Wagner's monumental drama are seldom prone to study such detail as who is mortal and who is not. Such an audience is well aware that if the societal standards, that is, the logic of mortal life as it is viewed in modern society, are applied to Wagner's characters, the intricate web that the composer wove as a story for his work immediately dissolves, and the drama *per se* ceases to be. The concern in such cases is laid upon a matter that is incompatible with the transcendency of the theme.

A comprehension of Wagner's *Ring* can be attained only when the viewer has invoked a suspension of disbelief. When such a state is achieved, there is no sensed intellectual uneasiness about who is mortal, who is god, who is giant, who is dwarf. Such a state allows for no mental discomfort, and there is no emotional standard to dissuade the viewer from full association with Wagner's argument. Once that suspension of disbelief is effected, the powerful impact of the drama will unfold, and the viewer will then be able to view himself within the argument and to attach his personal understandings and interpretations to the tale that is so universal in concept and development. Such an understanding gives no heed to the physical matters of existence, but rather allows that of the human condition to become the experience of time.

_____

NAMES (in the *Ring*)

It is not unusual that often the most seasoned followers of Wagner's *Der Ring des Nibelungen* seldom have even a partial understanding of the names that the composer brought into his drama. Such an understanding can include a linguistic and a semantic comprehension of a word, as well as the history, the significance, and the full meaning of each of the characters, places, groups, and objects that is named in the drama.

Wagner's monumental drama is replete with proper nouns, that is, words that serve as names. An examination of the meaning of each of these words, and a study of the origin of each term, when such data is available, combined with a serious consideration of other pertinent linguistic matters, will reveal almost immediately that most of the names that Wagner used are not merely names that are used solely for purposes of identification. These names will reveal, or perhaps convey, some aspect of the characters to which they have been attached, or the nature of the figure or figures, or that of the property that bears the name. Such a total examination will also show how deftly each of these expressive names makes its own individual contribution to the mythical ambience that pervades this musico-dramatic landmark. Indeed, the names that Wagner used within his *Ring* are so compatible within the context of the drama, and they are so appropriate to the actions in which they are a part, that any substitution, or even an alteration, could radically disturb the dramatic coloration that the composer so skillfully painted into the thematic canvas of his work.

The majority of names that Wagner placed in his *Ring* drama perform, in the main, two important functions other than that of identification. In the first regard, most of the names convey, in one way or another, a sense of antiquity, the aura of another age, an era that is apparently timeless yet somehow vital and pertinent in the present day. Such an ambience was one of the composer's primary intents. At the same time, these names usually project, in the minimum, a generic aspect of the figure, figures, or object with which they are associated. In the maximum, these names offer signification of a fundamental attribute of the holders, a certain quality (or qualities) that in turn subtly enhances the respective role in the thematic development of the drama.

The linguistic story of the names in the *Ring* is multifaceted. There are those names that Wagner carried over from an earlier day, names that are found in the myths, legends, sagas, songs, and poems of the ancient Teutonic world. For the most part, these names exist in two forms: one that is part of the Southern or German version of a story, and a variation that is used in the Northern or Scandinavian version of a tale. All of the names that Wagner used are the German varieties. On occasion, however, he would make some slight modification to a name, usually the more to bring it into the mainstream of modern language.

There are, then, those names that the composer himself created. Some of these names contain terms that he extracted from early Germanic language, ancient words to which he frequently gave a hue of linguistic modernity which allowed them to be acceptable as contemporary language, although such names were not always completely understood. Some of Wagner's creations contain words that are drawn from contemporary vocabulary, but which are then used in such a manner that their meanings deviate slightly from those of modern usage. Curiously, the varied linguistic techniques that Wagner employed permitted his created names to be acceptable as current language, while all the while somehow reflecting a hint of the Germanic mythico-legendary past.

The names that are found in the *Ring* are singular, regardless of how, or in what manner they are used. They seem unbound by any limits of time. They are at once ancient, yet they are also modern. They are, above all else, wholly Teutonic, and more specifically, German. Through it all, however, these names are products of a total culture, a total people, with a thoroughly German essence that Wagner considered imperative to a national work of art. These names are also another tangible means by which the drama becomes a full and complete work, one of the means by which Wagner's story seems to develop and expand so appropriately within the mythical ambient setting that they help to create. Finally, these names that Wagner put into his four-part drama are yet another segment that contributes to a more comprehensive understanding of his story.

See also: *Notes*
(*Each of the proper nouns that is to be found in the* Ring *is included in this volume, arranged alphabetically along with other matters pertinent to the drama. Each entry presents an appropriate linguistic and semantic analysis of that specific name.*)

NEIDHÖHLE See: *Fafner's Cave*

NEIDHÖHLE (Name)

In the first drama of Wagner's *Ring, Das Rheingold*, the giant Fafner slays his brother Fasolt and then gathers the gold hoard that the gods had given the pair as payment for their labors on Valhalla, flees to a forest, and seeks refuge in a great cave. In the cave Fafner changes himself into a dragon and in that form he will guard the great treasure that he has taken for himself. At some time much later and in the third drama of the *Ring, Siegfried*, Mime will lead the Volsung youth Siegfried to this cave in front of which the hero will slay the dragon and claim the treasure as his.

Wagner gave the cave into which Fafner carries the gold the name *Neidhöhle*, a German compound consisting of *Neid* and *Höhle*. The former word means "envy," "jealousy," or "enviousness," while the latter translates as "cave" or "cavern." Hence, Wagner's *Neidhöhle* can be translated in several ways, one of which is "Cave of Envy."

Wagner was prompted by some Eddic verses to give this lair of the Dragon a name. In the mythical tale that recounts a story similar to the one that Wagner prepared for his drama, the cave to which Fafner retires is named *Gnitaheid*. Although Wagner attempted to use the German form of whatever mythical names that were appropriate for his drama, there is every reason to understand why he did not accept the Eddic name or its translation for the name of Fafner's cave.

The word *Gnitaheid*, like Neidhöhle, is a compound term. The suffix *Heid* was derived from the Old Norse *heitr* and *heiti* which meant "moor" or "moorland" (Gothic – *haithi*; OHG – *heida*; MHG – *heide*; AS – *haed*; Swedish – *hed*; Danish – *hede*; English – *heath*). The verses of the *Edda* do not refer to Gnitaheid as a "moorland," however, preferring instead to speak of the site as a 'forest.' Wagner readily accepted the concept of a 'forest' as his dragon's lair, but he was quick to reject the prefix of this term. The ON *Gnita* became *Gnitte* and *Gnitze* in Low German (AS – *gnaet*; Low Dutch – *gnatt*; Middle – Dutch – *gnitte*). The word in English became *gnit* and *gnat*, both of which serve as translations of the prefix word, and the Eddic name thus inferred a place where swarming gnits congregated! Wagner's created name seems much more the mythical term than that of the *Edda*.

The geographic term *East* is frequently found in the Germanic myths. Early Teutonic beliefs held that the Land of the Giants, one of the nine worlds of the universe, was located "to the East." Donner traveled "to the East" quite often, for it was there that he fought and killed numerous giants who were the foremost enemies of the gods. The mythical cave in which Fafner guarded his treasure was also "to the East." Wagner rejected the mythical name of Fafner's cave, but he accepted its mythical location, and like its counterpart in the *Edda*, the *Ring's* Neidhöhle is to be found in a forest that is "to the East."

See also: *Fafner's Cave*

NEIDING

In the first act of *Die Walküre*, Hunding identifies himself as a Neiding, that is, a family member of the Neiding clan. This is the band that Siegmund describes as "cruel," the group that had slain Siegmund's mother, set fire to their house, and abducted his sister, all of which caused him and his father, Wälse (Wotan), to wander almost aimlessly at large and at length in the forest.

The custom of identification by means of a family or clan name was quite routine in early Teutonic society. That custom remains in several of the modern Germanic cultures. Wagner felt very much at ease as he included this type of name as he populated his *Ring* drama, not only with the mortal Neidings, but also the legendary, and at times mythical, Nibelungs, the Volsungs, and the Gibichungs.

NEIDING (Name)

The name *Neiding*, like so many other names in the *Ring*, is a compound of two words, *Neid* and *ing*. *Neid*, which is still in use in modern German, is a term that denotes "envy," or "grudge," or "jealousy," when combined with *ing* (See *Notes*), translates as "Child" or "Offspring of Envy." Indeed, either of the other two principal meanings of the term *Neid* can be substituted for "Envy," for the nature of Wagner's Hunding is so aptly developed that each term denotes an element of his character.

It should be noted that the other clan or family names that Wagner included in the *Ring* (Nibelung, Volsung, Gibichung) also include a suffix that translates as "Child" or "Offspring of." The semantic as well as societal and cultural distinction between the offspring of an *ing* and that of an *ung* is quite significant. Each of the suffixes makes its own inference as to type of family.

See also: *Notes*

NIBELHEIM

This word is the modern form of the mythical *Niflheim*, both of which refer to a kind of nether world deep within the earth. Both words can be translated as "Home of Darkness."

The original Niflheim, the land that is so frequently mentioned throughout the Teutonic myths, was not the home of the dwarfs, as Wagner depicted it in his drama. Rather, the mythical Niflheim (Nibelheim) was really the Land of the Dead, that is those who had not died a glorious and valiant death on the field of battle. In the minds of the early Teutonic peoples, Niflheim was of great importance and given that significance it is not unusual that it was thought of as one of the nine worlds that existed in early Germanic thought. Niflheim lay deep in the earth. In the center of this dark world there was a spring (some tales call it a *well*) that was called *Hvergelmir* ("Bubbling Cauldron"), and from this spring flowed all the rivers of the universe. The warder or guardian of this land was Hel (Hella), a daughter of Loge who had been assigned to her position by Wotan. On occasion, this dank subterranean world was called *Niflhel*, and at other times simply *Hel*.

(In addition to Niflheim, the eight other worlds that existed in the universe of early Teutonic beliefs were: Asgard (Land of the Gods), Vanaheim (Land of the Wanes), Alfheim (Home of the Elves [Dwarfs]), Midgard (Land of Mortals), Jotunheim (Land of Giants), Muspellsheim (Land of Fire [Giants]), Svartalfaheim (Land of Black Elves [Dwarfs]), and presumably Nidavellir ("Dark Fields"), which may have been the land of the Dark or Black Dwarfs.)

See also: *Hella*

NIBELHEIM (Name)

The prefix *nibel*, meaning "darkness," is discussed in *Notes*. The suffix *heim* means "home" or "dwelling." Together, this name can be translated as "Home of Darkness."

NIBELUNG

The follower of Wagner's *Ring* who has not familiarized himself with the several sources that served the composer as the basis of much of the argument of his drama may very well be surprised by the marked differences that exist between Wagner's use of the word *Nibelung* and the application of that term in Teutonic mythology, legend, and, in this case, history.

Historically, Charles Martel, the Frankish ruler who, in 732, defeated the powerful Moors in their northward trek out of Spain, had a relative whose name was *Nivelongus*. This name, in varied forms (*Nibelungus, Nebulunc, Nevelungus, Neuelunchus, Nevelongus*), continued to appear, if infrequently, as a family name throughout the region well into the thirteenth century. At all times the name belonged to those who, in one way or another, had some royal association.

The name *Nibelung*, in any of its distinct forms and for whatever reason or reasons, also began to appear in the early Germanic writings, as well as in a later body of dramatic and legendary works. As found in these several works the word was used as a name, but in a manner whose associations were quite different from the historical past. If indeed there had been living beings that bore the name, it is also fact that from an early date Teutonic beliefs held that there was a body of beings with that name, and it is possible that these same beliefs considered this race to be supernatural, either giants or dwarfs. There is no specific evidence to support this mythical possibility, and, as a result there has always been the question of exactly who were the Nibelungs (Niflungs), if indeed there was such a clan. That question has been a subject of much discussion and conjecture among mythologists and students of Germanic literatures.

There is, however, general agreement among scholars that this name, in the beginning, was attached to a literary family of related beings that was the possessor of a vast treasure. As the story of the Nibelungs and their treasure became more widespread and as it increased in popularity, new and different versions of the tale came into existence. In time, it was not unusual to encounter as varied a depiction of this race as there were versions of the Siegfried story.

The *Nibelungenlied (Song of the Nibelungs)* was the Southern or German version of the legend. There are extant no less than ten complete codices and three fragmentary manuscripts of this epic of the German people, and these writings clearly reflect the confusion as well as the inconsistencies that plague the matter of the name *Nibelung* and the race or group or clan that it represents.

The first chapters (*aventiuren*) of this poem, as it is usually reproduced today, present the Nibelungs as a group that lived in *Nibelung Land*. The king of this land is named *Nibelung* and he has two sons, Schilbung and Nibelung. These Nibelungs possess a treasure that lies deep within a great mountain. These individuals are not depicted as supernaturals, although the guardian of the hoard, Alberich, is said to be a dwarf. Siegfried, who is a Prince of the Lower Rhine and from Netherland, conquers the Nibelungs and becomes master of the people, their lands, and the treasure. At this point, in addition to the people that Siegfried conquered, he as well as those who came with him to the land of the Nibelungs now were known as Nibelungs. The Nibelung Siegfried and his Nibelung vassals soon journey to Burgundy, a kingdom on the Rhine. Siegfried marries Kriemhild (Grimhild), the sister of the Burgundian king, Gunther. In time, Siegfried is killed by Gunther's vassal, Hagen, and the Nibelung (Siegfried's) treasure is brought to Worms, the Burgundian capital. When Hagen learns that Siegfried's widow, Queen Kriemhild is distributing the treasure, he seizes the hoard and sinks it in the Rhine. At this point, the warriors (Nibelungs) who had served Siegfried joined forces with the Burgundian forces of King Gunther, and all were now known as Nibelungs. Long after the death of Siegfried, Gunther,

Hagen, and the 'Nibelung' forces engage in a furious battle with the forces of Attila, the Hun, and are defeated. A segment of the last line of the celebrated epic translates as "This is the fall of the Nibelungs."

Variations of this story, most of which endured by means of oral accounts, began to surface and to circulate. There were, however, some versions that were recorded in several sections of Teutondom. One of the most interesting is that of Hans Sachs (who was to become a figure in Wagner's *Die Meistersinger*) who dramatized a poem about the "horn-skinned" Siegfried. Sachs penned his work in 1557 and titled it "Der hürnen Seufrid." This drama and the original were expanded into a prose version that appeared in a seventeenth-century chapbook. In this latter work, the treasure that came into Siegfried's (Seyfrid) hand after he killed a dragon is called the 'Nibelung's hoard,' and, curiously, it is Siegfried himself who sinks the treasure in the Rhine when he hears that possession of the hoard will cause him to be quite short-lived. (It should be noted that from early in the thirteenth century until well into the seventeenth century the use of the word 'Nibelung' was essentially restricted to an association with the treasure that lay at the bottom of the Rhine River.)

The Eddic version of the Nibelung matter, as well that which is contained in the Norwegian work *Thidrekssaga*, can readily be associated with the southern version that was its source. The *Niflungar* are the vassals of Gunther (Gunnar), whose kingdom 'south of the Rhine' is known as *Niflunga Land*. In the main, however, the Nordic tradition associates the word *Nibelung* with a great treasure that had belonged to Gunther, one that had been demanded by Gunther's conqueror, Atli (Attila), but which had been sunk in the Rhine. In all of these northern myths and legends that deal with this matter, that is those that make reference to the name 'Nibelung' and also to Siegfried, continue to associate the youth with the original treasure that came into his possession early on, and the association of Siegfried and a treasure that he gained after slaying a dragon is not to be found.

Wagner seemed to voice no serious concern regarding the enigma of the Nibelungs, that is, the mystery of who, what, where, and even the when that surrounded the figures supposedly represented by that name. He could have been aware of the many questions about the Nibelungs that had gone unanswered in the past, and which remained unanswered even in his own time. He could also have been aware of the numerous associations, some of a conflicting nature, that had been made for this name. Yet, there could be no doubt that he was aware that the name was a familiar one in German societal culture, and that this was a name that was closely associated with the Siegfried, the Gunther, and the Hagen who were to figure highly in his *Ring* drama. It may very well be, then, that he felt that the name Nibelung was one that had a rightful place in his poem and therefore should be incorporated into his work, at whatever cost. Wagner made that incorporation, and in so doing, it would seem that he disregarded much of the historicity that enveloped the name and, rather, took careful notice of the basic semantics of the word, and adhering to the concepts that those meanings projected, applied the name to those of his dwarfs who inhabited the dark and misty inner-earth of his drama, the Nibelungs of Nibelheim.

NIBELUNG (Name)

The meanings of the two words that form this compound, *nibel* and *ung*, are briefly discussed in *Notes*. The compound word will render a meaning of "Offspring of" or "Child of Darkness."

The modern word *Nibelung* is derived from a Nordic antecedent, *Niflung*, whose prefix was to be found in several Germanic tongues: OHG – *nebul*; MHG – *nebel* and *nib*, Old Frisian – *nevil*; Middle Dutch – *nevel*; OS – *nebal*, OE – *nifal* and *neowal*. Each of these several words meant "mist," "darkness," "dark," and there was the ON word - *Niflheimr* ("underworld").

NIFLHEL (HEL, HELLA)

Niflhel, in the ancient Teutonic myths, denotes one of the nine worlds that constituted the universe. (In some of the early myths, the word *Niflhel* becomes *Niflheim* or *Nebelheim*.) Niflhel is not a factor in Wagner's *Ring* except that it served as a basis for the composer's use of the word *Nibelheim*, which he assigned as home for the Nibelungen dwarfs, and after which he patterned much of the ambience and atmosphere of this land in the bowels of the earth. The old word *nifl* meant "fog" or "mist" or "haze" in the sense of 'darkness.' In time, the variation *Nibel* came into use.

In mythical beliefs, Niflhel, often shortened to *Hel* and *Hella*, was the Land of the Dead. All the women and children who had died, as well as those men who had died of illness, accident, old age, or of an inglorious death in combat, were destined to live out their afterlife in this dark and eerie place that was located deep in the earth, at the root of the World Ash Tree.

The guardian of the dead that were destined for afterlife in Hel was also known as *Hel*, and often called *Hella*. Hel, or Hella, was one of the three monster offspring of Loki (Loge) and the giantess Angrboda. She had been condemned to life in the netherworld by Wotan who, acting upon the council of the gods, had feared that she would bring great harm to the land of gods and mortals if she were not sent far from those worlds.

Although Wagner makes no dramatic use of the word *Niflhel* or *Hel*, he does recall the name Hella on at least three occasions. It is Siegmund who first uses the name, declaring that he prefers Hella (Hel) to Valhalla if he must be separated from Sieglinde. Then it is an angered Alberich who says that with Hella's army he will one day conquer Valhalla and the gods. The last usage in the *Ring* of this term comes when Brünnhilde, faced by Siegfried who, in the disguise of Gunther, has come to take her as wife for the Gibichung. The fearful Brünnhilde, on seeing the unrecognizable figure who has emerged from the fire that surrounds the mountain top, cries out in fear, asking if he is human or if he is one of Hella's army.

NIGHT See: *Moon*
           Sun

NINE

It is not mere coincidence that Wagner placed nine Valkyries in his *Ring* drama! The number nine was the favored number among the early Teutonic peoples. It was considered to be the holiest, the most sacred of numbers, the number nine could bring good fortune. This number could make possible the most advantageous of opportunities, it could signal the coming of joy and happiness, it could bring about wealth and riches, and in the appropriate situation the number nine could also be a prelude to disease, degradation, and even death. Nine, in the minds of the ancient Germanic was indeed the most powerful and the most magical of all numbers.

The myths of Teutondom are replete with situations in which the number nine is a prominent factor. There are adventures, deeds, songs, charms, and runes that include the number nine in one or another manner. There are also cultural beliefs, concepts, ideas, habits customs, and religious practices that include the number nine as a basic focal point.

There can be no question regarding what is the most significant, and indeed the most prominent of Teutonic mythical matters that focuses on the beliefs concerning the number nine. This prominent mythical belief was one accepted by all the separate Germanic clans, that concept that held that the universe consisted of *nine* worlds, all of which were housed in the branches of or beneath the surface of the earth, in the roots of Yggdrasil, the World Ash Tree. All matter, living or dead, was housed in one of these nine worlds, each of which had a specific name. It would also be from this tree of all life that the Supreme God of Teutondom, Wotan, would hang, head down, for *nine* nights, after which he would see the runes of the universe, take them up, and then learn *nine* mighty songs that would contribute to his divine authority as the Allfather of the universe. As the number nine includes the gods in what can be considered the beginning of all time, so too would it be a factor in *ragnarök*, the fated downfall and destruction of the gods of Teutondom. In that mighty final struggle that places the deities in combat against their many enemies, Donner, the God of Thunder and Lightning, fights with one of the monster offspring of Loge, Jormungdandr, who is perhaps better known mythically as Midgardsorm, the World Serpent. Donner slays the monster, but as the god takes his *ninth* step away from this beast, he falls dead, killed by the poisonous slaver that the serpent had breathed upon him.

There are yet numerous other mythical matters that include the number nine as a fundamental factor in the life and activities of the gods. Draupnir, the gold ring that belongs to Balder, the favorite son of Wotan and his wife Fricka, drops eight other identical rings every *ninth* night. (It is this ring and this act that accounts for the wealth that frees them from any need to struggle to obtain any item that they desired.) When the god Froh (Freyr) falls in love with the giantess Gerd, he seeks her so intently that finally she agrees that she will meet the god *nine* nights later. Heimdall, the god that is charged with guardianship of Bifrost, the Rainbow Bridge, was born of *nine* women, who, in some myths are said to be sisters. Menglod, who is thought by some scholars to be the goddess Freia (Freyja), has *nine* virgins who kneel before her and who serve her. On one of his many journeys, Wotan (Odin) descends from the heavens to earth and first sees *nine* laborers who are mowing hay. Germanic concepts also held that Wotan played a game to entertain himself, a game that was called "Nine Pins." Ran, the wife of the sea-god Aegir, had *nine* daughters, each of whom is named in *The Poetic Edda*. Njorth, the god who was father to Froh and Freia and who was one of the hostages that the Vanir (Wanes) gods surrendered to the Aesir in the first battle of the universe, married Skadi. Skadi wanted to have her home in the land of her father, in Thrymheim, which was in the mountains. Njorth wanted to live in his home Noatun which was located near the sea. The couple finally decided that each would live for *nine* nights in the home of the other, and then they would decide where they would live. (Each hated the other's home, and so they decided to live apart, each in his original home.) Hermod, another of Wotan's sons, rode for *nine* nights, in dales so deep that he could not see anything, as he rode from Asgard, the Land of the Gods, down into Hel, the Land of the Dead, a world that existed beneath the earth, among the roots of the World Ash Tree.

Not all matters that included the number nine pertained specifically to the gods. Loge (Loki) has forged the only weapon that can kill the rooster that will awaken the gods at *ragnarök*, the time of the downfall and destruction of the gods. This weapon is named *Laevatein* ("Wounding Wand"), and it is kept in a chest that belongs to the shrewd and cunning supernatural, a chest that is held fast by *nine* locks. It is again Loge who is involved in a related tale. It is he who has built a large hall that is surrounded by fire and flame, Loge that is, with the aid of *nine* dwarfs.

The heroic literature that is contained in *The Poetic Edda* also reveals the significance of the number *nine* among mortals. Granmar turns herself into a Valkyrie and bears *nine* wolves to Sinfjotli. Helgi, the great hero of Denmark "sees" *nine* Valkyries. (Mythical beliefs held that the Valkyries were not visible to mortals, although Wagner's Brünnhilde states that those heroes who are marked for death and afterlife in Valhalla can see these Wishmaidens.) A curse is laid upon Atli, a jarl who captains his huge sailing ship, when an unknown speaker utters: *"Nine* miles deeper down may thee sink."

It was not only in myths and legends that the number *nine* was a matter of some importance. The early Teutonic society also conducted itself, in the daily routines of its life, according to the numerous beliefs that revolved around this number. There was at one time a tree on the outskirts of what is today Uppsala, Sweden, that was considered to be a most sacred tree. Every *ninth* month the people conducted a festival at the base of that tree. The celebration lasted for *nine* days, and *nine* animals were sacrificed, one each day. There was also a time when the people of the Germanic coasts believed that a seal sheds it skin every *ninth* day, and then for one day becomes a mortal man. There was also the widely held belief that a man could change himself into a wolf, and remain in that state for *nine* days, and on the tenth he could revert to his human form. There was also a religious practice that was carried out in some of the churches of modern Teutondom. This act included a prayer that was read by *nine* women on each of *nine* consecutive Sundays!

These are but a few of the Teutonic mythical, legendary, and societal incidents in which the number *nine* plays a key role. Given the numerous examples that occur so frequently, and which are collected with relative ease, it is probably safe to assume that the number *nine* was without doubt one of the major factors in the daily life of the Germanic peoples. Indeed, the significance of the number *nine* was so extensive and so profound that some of that concept has carried over to the modern day. *Nine* was without doubt the potent, the preponderant, the most prominent number within the society. It was, then, no matter of fortunate circumstance that caused that Wagner to include nine Valkyries in his *Ring* drama! His action in that regard could only have been intentional, and thoroughly mythical.

See also: *Nine Worlds*

NINE WORLDS

Although there are variations, often conflicts, in the details that the Teutonic myths reveal, in essence, the early Teutonic peoples conceived a universe that consisted of nine distinct worlds. Each of these worlds was housed within or at the roots of Yggdrasil, the World Ash Tree as it is more regularly called. Each of these worlds was inhabited by a different race of beings.

The nine worlds were:

1. Jotunheim – The Land of the Giants
2. Alfheim – The Land of the Elves
3. Muspellsheim – The Land of the Fire-Giants
4. Svartalfaheim – The Land of the Dark Elves
5. Niflheim – The Land of the Dead
6. Asgard – The Land of the Aesir Gods
7. Vanaheim – The Land of the Vanir Gods
8. Midgard – The World of Men
9. Nidavellir – (?) – The World of the Dwarfs (There is some question about the existence of this world in Teutonic mythical thought.)

Wagner brought four of these worlds into his *Ring* drama. One of his worlds is *Nibelheim*, which is a name of his own creation but borrowed from

Niflheim, the Land of the Dead. Wagner made this world the Land of the Dwarfs. A second world that makes its way into the drama is *Riesenhiem*, the *Ring's* Land of the Giants which, in turn, corresponds to the mythical *Jotunheim*. Wagner's Riesenheim is more mentioned than actually viewed. A third world of Wagner's drama is, of course, the Land of the Gods. Wagner does not name this world, but reference is made to it frequently, and the great fortress Valhalla, which the giants have constructed, is located in that divine world. Wagner's Land of the Gods would refer to the mythical Asgard rather than to Vanaheim. The fourth of the *Ring's* worlds is that of mortal man. As with the Land of the Gods, Wagner does not name this world, but reference to it is inferred when it is learned that Wotan descended to that world for his union with Mortal Woman and the resultant creation of the Volsung clan.

NIXIE

The first words that Alberich utters when he appears in the opening scene of *Das Rheingold* are "Hehe! Ihr Nicker!" This single utterance makes reference to the three Rhinemaidens with the word "Nicker," which translates as *nixie*. With that one word, Wagner was able to set the mythical stage for the powerful ambience of mythicalness and legend in the drama that was to follow.

In the beliefs of the early Teutonic peoples, there were sprites that inhabited all bodies of water. Each of these figures was given a generic name that essentially denoted the type of water that served as a home. Perhaps the most familiar name of such sprites in English is *mermaid*, those half-woman half-fish creatures that lived in the oceans and seas of the world and lured sailors to their deaths by means of their haunting song.

The *nix* or *nixie* was a water sprite that lived mostly in or near rivers, and on occasion, in streams, or lakes. The word was derived from ON *nykr* (AS – *nicor*; OHG – *Nichus*; MHG – *Nickes*; Mod G – *Nixen*). (It should be noted that Wagner's word *Nicker* imitates in sound the original Old Norse term *Nykr*.)

The nixies of the early Germanic culture were beautiful creatures. They were human in form, usually with long, golden hair which they combed while they sunned themselves on the shore of the river in which they lived. It is perhaps because of that beauty that nixies were usually seen only by men. The beauty of these nymphs was complemented by exquisite voices with which they sang their songs. The combination of their beauty and their lovely songs was an enticement to men, but it was a dangerous lure. These water sprites were, in reality, cruel spirits who took delight in tempting men into their arms and then doing great harm to them, even that of dragging them to their deaths in the water.

The most celebrated nixie of Germanic legend is Lorelei, the nymph whose songs reportedly caused many sailors to wreck their boats on her rock. This legend is kept alive today by the name of a prominent rock that juts out into the Rhine River, near Coblenz, in Germany, and by a well-known piece of music that bears the name of this siren. The story of Lorelei was told by the German author Clemens Brentano, which in turn was popularized by the poem "Die Lorelei" of Heinrich Heine.

See also: *Rhinemaidens*

NORNS

The most absolute of all spirits of the heathen Teutonic world, frequently mightier even than the gods, was the *Norn*. This being was the divine virgin female who possessed the threads of destiny and who, guided by her vast and unlimited wisdom, carefully spun those threads into a term of life for each being of the universe, including the deities. The cultural concept that allowed the Norn to exist was developed quite early and, curiously, that initial concept that gave rise to the Norn was originally the mythical concept of the Valkyrie. This early depiction that ultimately allowed two thoroughly mythical Teutonic figures, the Norn and the Valkyrie, to emerge into the mainstream of mythical thought is to be found in a work that bears the title *Njal's Saga*. The description of the original Valkyrie that this work presents is quite vivid. The Valkyrie determines the fate of men and then, with their swords, these creatures weave those words into their loom of slaughter. As the figures weave, they sing, and the heavens are splattered with blood. The blood drips and falls onto the loom whose shuttles are arrows, whose shafts are ironbound, and whose treadles are spears that are wet with blood. The weights of this loom are human heads, and the web is human entrails!

The early concept of a supernatural eventually evolved into two distinct figures in the Teutonic mythical thought, one of which was the Norn, the Germanic figure that determined the destiny of all things. So integral did this figure ultimately become in Germanic beliefs, and so widespread was its influence throughout all of the early Teutonic territories that, in time, the single word Norn was used in each region of the Teutonic world without any of the variations that would seem to rise naturally within the several languages and dialects that were developing.

The Norn, collectively they were called *Nornir*, was an obvious conceptual outgrowth of two fundamental aspects of the ancient Germanic thought. Firstly, the heathen Teutonic mind believed that the world was inhabited by countless spirits, supernatural beings who, in one manner or another, possessed certain magical powers with which they could control or otherwise exercise some degree of control over certain specific activities of the natural world. These spirits, whatever their form – which was usually patterned on human life – and whatever their powers, were looked upon with deep respect, even reverence, while at the same time these spirits were greatly feared by the same people. In the second regard, faced with the realization that ultimately death came to every living thing, there existed, again throughout the entire Teutonic world, a belief that there was an inevitable but unknown fate that existed for every being, a fate that was always foreordained. These two tenets of heathen Teutonic thought, each so rigorously accepted by the Teutonic mind, complemented each other and, early on, fused and took conceptual shape as the Norn, that spirit who cast the destiny of each and every being.

Extensive studies by mythologists of this spirit of the Teutonic world reveal that in the beginning there was but a single Norn. This reality had been based on the known existence in the cultural world of the *volva*, the "wise-woman," sometimes referred to as the "prophetess." The *volva* was a mortal woman who was thought to be versed in the ways and customs of the culture itself as well as life in that culture, and who had great wisdom in all matters. This woman counseled and prophesied for those of her community. The *volva* lived apart from others and was a solitary figure who practiced her art unaided by others of similar character. As the mythical counterpart of the mortal *volva* emerged in the heathen Teutonic mind, she too was a single figure who functioned alone. This was the Norn, a powerful spirit who, like all other significant figures of the ancient supernatural world of the Teutonic peoples, acquired a name.

The first references to the Norn were by means of the word *urd*. This Old Norse word can be translated as "destiny" or "fate." In time, this word ceased to be a generic term and was accepted as a proper noun, that is a name, for this female figure. As time passed, Urd, the first Norn, became three in number. This development was especially prominent in Scandinavia where the trio was viewed as sisters. Scholars have concluded that the change in number of Norns from one to three was the logical result of the influence on Teutonic thought of classical mythology, specifically that of the three goddesses who were regularly referred to as *Past, Present, and Future*. The names for the other two Norns became *Verdandi* and *Skuld*.

The three Norns of Teutondom had their dwelling at the foot of Yggdrasil, the great ash tree that housed the nine worlds of the universe. It was under the third root of the World Ash that this trio, in addition to setting the fate of men, carved runes on the wood of the tree and made certain laws. Urd tended there her spring from which the Norns daily took water to sprinkle on the tree, to keep it green and in full bloom. The water that fell from the tree was the dew that covered the earth. (There is a second concept that holds that the dew that is found on all things every morning is the sweat that falls from the brows of the horses that are ridden furiously by Valkyries as they raced from earth to Valhalla, the home of slain heroes.)

The three Norns of the ancient Germanic world possessed the golden threads of life and it was with these threads that they wove the Cord of Destiny, sometimes called the Web of Fate. As they wove, they cast the ends of the Cord to the East, to the West, and to the North. (The use of the direction *South* is carefully avoided in the Teutonic myths, probably because it is "in the South," which was called *Muspellsheim* ("Muspell's Home"), that the giant Surt and his fire-giants lived. It was ordained that these giants would invade the land of the gods at the moment of the downfall and destruction for these deities, and the giants would bring with them the fire that would consume the corrupt universe.) Once the Cord of Destiny had been spun and the Norns had made their pronouncements, the fate of the being involved was determined. The declaration of the sisters was irrevocable, it could not be altered in any way. It is curious to note that the pronouncements of the Norns were equally valid for the gods and other supernatural beings as they were for mortals. (The concept that the Norns weave a Cord of Destiny is not general to the myths of the gods as found in *The Poetic Edda*. In those myths, the Norns determined the fate of each newborn child, and then carved that fate into the trunk of the World Ash Tree. The matter of their weaving the Cord of Destiny is found, however, in the "Lays of the Heroes" that is usually included with those of the gods. More specifically, it is at the birth of the Danish national hero Helgi that the Norns appear and at that time weave the fateful web.)

The Norns of Teutondom and the *volvas* that were found in every community were essentially mythical and mortal counterparts. The numerous *volvas* that existed in the culture slowly gave rise to the thought that there were also numerous Norns. Albeit that these lesser Norns were minor figures, they were nevertheless consulted and involved in shaping the lives of the people. It was these Norns who were called upon to look favorably upon the birth of a child, to make pronouncements regarding the health, now and in the future, of the newborn, and it was the Norns who were called upon to protect the newborn as he grew and traveled about the world. It was these lesser Norns who were the cause of whatever minor misfortunes that befell a person, for if there were good Norns, there were also bad ones, and woe to the mortal who chose as his life's Norn one of the evil ones!

The lesser Norns literally numbered in the hundreds, if not thousands, in ancient Teutondom. Inasmuch as the heathen Germanic peoples conceived of their gods as human in body and basic nature, so too were the Norns of that world human in form and nature. It was because of these concepts that there were Norns that existed for all levels of life, that is, in addition to those that lived in the world of man, there were those who were natural to and who tended all the races of the Teutonic universe, which included the gods, the giants, and the dwarfs.

The three Norns that Wagner incorporated into the argument of his *Ring* drama are, essentially, that celebrated trio of supernatural spirits that exerted great power within the world of heathen Teutonic thought. As in the Eddic literature, so too in the *Ring*, where the Norns are referred to no less than six times in the first three music-dramas, there is an appreciation of the integral role that these figures played in the continued existence of all living things, an awareness of the ever-present control that they had in the destiny of all life. In the fourth drama of the *Ring*, in what can only be termed a subtle revelation of a keen sense of theatricality, Wagner caused the Norns to appear, alone, as a trio that ponders what has been, what is, and what is yet to come, including a pronouncement of the downfall of the gods.

Wagner gave to his Norns much the same role that these figures had exercised in early mythical beliefs. They appear in the darkness of night, to weave and to spin the threads of the Cord of Destiny. At one time, they cast an end of the Cord "northward." They refer to their life beside the World Ash Tree, and they speak of the spring whose waters kept the tree lush and green. Like the Norns in the mythical literature, Wagner's Norns infer an analogy to the classical Fates, and in such a fashion that there is no violation of their thoroughly Teutonic character, their Teutonic uniqueness that is so evident in the Eddic literature.

Wagner's Norns, like the mythical creatures, were endowed with the power to determine a term of life for all beings, for gods as well as for man. It is in *Siegfried* that Wotan, in the guise of Wanderer, who admits that the Norns control the destiny of the universe and that they weave into their Cord of Destiny what they must. Then, as he questions how their judgment may be undone, he infers that their power is great, greater than that which he, the

Supreme God of all Teutondom, has, and that not even he can undo their decisions. It is in the "Norn Scene," that scene of the "Prelude" of the fourth drama that Wagner then causes the three sisters to speak of the gods and the ultimate fatal end that is to be theirs, the end of them and all that they have created.

The control that Wagner's Norns have on the fates of mortals is revealed in two separate scenes of the *Ring* drama. It is Hunding, in *Die Walküre*, who tells Siegmund that the sorrows that he has known in his solitary and lonely life have come to him because the Norns have not looked favorably on him. It is later, in *Siegfried*, that Brünnhilde, now a mortal whose passions have been stirred by Siegfried, calls upon the Norns to destroy the Cord of Destiny that they have woven for each of the pair, thus allowing her and the hero to know the fullness of the love that has flowered between them. It is evident that these separate references to the Norns and their powers are specific to given situations, yet, in light of the future events of the drama, there is present in each scene a subtle inference, or perhaps it is a prophetic signal, of a darker fate that is to come. It is thematic fact that shortly after Hunding's remarks that the Norns have not shown favor to the sorrowed Siegmund, the latter dies in combat, killed by the very person who made reference to the baleful Norns. In Brünnhilde's plea to the Norns that they undo the Cord of Destiny that has been woven for her and Siegfried, she hints that their love is not to be enjoyed, that there is in the Cord of Destiny the thread of a sinister fate that is awaiting them. As with the Siegmund incident, so too shortly after Brünnhilde addresses the Norns, Siegfried meets his death at the hands of Hagen, and the daughter of the Allfather Wotan then perishes by her own hand.

Wagner's inclusion of the Norns in his *Ring* is an obvious indication of his dramatic awareness of the significance of these spirits in the heathen Teutonic mind. If Wagner sensed that these figures had a rightful role in his argument, along with other prominent mythical beings and properties, he also felt that if he was to maintain the dramatic continuity in his work, this trio and its activities must relate directly to the story as he was writing it. Wagner worked to this end, all the while trying not inject into his Norns the mythical essence that was theirs in the ancient culture.

Wagner worked carefully to depict his trio of Norns much as they were in Eddic times, yet he attached to the sisters certain dramatic aspects of his own creation. Wagner's personal dramatic contributions to the Norns were essentially factors of a thematic nature, but factors that he obviously felt were also compatible with the overall concept of these spirits.

The first of these Wagnerian exceptions to the mythical Norns, and the drama's first reference to these spirits, appears in *Das Rheingold*, in words that Erda pronounces. This spirit of the mother-world warns Wotan to beware the curse, Alberich's curse of death, that will come to the possessor of the gold ring. Erda's words reflect the nature of a *volva*, the All-Wise, the All-Knowing being of ancient times. It is, in fact, Wagner's Erda who has great wisdom, the being to whom Wotan turns when in need of counsel. In his dramatic mind Wagner believed that it would have been dramatically unwise for the supreme god of the universe to seek counsel from any figure less than the wisest and most knowledgeable of beings. Thus, the Norns, as important as they were in the Germanic culture, become in the *Ring*, the daughters of the Wala (Erda), from whom they gained only that knowledge that she passed on to them. If Wagner's Norns spun the Cord of Destiny, as did their counterparts in the myths, it was with the threads of fate that Erda had given them. If the Norns of Wagner's *Ring* made their pronouncements and informed Wotan of their judgments, both those pronouncements and those judgments had been formed for them by the all-wise Erda.

There were other adaptations that Wagner made as he placed the Norns of Teutondom in his drama. He did not give them names. He rejected the names that he had encountered in the myths, and he did not create names as he had done for several of his *Ring* figures. Rather, he simply called them "First," "Second," and "Third." There are some scholars who believe that this action was prompted by the brief appearance of the Norns in a single scene, so brief that they could not be considered as major figures of the *dramatis personae*, and therefore did not warrant names. These students of the drama cite the appearance of Forest Bird as a parallel action. Such reasoning fails when that same thought is applied to the situation of seven of the nine Valkyries who make a brief appearance in *Die Walküre*, each of whom bears a specific proper name. Wagner is not known to have spoken to the matter, yet it seems most probable that he deemed that if his Norns did not have proper names, perhaps they could reflect that late Teutonic thought that associated the Norns with the classical Fates. By such means it would be possible to retain the basics of early Teutonic thought yet, at the same time offer a matter with which an audience of the nineteenth century had some greater familiarity and, hence, the probability of a greater acceptance of the role as he had created it. It is also entirely possible that Wagner did not give his Norns names because the original names had no counterparts in the German language, and he was unable to find or to create German names that either suited him or were appropriate to the figures.

Wagner made yet another modification in the Teutonic Norns as he placed them in the argument of his drama. As depicted in the Eddic literature, these Norns lived at the base of the World Ash Tree. Wagner's stage instructions direct that the Norns spin their Cord of Destiny beside a giant *fir* tree. This deviation from mythical thought became necessary because of certain thematic factors that Wagner had included in his argument, factors that are not to be found in the mythical past, and which are explained by the Norns. As the first daughter of Erda fastens an end of the Cord of Destiny to the fir tree, she reminisces about the distant past. She recalls how once she spun and wove beside the World Ash, but when, at the beginning of time, Wotan had broken a limb from its trunk to fashion a spear of authority, the tree of life began to wither, to die. She recalls how the spring that she tended at its base, and whose waters she presumedly sprinkled on the tree, began to flow less. Wagner's Second Norn then continues the story, relating how the great god's spear had been shattered and because his authority was now shattered also, he was greatly tormented, so tormented that he ordered that the World Ash be felled and cut into boughs. When the tree had been cut down, the spring at its base then flowed even less than before. The Third Norn completes the account when she tells that Wotan then ordered that the boughs of the World Ash be placed around Valhalla, there where the gods forlornly awaited the torch that would set all ablaze and signal that the fated end of the gods and the universe that they had created had arrived.

The thematic modifications that Wagner induced into the Norns of Teutondom, as he incorporated them into their role in his drama, are relatively minor in character. Obviously, these changes relate to his argument, and they are such that in that relationship they do not detract in any substantial manner from the basic nature of the Norns conceived in early Teutonic thought. Wagner's Norns are essentially those of the ancient culture, and in that capacity they fulfill a thematic need in his argument and also contribute to that ambience of supernatural quality that was so necessary to his drama. If there is any question regarding Wagner's Norns, it is not *how* they appear or *how* they function in the *Ring*, but rather *when* they appear in the argument. The "Norn Scene" opens the "Prelude" of *Götterdämmerung*, a drama which is one whose *dramatis personae* is essentially one of mortals. This situation represents the opposite cultural extreme from that of *Das Rheingold*, the first drama of the *Ring*, which is totally a divine world of gods and other supernaturals of the Germanic mythical world. As the argument of the drama progresses from that initial ambience, mortals--or at least semi-mortals–are introduced and, at the same time, there is a slow dissolution from the divine world into one which is of men. Once the fourth drama is reached, the scope of action is centered in the world of mortals. Curiously, Wagner opens that drama of mortals with the scene of the mythical Teutonic Norns. In the minds of some followers of the *Ring*, the "Norn Scene" with adjusted dialogue, of course, would have been more effective if it had appeared earlier in the drama, that is as a part of the supernatural world. It must be remembered, however, that the "Prelude" to the fourth drama of the *Ring* was a dramatic afterthought, suggested to Wagner and written by him after he had completed the body of that drama's three acts. At the time, the "Prelude" was intended to explain certain events that had occurred prior to the action of *Götterdämmerung*, events that were primary to the argument and which perhaps the audience would not truly comprehend if only the three acts were presented. It should also be remembered that in 1848, as Wagner was writing the sketch for his drama and the actual poem, he was concerned with a single drama, one that dealt with the death of Siegfried, the Volsung. The idea for another drama, or then a series of other dramas, was to come later, and would necessitate that the text of the dramas be written in reverse order of intended presentation as music-dramas. The appearance, then, of the Norns was determined at a time when the thought of a second, or even a third or fourth drama, had never yet surfaced. By the time the case for three additional dramas had been determined and Wagner had arrived at the composition of *Das Rheingold*, the "Norn Scene" had long been a fixed part of *Götterdämmerung*, and despite the numerous revisions and changes that were required because of the reverse order of composition of the poems, the appearance of the Norns remained as originally conceived, despite the fact that much of what the trio relates now had been included as part of the dramatic argument. It is because of this latter circumstance that, on occasion, when cuts in performance times must be made, the "Norn Scene" is deleted from a production of *Götterdämmerung*.

There can be no doubt that the question of *where* in the *Ring* the appearance of the Norns would have been most effective theatrically is, at most, a conjectural matter. The scene, as it remained in the drama, has both a dramatic and a theatrical result. What is more significant, however, is the integral role the Norns have in Wagner's drama, as well as the essential qualities of their Teutonic nature that he was able to include and to project despite the brevity of their scene and the several thematic deviations that he created for these celebrated spirits of the Germanic past.

NORNS (Name)

At the outset of Teutonic mythical life, there was but a single *Norn* (German plural – *Nornir*). In time, however, the number became three, that is, a trio of sisters which, according to numerous scholars, was the Nordic adaptation of the three classical Fates. The history of the Germanic mythical figures was of no thematic consequence to Wagner. Rather, he was interested in their functions and their status within the early Germanic scheme of things. He was, therefore, to pattern his figures after those that existed in mythical beliefs, and the Norns of the *Ring* are essentially reflections of those of the ancient past, with one major exception. Wagner's Norns do not have names!

The Norns of Teutonic mythology have names. For whatever reasons, Wagner neither Germanized those names, as he did with numerous other names in his drama, nor did he devise names of his own creation. Wagner identified his Norns with numbers!

A brief glance at the mythical names of Teutondom's three Norns allows the possibility of a greater understanding of the nature of these spirits and their powers. The first of the Norns who, in the beginning, existed alone, was called *Urd*. This name was derived from the ON *urdr*, which meant "fate" or "destiny." Jakob Grimm, the German mythologist, suggested a different meaning for the word. In his monumental study of Teutonic mythology, Grimm associated the original word *urd* with *vard*, which was a preterite form of the verb *verda*, which meant "to become." According to Grimm, *urd* thus signified "what was." (The original Old Norse *urd* became *wyrd* in Anglo Saxon, and *wirde* and *werde* in Middle English and the word remains in modern English as *weird*. In Low German the word became *wurd*, and in Old High German *wurt*, which associated with *wirt*, a 'hostess' or 'wife of the household,' and *wirtel*, the spindle of a spinning wheel.)

The need for other figures to represent times that were complementary to that of "what was" was obvious. Scholars are convinced that it was at this point that the influence of the Fates became primary. The two other names of Norns, *Verdandi* and *Skuld*, then became mythical fact.

The word *Verdandi* is often rendered in English as *Being*. Grimm, however, also expressed his ideas regarding this name. The German scholar maintained that the word used here as a name was really the present participle of the same verb from which Urd had been derived, *verda*, and therefore, the name of the second Norn meant "what is."

The name of the third Norn, *Skuld*, is frequently translated into English as *Necessity*. Grimm, as well as others, believed that this name was a form of *skula*, the auxiliary verb with which the ancient language formed the future tense. *Skuld* thus meant "what shall be."

This trio, Urd, Verdandi, Skuld, was now Teutondom's trio of spirits that determined and controlled the destiny of all life. Each Norn represented a period of time in that life, and the forces of each Norn were so great that no god could counteract them, not even **Wotan**. These three Norns were, in their own way, an accurate reflection of another mythology in which the figures are known as *Past, Present,* and *Future*.

NORTH See: *Compass Points*

NOTUNG See: *The Sword* (Vol. I)

NOTUNG (Name)

The word *Notung*, the name that Siegmund gives to the sword and the name that Siegfried learns from Mime as he reforges its broken pieces, is another of the several proper nouns that Wagner created for use in his *Ring* drama. To form this compound, the composer joined the old Germanic word *Not*, which is still a part of modern German, with the suffix *ung*. A rather generic translation of the term *Notung* would then be "Offspring of" or "Child of Need," in the sense of "Born of Need." (The meaning and the use of *ung* are explained in *Notes*.) Wagner was aware that this meaning of the word *Notung*, as applied to the sword of his *Ring*, could also be interpreted literally as well as figuratively. After all, it was in the weaponless Siegmund's hour of greatest need that he came upon this weapon which, in time, will belong to his son who in turn will have it for his time of need as he ventures forth to slay the dragon Fafner.

The modern German word *Not* ("need") was derived from ON *naud*. (Modern English *need* is also derived from the ON *naud*: OE – *neod, ned, nyd,* and *nied*; ME – *ned, nede*.) Early pronunciation of the ON word was similar to "noth" which accounts for an occasional pronunciation and spelling of the name of the sword as "Nothung."

The word *Not* has several distinct meanings, each of which falls into one of three categories. All of these meanings, however, have a definite semantic kinship. The primary meaning of the word is "need," in the sense of "necessity." A second set of meanings of the word interprets the term "need" as "exigency" or "emergency." A third set of meanings, which derived from the first two, allows the word to connote "distress," "misery," or even "destruction." Any of these several meanings of *Not* can be read into the name that Wagner gave to the all-important sword, and in combination with the meanings of *ung*, the word *Notung* has several acceptable semantic possibilities, not the least of which is "Child of Need."

The original ON *Naud*, which in time became *Not*, was of special interest to the early Teutonic peoples. In addition to its obvious semantic value, the term was of significant importance in the cultural lives of these people. The term *Naud* also the name of one of the Germanic runes, those mythical bits of magic that could produce some wonder if properly 'worked' by one who knew the 'secret' that unleashed the powers of the runes! One facet of *naud's* power as a rune was that it could prevent a wife from betraying her husband's trust. The mark of this rune was ⸕, which later developed into the letter *N* of the alphabet.

The word *Not* was also a term that was quite familiar to the German people. It is prominent as part of the original title of the German epic poem *Nibelungenlied*. That title, *Nibelunge Not*, is routinely interpreted as *Fall of the Nibelungs*. The word *Fall* is used here in the sense of "destruction" or "defeat." This translation is approximate in light of the end (death) that befalls each of the Nibelung figures in the work.

See also: *The Sword* (Vol. I)